Syria

From Revolution From Below to Holy War (Jihad) 2011–2018

Munzer Eid Alzamalkani

Grosvenor House
Publishing Limited

This book is published by
Grosvenor House Publishing Ltd
Link House
140 The Broadway, Tolworth, Surrey, KT6 7HT.
www.grosvenorhousepublishing.co.uk

A CIP record for this book
is available from the British Library

Paperback ISBN 978-1-80381-582-4
Hardback ISBN 978-1-80381-583-1
eBook ISBN 978-1-80381-584-8

CONTENTS

ACKNOWLEDGMENT

To my mother Hadiyah Kabbara and my father Eid

I miss you so much and may Allah bless you

To all the children, women, and men got killed in Syria by Assad, Iran, Russia, and Nato

To all the children, women, and men in Assad's jails and torturing chambers

To all the Syrian children, women, and men drowned in the sea or got killed by the Turkish Gendarmerie on the borders fleeing the Assad's and the Russian airstrikes and missiles.

To all the displaced Syrian people living in poor tents under the ferocity of heat and cold or suffering from hatred and exploitation in diaspora, but not to return home accepting Assad

To everyone has helped the Syrian people at home or in diaspora

To all the people fighting against aggression and oppression

To all the people suffering from and struggling against the Western arrogance and hypocrisy

To the Arab Spring Revolutions and to heroes of the Syrian Revolution

To my beloved captive cities, Mecca, Jerusalem, and Damascus, suffering from the same ordeal

To Ghouta, was ever the heaven on Earth before the thuggish rule of savages Assads. And to Gaza, and the children of Gaza.

Also with love and respect:

To Kadee and the genius children

To my precious sisters and in the memory of my brothers (Mouaz, Muhammad, and Ghiath)

To my adored nieces, and nephews

To my uncles and to my dearest brothers in law

To my creative father, mother, sisters, and brothers in law

To Ayman, to all my teachers, especially, Mr. Haj Ali, to my friends, relatives, and to all my people around the world

PREFACE

Neutrality is an honor in academia and journalism even though it is impossible in reality. However, when it comes to talking about criminals killing and slaughtering children, raping women and torturing people to death, neutrality becomes a shame and disgrace. You cannot avoid your strong emotions and wiping up your own tears falling on your words while observing tragedies and calamities taking place against children and women while the world is silent.

I have been a victim of such a big dilemma trying to balance being a neutral academic and an emotional Syrian caring for his people and his country, watching and analyzing the situation in Syria and hearing about the massacres that were committed by the Assad regime, and his allies from Russia and the Iranian militias, against the Syrian people. However, I escaped this dilemma gradually when realizing that sticking to neutrality and reflecting the real picture in Syria would indeed bring the whole world to a conclusion that what is happening in Syria is a crime against humanity, and Bashar Assad is a child killer, and the Syrian people have been left alone and let down by the international community facing their greatest ordeal ever.

Therefore, I seized the opportunity of being a Syrian benefiting from new communications technology and worked very hard trampling over my feelings in order to establish great links with the people on the ground, with the opposition and with various armed and Jihadist groups in order to get the unique, righteous information that readers never had before and put it in their hands, displaying my analysis before their judgments.

Writing this book made me acquire expectational skills, from being an academic in Chapter One to a political historian in Chapter Two, to a journalist in Chapter Three, Four, and Five, and a politician in Chapter Six, implying that this book is for all: for academics, students, journalists, politicians and everyone is interested in Syria and in the Middle East complexities.

Finally, this book is based on my PhD thesis at the University of St-Andrews in Scotland in the United Kingdom. I have tried to publish this book before through some other publishers, but apparently some of its contents are inconsistent with their policy approaching and observing the situation in Syria. I decided not to compromise my views and hence not to betray my readers, but to go with a reputable self-publishing company revealing the facts and the reality about the war in Syria; its origins and its developments. I am so confident that readers will observe by themselves the boundaries that I have crossed in this book and the unique approach I am adopting here observing the holocaust against the Sunni Muslims in Syria.

Munzer
November 2023, England

INTRODUCTION

Syria is a central and pivotal country in the Middle East, where geography, history, identity, religion and politics overlap. The unique geopolitical importance of Syria made it the heart of international struggle in the Middle East, in the present as well as the past. Saint-Marc Girardin, writing in the nineteenth century, stated in 1860: "The Syrian dilemma is the core of the whole Orient's dilemma."[1]

Almost fifty years after Syria's Eighth of March Revolution in 1963, which was described by Raymond Hinnebusch as a revolution from above, in March 2011 Syria was struck by a different type of revolution; a popular, non-partisan, non-hierarchical and elite-less revolution. In other words, Syria was enduring a revolution from below. It was an aspect of the Arab Spring revolutions that stormed many other Arab countries such as Tunisia, Egypt, Libya, Yemen and Bahrain. The social basis for this revolution was overwhelmingly Sunni Muslim, both rural and urban. Nevertheless, it did not start as an Islamic revolution or as a holy war. The ideology was immaterial; in fact, the political, economic and social grievances were the real instigators for the uprising. It was the people's revolution or, as they described it, the Freedom and Dignity Revolution. However, this revolution developed into a destructive internal war between the regime and its allies on one side against the revolutionaries and their allies on the other side, turning the struggle into a prolonged, outrageous and interlocking conflict. The struggle has developed further into Jihad, threatening the security of the entire Middle East.

[1] Josef Hajjar, *Syria: Belad Asham*, Dar Tlas, 1999, p.22.

CONTRIBUTION OF AND BACKGROUND TO THIS BOOK

The importance of this study is, in fact, derived from several factors: First and foremost is the great importance of the Arab Spring as an unprecedented event taking place in the Middle East and North Africa. The Arab Spring (if successful) would break the nature of international politics in the Middle East that has prevailed since the second half of the 20th century. Consequently, great changes will occur in the international political system and lead to a new phase in the relationship between the north and the south, or more accurately between the core and the peripheries. Second, it comes from the great importance of the Middle East for the United States and other great powers for its rich resources, as well as its importance to Israel and Islamism. Resources mean survival and dominance, whereas the security of Israel can mean world security, but it is Islamism that has turned out to be the real danger for the international system. Therefore, such changes in the political order of the Middle East will undoubtedly create a great concern among the great powers and hence urge them to interfere in order to protect their national interests by manipulating the undesired but inevitable far-reaching changes. Third, it comes from the great importance of Syria as the most vital country in the Middle East, in Zisser's words:

> Syria plays a crucial regional role and may even decide the fate of the region for better or worse, for peace or war. The vacuum [if] created at the top of the ruling pyramid in Damascus presents problems, not just for Syria, but for the region as a whole.[2]

The problems have no doubt spilled over beyond the region as well. Moreover, the internal war in Syria is not only a threat to the political system of the Middle East, but, additionally, a great

[2] Eyal Zisser, "Does Bashar Assad Rule Syria?" The Middle East Quarterly, Winter 2003, Volume X: Number 1, pp.15–23.

threat to the Sykes–Picot Agreement, a document in which the Middle East was shaped during and after the Great War. Such a threat is looming because Iraq and Lebanon, as two of Syria's neighbors, have turned into failed states and suffer from internal social and political disharmony. They are divided into sectarian and ethnic communities. The social contract among their citizens has been broken away and seems irreparable in the short term. These territorial states might collapse in front of the overwhelming forces of identity. Borders may be abolished in between these three countries, knowing the fact that western Iraq and northern Lebanon are Sunni, the same as the majority of Syria. In other words, the internal war in Syria may reshape the entire Middle East geographically and politically, breaking long-term alliances and changing the political game in the region, leading to endless conflicts and wars.

The main aim of this book is to provide a deep analysis to the causes, dynamics and developments of the Syrian Revolution from phase to phase since its beginning in March 2011 until the end of 2018, when ISIS was defeated by the international coalition. It is very important to begin from the very early events in Daraa and Baniyas in close detail to observe how this complicated crisis could have been avoided through very modest policies if there was wise leadership in power in Syria. Works by prominent scholars on the Middle East and Syria such as Roger Owen, Oliver Schlumberger, Fred Halliday, Raymond Hinnebusch and Simon Bromley are essential resources in this book. Their theories and analysis on the history and the politics of the Middle East since the early days of the 20th century until the post-independence period support this book, and in particular when grasping state formation in the Middle East and establishing the nation-sate system in the region. They have recorded the transition of the region from an empire into independent states, paying great attention to the role of the Western powers in shaping the region and building the new states. It is important to examine that period in order to understand the roots of authoritarianism in the Arab world, and to understand the possible collapse of the state system in the region due to its frail nature. There was also reliance on many Arab sociologists such as Burhan Ghalioun and Khaldoon al-Naqeeb. Their views on the roots and the resilience of authoritarianism in the Arab world have been especially insightful resources. Moreover, Steven Heydemann's theory on authoritarian upgrading occupies a key position in the first and second chapters of this book. Additionally, works by prominent revolution theorists such as Samuel Huntington, Ted Gurr, Eric Selbin, Jeff Goodwin and Crane Brinton are fundamental pillars. Their works and hypotheses on the definition of revolution and its causes are well relied on. Jeffery Goodwin's important work, for instance, on the causes of revolution was a fundamental piece that I relied on to explain the Arab Revolutions in 2011 and the Arab Spring in general.

Jawdat Sa'id's work on non-violence as a way to deal with opponents and enemies for the sake of change or reform was a great source in this book in order to explain the peaceful phase in the Syrian Revolution. Considerable numbers of peaceful activists in Syria were adopting Sai'd's views. On the other hand, Lawrence Stone and Samuel Huntington's definition of the revolution as a "change through violence" has helped me to understand the transition of the Syrian Revolution from a peaceful uprising into a violent revolution. Similarly, Eric Selbin's views on the role of ideas and symbols in revolution have led to a large extent a better understanding of the transition of the Syrian Revolution into a holy war (Jihad). I have also relied on some Quranic text, some speeches of the Prophet Muhammad (Peace Be Upon Him), and on some Jihad theorists such as Abu Qatada in order to explain the immigration of Jihadists from around the world to Syria to participate in Jihad.

The aim of this book is to provide missing details of the Syrian uprising, and to offer a different approach to studying the Syrian Revolution by dividing it into phases, and using more precise terms. Thus I have divided the Syrian Revolution into three phases:

1) *Revolution from below*, where popular and peaceful uprising was the mainstream character of the Syrian Revolution;

2) *Internal war*, where mutual violence was spread formally and nationally after the formation of the Free Syrian Army (FSA);
3) *Holy war (Jihad)*, where most revolutionaries have turned into national Jihadists and monitoring the arrival of global Jihadists to Syria to fight the regime and to establish an Islamic State (Khilafa).

In this book I use the term *internal war* rather than *civil war* for many reasons. First, Harry Eckstein's view is that "internal war denotes any resort to violence within a political order to change its constitution, rulers, or policies."[3] This is the most appropriate image for what is happening in Syria since March 2011 until the moment when the internal war turned into a holy war. Second, the definition of civil war is a controversial issue and in many cases does not reflect a correct image about the war in Syria. Third, talking about civil war in the Middle East suggests a portrayal of the Lebanese civil war from the 1970s to the 1980s, or the Iraqi sectarian war after 2003, but such events occurred as a result of a foreign occupation and state collapse in Iraq, or as a result of a state failure in Lebanon. In Syria the situation is very different. There are two parties at war in Syria: pro-regime fighters and their allies against anti-regime fighters and their allies. This would challenge allegations of a purely sectarian war in Syria. Nevertheless, identity remained a relevant factor, and represented one side of the conflict. It is a factor that some elements in both parties have invested in greatly, but the war in Syria is much broader. In fact, the identity factor was used as an instrument to mobilize the loyalists in both parties and fuel up the conflict. There is no open fighting between Sunnis and Alawis, Sunnis and Druze, or Sunnis and Christians. Fourth, there is a lot of relevance to Stathis Kalyvas' comment: "Internal war is more precise, but civil war is by far the most

[3] Harry Eckstein, "On the Etiology of Internal War", in *Why Revolutions*, C. Paynton and R. Blackey(eds), Shenkman Publishing, Massachusetts, 1971, pp.16–22.

familiar term".[4] Analyzing the Syrian conflict requires precision and meticulousness, using very careful terms and expressions in order to convey the clearest picture about the situation in Syria. In this book, it is also important to mention how identities constituted a substantial burden on the revolution in Syria since day one.

As identity is one side of the conflict, it will occupy limited attention in this book because sectarian and ethnic war in Syria at this stage is still a prospect rather than an established scenario. Sheikh al-Hamwi, a prominent figure in the Syrian Revolution from the city of Hama commented:

> Everyone speaks about a sectarian war in Syria!! Do we target only Alawis? Do we ask for ID when targeting the regime's check points? Indeed no, anyone [who] does pose a threat towards us is a legitimate target regardless of his identity or his affiliation. Our revolution is not against a certain sect or a certain group. It is, indeed, against an authoritarian regime in the country.[5]

There is a good bit of truth to Darwisheh's observation, "The tendency of the international media to play up a Shia–Sunni civil war obscures the regional reality that forms the big picture of the conflict".[6]

There are no recent formal reliable figures that can reflect the real size of every sectarian or ethnic community in Syria. According to the CIA Fact Book:[7] Sunni Muslim 74%, other Muslim (includes Alawi, Druze) 16% and Christians 10%. In relation to

---

[4] Stathis Kalyvas, *The Logic of Violence in Civil War*, Cambridge University Press, Cambridge, 2006, p.17.

[5] Interview with author via Skype on 13 April 2014.

[6] Housam Darwisheh, "Trajectories and Outcomes of the Arab Spring", Institute of Developing Economies IDE, Discussion Paper No. 456, March 2014.

[7] There is no real evidence to support these figures. Some other figures which are more reliable show Muslims 80%, Christians 10%, Alawis 6%, Druze 3% and 1% others such as Ismailis. There is no authentic credible figure reflects the real ethnic and religious mosaic in Syria.

ethnicity: Arab 90.3%, Kurds and Armenian 9.7%. However, this figure excludes the Sunnis who left the country in the aftermath of the March Revolution of 1963 and after the Islamic rebellion in the 1980s. On the other hand, the Turkmen community is a relatively large community in Syria and the vast majority of them are Sunni Muslims. It is important here to speak briefly about Alawis, Druze and Ismailis in Syria. However, the current stance of these groups, including Christians, toward the revolution is more fully discussed in Chapter Three.

Alawis

Stephan Prochazka pointed out that Alawis (Alawiyyun) means adherents or descendants of Ali Ibn Abi Talib, the Prophet Muhammad's cousin. Other Muslims regard them as heretics. For centuries, the Alawi sect was called Nusayria after its founder Ibn Nusayr.[8] It is important to differentiate between Alwais and Alevis; so while the Alawis are Arabs, Alevis are Turkish, Balkan and Kurdish. Both names are derived from Ali, the Prophet's cousin, but their religious practices are different. However, both define themselves as minorities, and claimed they were historically persecuted by Sunnis. Alawis historically are located centrally in the countryside of the Syrian coast, and there are many Alawi villages in Homs, Hama and in Al Qunaitra, south Syria.

Druze

Hussam Timany explains that the emergence of the Druze faith occurred in 1017 CE when the Fatimid ruler al-Hakim bi Amrillah (r. 996–1021 CE) instructed missionaries to propagate for a new era of Tawhid (Unitarianism). Although the call originated in North Africa, the Druze can be found today in Lebanon, Syria, Israel and Jordan. The Druze have a distinct set of beliefs

---

[8] Stephan Prochazka, "Alawis", www.oxfordbibliographies.com http://www.oxfordbibliographies.com/view/document/obo-9780195390155/obo-9780195390155-0175.xml, viewed on 15 March 2014.

and practices, and their manuscripts, *kutub al-hikma* (wisdom books), are a collection of epistles and correspondence between luminaries.[9] Druze are concentrated in As-Swayda province in the south of Syria, and there are many scattered Druze villages in Aleppo and Idlib. Jaramana in the suburb of Damascus also is a large Druze town, and was originated from Durze workers from As-Swayda who came to Damascus for work since the collapse of the Ottoman Empire.

Ismailis

According to the official website of the Ismaili community,

> The Shia Ismaili Muslims are a community of ethnically and culturally diverse peoples living in over 25 countries around the world, united in their allegiance to His Highness Prince Karim Aga Khan (known to the Ismailis as Mawlana Hazar Imam) as the 49th hereditary Imam (spiritual leader), and direct descendant of Prophet Muhammad.[10]

Salamiya town in the eastern countryside of Hama in Syria constitutes the most important town for Ismailis historically as well as in the present. There are also scattered Ismaili villages in Masyaf in west Hama.

The complicated internal situation in Syria does not come only from the ethnic and religious diversity in the country, but moreover, the ethnic and religious groups are geographically unbalanced across the country. Alawis for instance, are mainly in the coast mountains, Kurds are mainly in the north and north east and Druze in the south. Such situations undoubtedly threaten the unity of Syria and make a divided Syria one of the possible scenarios at any time.

---

[9] Hussam Tamini, "Druze", www.oxfordbibliographies.com http://www.oxfordbibliographies.com/view/document/obo-9780195390155/obo-9780195390155–0104.xml, viewed on 15 March 2014.

[10] http://www.theismaili.org.

THEORETICAL OVERVIEW

Revolution is still a controversial concept among scholars. However, all of them indicate one common connotation, which is *change*. Revolution, according to Crane Brinton, "is more than an emphatic synonym to change, it is perhaps with a suggestion of sudden and striking change."[11] Nevertheless, Lawrence Stone stresses violence as the way for that change. He wrote that revolution is a "change affected by violence in government and/or regime, and/or society",[12] and caused by two factors. According to Chalmers Johnson:

> Revolutions have two general causes: a dysfunctional social system and inflexible elite... If the elite, instead of being intransigent responds to the crisis by allowing for peaceful changes in the system, by introducing the requisite reforms, then the dysfunction will be relieved and no revolution will take place.[13]

On other hand, Samuel Huntington applied more weight to the political causes for revolutions. He stated:

> The political essence of revolution is the rapid expansion of political consciousness and the rapid mobilization of new groups into politics at a speed which makes it impossible for existing institutions to assimilate them. Revolution is the extreme case of the explosion of political participation. Without this explosion there is no revolution.[14]

[11] Crane Brinton, *The Anatomy of Revolution*, Random House, New York, 1956, p.3.

[12] Lawrence Stone, *Theories of Revolution*, World Politics, Princeton University Press, Princeton 1966, pp.159–176.

[13] Chalmers Johnson, *Revolution and the Social System*, Hoover Institution Press, Stanford, 1964, pp.6–7.

[14] Samuel Huntington, "Revolution and Political Order" in *Revolutions*, Jack Goldstone (ed), Thomson, USA, 1986, pp.37–40.

Based on the factual importance of the nation-state, where the state represents the revolution's "field of action",[15] it is very essential in the era of globalization to find out the new circumstances that influence revolutions, and how the forces of globalization may obstruct or promote revolutions and revolutionaries. The Arab Spring is not a unique historic global event. In fact, Europe had a similar spring, where political upheaval started in France and spread to many countries in Europe. Hoverer, the Arab Spring has the potential to be more disruptive to the international system. According to Mark Katz, "what is disruptive is not just an ideological revolutionary regime seeks the establishment of regimes similar to itself elsewhere, but that the revolutionary idea resonates in other countries, and significant forces appear that seek to implement it."[16] After the Tunisian Revolution in January 2011, the revolutionary idea resonated in some other Arab countries, which led to revolutions in Egypt, Libya, Yemen, Bahrain and Syria. Such an idea may spread further in the region in the future. Some of these revolutions were suppressed immediately, such as in Bahrain. Some others were contained, such as the case in Yemen. In Libya, the revolution was turned into international military intervention. But in Egypt, powerful counter-revolution forces defeated the revolution on 3 July 2013. Meanwhile, the revolution in Syria turned out to be a long destructive war, and one with great regional and international dimensions.

HISTORICAL BACKGROUND

Syria (including Lebanon) as a state was formed after the collapse of the Ottoman Empire in the aftermath of the Great War. Many Western (France, Britain, and Russian) agreements took place, dividing and ruling the pre-Ottoman territories, drawing a new map for the Middle East. The Sykes–Picot Agreement between Britain and France in 1916 was the foundation for subsequent

[15] Phrase of George Pettee.

[16] Mark Katz, "The Diffusion of Revolutionary Waves" in *Revolutions*, Jack Goldstone (ed), Thomson, USA, 1986, pp.150–146.

Western agreements to reshape and colonize the Middle East. The French Mandate was imposed on Syria in July 1920, and the formation of Lebanon was completed in 1925. During the phase of colonization, the French started to establish a nation-state in the country with a secularist nature. Eventually, the French departed from Syria in April 1946.

Since immediately after independence, Syria encountered a significant problem in the form of the state-formation dilemma. Syria found itself as a territorial state, but not a nation-state. It was an inharmonious political entity. Class conflicts, military coups and political instability prevailed from 1946 until 1963. During this period, no ideology was able to assemble the people, and a collective identity was missing. The Baath Party after the revolution of March 1963 was able to impose an ideology and identity for the state: Baath ideology and Arab identity.

After the 1963 revolution in Syria, a phase of populist authoritarian rule began through concentration and expansion of power. According to Hinnebusch, "Power was concentrated through an ideological movement and a revolution from above, expanded through party-building, and consolidated through patrimonialsation, at the cost of a later contraction in power."[17]

Hafiz Assad ascended to power in November 1970, and his power was consolidated by relying on clan and sectarianism in the army. He was able to suppress the Islamic revolution in 1982, which made him the absolute ruler. In the 1990s, the Baath Party started suffering from bankruptcy, the state was overburdened, and the economy was struggling. However, the military was concentrated totally in the hands of loyal Alawi officers.

A phase of authoritarian upgrading started in Syria in the early 1990s, facing the new challenges of globalization and the new world order. The regime also engaged in a reconciliation process with some exiled Islamists and some Muslim scholars. In 2000 Hafiz Assad died, and his 34-year-old son Bashar Assad

[17] Raymond Hinnebusch, *Syria: Revolution from Above,* Routledge, New York, 2002, p.5.

inherited the power under the absolute and fiercely loyal Alawi military influence in the country. He presented himself as a modernist and a reformer. However, after more than decade of his rule, social and economic inequality prevailed in society as result of neo-liberal economic policies. Meanwhile, political persecution and oppression continued and reached an unprecedented level, making it hardly surprising for large numbers of Syrian people to respond positively to the Arab Spring revolutions in 2011. In March 2011, Syria witnessed a revolution from below, but the regime's violent and brutal response turned it into a prolonged internal war and later into a holy war (Jihad).

METHODOLOGY

This book represents a single case study focusing on the Syrian Revolution in 2011 since the early days of the failed mobilization in February 2011. A qualitative book method is adopted in this book because collecting data serving the purpose of this book cannot be based on quantified categories. Moreover, this book focuses on identifying underlying causes and other contributing factors.

The main sources for this book are scholarly books, journals, studies and reports, as well as internet resources, and some websites and videos on the internet and television documentaries. Interviews are also a very important source of information in the empirical work, especially where the academic sources are lacking. More than 70 interviews were conducted, mainly through Skype conferencing, in order to be based on the genuine events during the uprising and later during the internal war and the Jihad phase. A few interviews can be traced back to the mid-1990s, when the author was investigating the possibility of inheriting power in Syria. The majority of interviewees were members of the Free Syrian Army, military and political defectors, activists, opposition figures and members of Jihadist groups. Several of the interviewees were known personally, and this included opposition figures and the founder of the Free Syrian Army, but reaching activists and fighters was made through mediators, mainly in the form of close friends or relatives arranging Skype meetings with them. I have tried to conduct interviews with the most relevant people, so choosing the interviewees was not done randomly, but was done through careful selection, taking their positions and activities into consideration as important factors. Therefore, the result gained from these interviews was information from original sources, so the possibility of error or fabrication was limited. As the uprising in its peaceful and violent phases was overwhelmingly a male responsibility, there has been reliance mainly on men rather than women in the interviews. The age of the interviewees was between 25 and 70 years old or over; the interviewed activists and fighters were as young as 25 years, while the age of some interviewed figures in the opposition was nearly 70 years old or over. As a matter of security and safety, and on the demands of the interviewees, names here are only the first names of the interviewees; a few preferred their initials only, but some figures in the opposition and the Free Syrian Army did not demand certain privacy, so their names were listed fully. Nevertheless, all the interviewees' details such as their locations and their contact details were wiped out and would not be passed over to a third party under any circumstances. The people interviewed here belong to the revolutionary side. The regime's loyalists do not believe in the revolution as such, and their discourse is still the same since the beginning of the uprising in March 2011, matching the regime's discourse, which is labeling the uprising as a conspiracy from the West against Syria for its brave stance against Israel, and labeling the revolutionaries as Islamic militias or terrorist groups. However, the regime stance toward many events during the uprising from its loyalist sources is conveyed.

Finally, being a Syrian and well acquainted with many opposition figures, as well as a relative or friend to many members of the Free Syrian Army and the national Jihadist groups, has made conducting the interviews an uncomplicated process despite the great concerns that the interviewees had regarding their security and their safety. Still, conducting qualitative work during the conflict situation requires more time as the candidates might cancel or postpone the meetings due to security concerns. Moreover, being a relative or friend to many victims of the

Assad's regime brutality makes my narrative in this book more authenticated.

Five main terms are used throughout this book: the Syrian Uprising, the Syrian Revolution, the Syrian Conflict, the Syrian Internal War, and the Syrian Crisis. All these terms refer to the political disorder in Syria after March 2011 and are explained as they come up in discussion. I have adopted Google Maps when referring to cities' and villages' names in Syria in order to make it easier for the reader to track the events in Syria geographically. In addition, this book contains some distressing and disturbing images showing the brutality of the Assad's regime.

BOOK STRUCTURE

This book poses two main questions: 1) Why is there a revolution in Syria? and 2) Why is the revolution in Syria taking such a long time in comparison to its counterparts in the Arab Spring?

In the first chapter, three main issues are covered: authoritarianism in the Arab world and Syria; authoritarian upgrading in the Arab world and Syria; and theories of revolutions and revolution analysis in relation to the Arab Spring and Syria. This will include a discussion of the consolidation of authoritarianism since the collapse of the Ottoman Empire and the rise of state formation, as well as the important roles of tribalism and religion. Other factors such as the link between Islam and authoritarianism, creating a culture of fear, supra-state ideology such as Arabism, and the struggle with Israel are also considered. Heydemann's theory on authoritarian upgrading is well discussed in this chapter, including his five elements of authoritarian upgrading: 1) appropriating and containing civil societies; 2) managing political contestation; 3) capturing the benefits of selective economic reforms; 4) controlling new communications technologies; 5) diversifying international linkages. The concept of revolution is the main issue discussed in this chapter. This includes its definition and causes in both deprived and modern societies, as well as violence or peace as a means of change. Revolution in the age of globalization is very much considered too, as are the obstacles of revolution. Moreover, the international dimensions of revolution, and Mark Katz's valuable works in this field, are also included.

Chapter Two contains an overview evaluation of Bashar Assad's era from 2000 until 2011, when the revolution erupted. Starting with a review of inheriting power in Syria, it considers the circumstances surrounding Bashar Assad's ascendency to power, and the military loyalty that guaranteed the succession process. The domestic political developments and the opposition status from the Damascus Spring to the National Salvation Front are particularly observed. The economic developments in most sectors such as free trade, agriculture and business networks are also carefully examined, as well as the changes in the services sector, such as the education and health systems. Other issues such as new legislation cannot be ignored when evaluating Bashar Assad's era. All those changes and developments had great social implications, which are addressed here too. The status of the religious institutions and the Jihadists' challenge are also covered. Syrian foreign policy during Bashar Assad's era regionally and internationally is also carefully examined in order to understand the changes that occurred after the beginning of the revolution on one hand, and to understand the regional and international dimensions of the Syrian Revolution on the other hand.

Chapter Three covers the circumstances of the Syrian Revolution in the first six months, and this phase is called a revolution from below. The discussion begins here with conveying the circumstances of the Arab Spring and a brief representation of the revolutions in the Arab Spring countries: Tunisia, Egypt, Libya, Yemen and Bahrain. The pre-revolution conditions in Damascus are also covered, as well as the spark in Daraa, and the regime response to the early events in this city, all examined closely in order to stand on the developments of the uprising trajectory. The circumstances in the major cities and towns such as Baniyas, Damascus and its suburbs, Homs, Latakia, Aleppo and the other cities are also considered. Bashar Assad's first speech after the uprising is also looked at, along with the major events that took place immediately after his speech, which made the situation in Syria very bleak. The role of information technology and telecommunications as well as the engines of revolution in Syria are also well explained in this chapter. There is great consideration for the Syrian opposition and its activities during this phase of the revolution. The stances of the religious institutions, the tribal community and the ethnic and religious communities in Syria occupy an important space as well.

Chapter Four covers the second phase in the revolution, which I call the *Internal War*, where the revolutionaries have adopted violence formally after the establishment of the Free Syrian Army. The discussion includes analysis of the reasons behind the failure of the peaceful uprising to make political change in Syria. Gurr's military loyalty theory is applied, and military defections and the mysteries surrounding the formation of the Free Syrian Army are also disclosed. The establishment of the Syrian Nation Council (SNC), and the factors behind its failure, are integrated into the discussion, with attention paid to the National Coordination Body for Democratic Change in Syria (NCB) as another opposition body with a different road map on the situation in Syria.

In Chapter Five, I focus on the third phase of the revolution, when it had transformed into a holy war. Starting with explaining why the revolutionaries have returned to ideology, Selbin's hypotheses on the role of ideas and myths in the revolution are applied. The concept of Jihad is analyzed using Abu Qatada and Qutb's theories, and also the roots of Jihadists in the Syrian Revolution. The most operative groups are mentioned in this discussion along with their affiliations, if known, and their differences.

Chapter Six reviews international relations vis-à-vis the Syrian Revolution. Countries are divided here into three groups: friends of Syria, friends of the regime, and countries that declared formal neutrality. The stances of sub-state actors such as Hezbollah and Hamas are also included, as is the use of chemical weapons in August 2013, and debating the notion of proxy war in Syria. Finally, Chapter Seven is the conclusion, where the main arguments are summarized and discussed as a whole. Findings are identified and considered, and the author's point of view on the conflict for the future is also expressed.

Chapter One

AUTHORITARIANISM AND REVOLUTIONS IN THE ARAB WORLD AND SYRIA

INTRODUCTION

Authoritarianism has existed as a form of governance after independence in the Arab world during or after the Second World War, and has consolidated itself through many means for decades. International support for these regimes, and their brutal nature, had to accompany some measures and policies in order to make them sustainable and resilient, and able to be prolonged. However, new internal and external forces have emerged particularly after the Cold War, and challenged authoritarianism, obliging the regimes in the Arab world to move to authoritarian upgrading, and to offer some concessions to the public and to the opposition in order to survive the challenges. Ironically, authoritarian upgrading has led to revolutions, risking the regimes' security and their survival.

AUTHORITARIANISM IN THE ARAB WORLD

There are three major crises which are rooted in every country of the Arab world, republic or monarchy, as observed by Abdullah al-Nufaisi, an Arab prominent intellectual from Kuwait: first, political authoritarianism; second, unequal distribution of wealth; and third, the dependency on the West through an unbreakable alliance between the ruling elite in the Arab world and the West.[18] Authoritarianism has built its nest in the Arab world after the independence, taking advantage of the weakness of the state. The Arab republics such as Egypt, Syria, Algeria and Iraq have used populism as the main tool to consolidate authoritarianism, while the concept of compulsory public and religious allegiance and loyalty (*Bai'a*)[19] was the key element for sustaining authoritarianism in the Arab monarchies such as Saudi Arabia and Morocco. To appeal to the people, for example, al-Hasan, the deceased king of Morocco, called himself *Amir Al-Moumineen*, the Prince of the Believers; Fahd Bin Abdul-Aziz, the deceased king of Saudi Arabia, changed the title in 1986 from His Majesty to *Khadem Al-Haramain Al-Shareefain,* the Servant of the Holly Mosques. Meanwhile, Jamal Abdul Nasser was called *Habib Almalaeen*, the Beloved of Millions of People.

In a republic such as Tunisia, the deceased President Bourguiba was an icon of authoritarianism in the Arab world. It was reflected in his brutal rule as well as in his views about the political system in Tunisia. "What system? I am the system".[20] This is how he replied when he was asked about the political system in Tunisia, imitating King Louis XIV of France, when he said, "I am the king I am the state".[21] However, that was almost three hundred years ago. In a monarchy such as Morocco, article 19 in the constitution of 1962 states:

> The King is the commander of the believers, and the symbol of the unity of the nation, and the guarantor for its survival, the protector of religion, and the guardian for the respect of the constitution, and to protect the rights and freedoms of

[18] M O H A M M E D, The Nation's Status, Posted on 05 February 2011, https://www.youtube.com/watch?v=wQwUc-BCm1U.

[19] The word Bai'a means agreement in the form of a pledge of loyalty. A Bai'a for the khalifa (ruler) e.g. means his induction into his office.

[20] Clement Moor "*Politics in North Africa: Algeria, Morocco, and Tunisia*", Little Brown, Boston, 1970, p.95.

[21] Khaless Jalabi, *The Contemporary Authoritarianism*, Madarek, Dubai, 2012, p.87.

> citizens, groups and institutions, and he is the patron for the country's independence and the kingdom's sovereignty over its territories.[22]

Consequently, authoritarianism is a common and inherent governing system across the Arab world (with the exception of Lebanon due to its semi-balanced sectarian structure and to foreign influence), making no vital difference between republics and monarchies. In fact, some republics have turned virtually into dynasties, such as the situation in Syria. Oliver Schlumberger argues, "Arab policies are homogeneous insofar as they are all characterized by an authoritarian mode of governance".[23] Steven Heydemann shares the same concern, stating: "Everywhere in the Middle East, authoritarianism has proven to be an adaptive flexible style of rule".[24] Most of the Arab republics before the events of the Arab Spring were involved heavily in the process of transferring power from the ruler to one of his sons in a clear challenge to the constitution. In Tunisia, Egypt, Libya and Yemen, the plan of inheriting power was evident and was the utmost concern for the state and its institutions. The plan was aborted by the Arab Spring revolutions, which have overthrown those leaders and their families. In Syria, such a plan had already been implemented in June 2000, when Bashar Assad inherited the power from his father Hafiz Assad. Moreover, there was a real concern among Syrian people that Bashar Assad might repeat the same scenario with one of his children in the future.

Authoritarianism in the Arab world has developed into upgrading authoritarianism rather than to democracy in the past few decades. In fact, the Arab regimes have never showed serious

---

[22] Idress al-Shamekh, *A Critical Reading in the Moroccan Constitutional Experience*, Hespress, 27 November 2009. http://hespress.com/opinions/16921.html, viewed on 11 October 2012.

[23] Oliver Schlumberger, "Arab Authoritarianism: Debating the Dynamics and Durability of Non- Democratic Regimes" in *Debating Arab Authoritarianism*, Schlumberger (ed), Stanford University Press: Stanford, 2007, p.1–20.

[24] Steven Heydemann, "Social Pacts and Authoritarianism" in *Debating Arab Authoritarianism*, Schlumberger (ed), Stanford University Press, Stanford, 2007, pp.21–38.

attempts to move toward democracy or any other form of governance that would imply some genuine political freedom such as *Shura*[25] in the Islamic governance system. The Arab world is the only region in the world that has not undertaken any cases of transition from authoritarian rule in the past few decades.[26]

The Origins of Authoritarianism in the Arab World

Great scholarly contributions were made analyzing the phenomenon of authoritarianism and examining its political, social and economic DNA, and exploring its elements of resilience and continuity in the Arab world. No political system in the world can survive and sustain without resorting to genuine or ungenuine legitimacy that maintain and prolong its life and guarantee its acceptance from the subjects. Mere suppression and oppression are insufficient to guarantee its continuation.[27] Therefore, there are great internal and external factors that have consolidated and prolonged the Arab authoritarian regimes. In the Arab world, there are internal factors such as culture and social considerations, and external factors such as the state formation and the persistence of foreign threat to the national security. All these factors have laid the ground for authoritarianism and supported its structure in order to get stronger and to live longer.

Imperialism

It is very important to cast light on the origin of the contemporary form of the Middle East in order to reach an insightful analysis of the current events in the Arab world and the Arab Spring prospects, and in particular the Syrian Revolution.

[25] Shura is an Arabic word means consultations.

[26] Schlumberger, op, cit, pp.1–20.

[27] Muhammad al-Khalefi, "A Historic Reading in the Authoritarianism Concept", in *Authoritarianism in The Contemporary Arab Regimes* (ed) by a Group of Researchers, CAUS, Beirut, 2006, pp.279–303.

The Collapse of the Ottoman Empire. The Great War was a crucial moment not just for Europe, but for the Middle East's history as well. The Ottoman Empire decided to ally with the Central Powers; it was a decisive but ill-fated decision which led to its collapse and its partition. The region was transformed from an extending Ottoman Empire into a states system by the leading world powers at the time

> Britain, France, and other entente powers entered into series of secret agreements that outlined plans for the orderly partition of the Ottoman Empire. One such agreement, the Sykes–Picot agreement of 1916, stipulated the division of the Arab provinces of the empire into areas of direct and indirect British and French control.[28]

The partition of the region was the concluding, but not the preferred, achievement of the Arab Revolution against the Ottoman Empire in 1916, which was fueled by cultural, economic and political motivations. The Arab nationalist elites, and mainly from religious minorities from Syria, Lebanon, Egypt and Iraq, had supported the Arab Revolution against the Ottomans in order to establish the Great Arab State based on the notion of Arabism. Antony Smith argued, "Throughout the nineteenth century and well into the twentieth century, nationalism was found wherever native elites fought to overthrow foreign imperial and colonial administrations".[29] The Ottoman Empire was not an imperialist administration, but had neglected the Arab provinces in many aspects, particularly in education and developments and relying on non-Arab in management and governance. However, it was conceived by the Arab nationalistic[30] elites as a foreign power and had to end. On the contrary and from an Islamic perspective, the

[28] James Gelvin, *Divided Loyalties*, California University Press, California, 1998, p.24.

[29] Andy Smith, *Nationalism and Modernism*, Routledge, London, 1998, p.1.

[30] The Arab Nationalism is a term that centralized on two pillars; Arab identity and Islam religion. The Arab Nationalists believe in building a modern untied

Ottoman Empire was not a foreign power as there is no difference between Arab and non-Arab, nor between White and Black in Islam.

Most of the Arab provinces stayed under the control of the Ottoman Empire for more than three hundred years. Some of them remained under the direct influence of the Ottoman Empire for four hundred years, such as Syria. Therefore, the dismemberment of the Ottoman Empire caused social, cultural and political crises for the people in the Arab provinces, especially *Bilad Asham* (Syria, Lebanon, Jordan, Sinai Peninsula and Palestine) and Iraq. Nevertheless, one of the most lasting crises was the identity crisis. The disintegration of the Ottoman Empire, which was the last Islamic state (traditionally) exploded the greatest identity crisis, most harming and long lasting in the history of the Arab world.[31]

Syria, which at time included Lebanon, was declared as an independent state on 8 March 1920 during King Faisal's short reign, but on 24 July 1920 the French Mandate forces entered Damascus, starting the colonization period. Meanwhile, Iraq and Palestine, including Jordan and many provinces in the Arab Peninsula, went under complete British rule immediately after the Great War. Egypt was under British rule since 1882. Tunisia, Algeria and Morocco were under French rule, but Libya was under the Italians.

The Colonization Period. The Arabs found themselves after 1918 not just divided, but ruled by external imperialist powers. They plunged into a triple dilemma: 1) They have been divided into territorial states rather than having their sought-after united Great Arab nation-state; 2) They were ruled by external powers; and 3) They had fallen under the direct influence of imperialism. The region was reshaped on the basis of a nation-state system, and values and institutions of the modern civil state were installed in these new states. Roger Owen observed:

Arab country in the region represents the Arab nation as a whole crossing the geographical and unoriginal boundaries.

[31] Burhan Ghaluion, *The Arab Ordeal: The State against the Nation*, CAUS, Beirut, 2003, p.58.

> The new states were also given new bureaucracies and a new emphasis on homogeneity and equality. There was now to be one center of authority, issuing standard rules and regulations which were supposed to be applied equally to all those who lived within its boundaries as citizens.[32]

Colonial powers such as France had given preference to some religious groups, mainly the minorities, and recruited them in *Les Armée du Levant,* and guaranteed their representativeness in the parliaments as well as in the governments. Les Armee du Levant constituted the core of the military institutions for the new states after the independence. Therefore, the new states went through fundamental transformation, it was the greatest in their history after Islam. Fred Halliday stated: "Although the colonial period was a matter of decades only, it nonetheless had significant impact on politics and society, building as it did on centuries of informal influence".[33] During the period of colonization, the colonizers tried to create modern state institutions, forging national identity and prompting secularism in the new-formed states.[34] The Europeans established institutions that were based on liberalism rooted in their own societies; that is, citizenship rule of law, and rational administration.[35] Despite promoting the values of a modern civil state, mass politics and real political representation was not genuine. The rule of oligarchy prevailed during this period. The influential families during the Ottoman Empire remained powerful and adapted themselves to the new political changes. In Syria, many families changed their loyalties from being pro-Ottomans to being pro-French in order to preserve their interests. Such conditions created an urban aristocratic and

---

[32] Roger Owen, *State, Power, and Politics in the Making of the Modern Middle East*, Routledge, New York, 1994, p.13.

[33] Fred Halliday, *The Middle East in International Relations*, Cambridge University Press, Cambridge, 2005, p.83.

[34] Ibid, p.87.

[35] Nicola Pratt, *Authoritarianism in the Arab World*, Lynner Rienner Publishers, USA, 2007, p.27.

rural land-owning class controlling the political power in these new states.

The Gulf States were under the direct influence of the Western powers, mainly Britain for almost half a century. They did not undergo any sort of ideological mobilization. In fact, there was no anti-colonization struggle in the first place. However, the wave of Arab nationalism that stormed the Arab world heavily pushed their movement toward independence from Western direct control. The Gulf Sheikhdoms have been established as rentier states. This was an important element of sustaining authoritarianism in their countries, particularly after the price boom of oil. In the words of Matthew Grey:

> The rentier state is supposedly autonomous from society. Provided it allocates a minimum amount of wealth to society—presumably a sum similar to what the domestic economy in a wealthy extractive state would produce—then the state is free to do what it wishes with the remaining wealth. Further, the state also need not concern itself with domestic bases of support or legitimacy either: the population in effect is "bought off", with democratic input sacrificed by society in exchange for a share of the rental wealth accruing to the state from abroad.[36]

Post Colonization. The Arab people, after a long violent and political struggle, were able eventually to purge their countries from the Western occupying forces, but they could not abolish the Western political social, and economic system that had been installed in their counties during the period of colonization. In fact, they were involved after independence in a complicated process of accomplishing and completing the state-building strategy, which had been initiated and engineered by the colonizers on the basis of

[36] Matthew Gray, *A Theory of "Late Rentierism" In the Arab States of the Gulf*, Center for International and Regional Studies, Georg Town University, Qatar, 2011. http://www12.georgetown.edu/sfs/qatar/cirs/MatthewGrayOccasional Paper.pdf

the nation-state system. It is a system has never been genuinely established. For instance, Syria since the independence in 1946 was a state without being a nation-state, a political entity without being a political community.[37] The colonizers left the new states after violent struggles (mainly in the rural areas) and political struggle through the urban-based class. However, the imposed state system has remained, and every state was suffering from critical internal crises such as weak civil and governmental institutions. Moreover, the class division and the rural-urban contrasts were deepening in the society. Jacques Weulersse wrote:

> The antagonism between urban and rural people reaches such an extent that one can almost speak of two different populations co-existed within the same political frame but without intermingling. The peasant pays all the costs of this antagonism, because the economic and social structure is based on the incontestable primacy of the cities.[38]

Moreover, the true freedom fighters that struggled against the colonizers have been disregarded and neglected politically after the independence. In fact, politics and power were centered in the hands of the urban-based class in alliance with the huge landowners in the rural areas. An alliance had huge Western support and influence. However, political instability has prevailed, threatening the failure of the newly independent states. In fact, the political turbulence in these new states reflected the enormous weakness of the state as a social political entity. There were great politics going on, but not great institutions nor strong parties. Syria established a constitution in 1950, but there were no strong institutions able to enforce it, so the military never had any respect toward the constitution. Nazih Ayubi believed that the Arab state was overstated, he argued:

---

[37] Moshe Ma'oz *Attempts at Creating a Political Community in Modern Syria,* The Middle East Journal, Vol.26, No.4, Autumn 1972, pp.389–404.

[38] Jacques Weulersse, *Paysans de Syrie et du Proche Orient*, Paris, 1946, p.85.

> The Arab state is not a natural growth of its own socio-economic history or its own culture and intellectual tradition. It is a fierce state has frequently resorted to raw coercion in order to preserve itself, but it is not a strong state because (a) it lacks—to varying degree of course—the infrastructure power that enables states to penetrate society effectively through mechanisms such as taxation; and (b) it lacks ideological hegemony that would enable it to forge a historic social bloc that accepts the legitimacy of the ruling stratum.[39]

The frequent military coups in Syria after the independence reflected the fact of a weak state in the country, so the Baath Party was able to hijack the country through a revolution from above, which was carried out by some officers in the army on 8 March 1963. This revolution from above tried to establish a strong state. It responded significantly to the rooted crises in the society for decades and maybe for a century. It also promoted social and secular values, minimizing the gap between the rural and urban areas, and between religious groups in the country. Significant achievements boosted its roots in the country such as land reform, free education and free health services. All these achievements, which were associated with loyal institutions, have sustained the states and the new regimes. Moreover, the regimes adopted a foreign policy that boosted their legitimacy internally and regionally. Thus, the new states became much stronger and more stable, but at the expense of civil liberty, democracy and religion. They imposed a dominant ideology strengthening the new ruling elite as well as the state.

After the independence, the state formation and power consolidation in the Arab world went through different means in the republics and the monarchies:

---

[39] Nazih Ayubi, *Over-Stating the Arab State*, Turis & Co Ltd, London, 2009, p.3.

> In the monarchies, rentier economies and tribal loyalty were the main instruments to consolidate the regimes, while in the republics, they consolidated power after concentrating it in the hands of the new ruling elite through a single-party rule and through a neo-patrimonial system, which implies informal clientelism. However, the military in both the republics and monarchies constitutes the safety valve for the regimes in the Arab world.

The formation of a state in Syria, for instance, went through big complexities such as different identities, lack of common ideology, unbalanced demography, social incoherence and economic centralization. Syria remained a fragile country and transferred to be an arena for regional and international struggle in the Middle East after the independence. The situation started to shift over since 1963, where the Eighth of March Revolution has laid the ground for a common ideology for the country, the Baath Party's ideology, but at the expenses of religion, ethnicity, plurality, liberty and democracy. Islamism and other competing ideologies were suppressed. The Baath Party somehow united the country on a common ideology. Such unity began to crack and wobble when the Baath ideology was found to be bankrupt. It started to be empty slogans rather than real policies and words rather than actions, so the needs for upgrading authoritarianism was crucial for regime survival at this stage.

The Cultural Factor

Is the culture of Arabs and Muslims a culture of authoritarianism? In other words, do Arabs and Muslims have social structural limitations that validate and vindicate authoritarianism? Are Arabs and Muslims susceptible to authoritarianism? The most prominent Muslim scholar Youssef al-Qradawi believes the opposite, and argues that Islam does not accept authoritarianism. However, there are two main loyalties prevailing among the Arab countries: tribal loyalty and religious loyalty.

Tribalism. People do belong to their tribes before belonging to their state and to their fellow citizens in the country. Citizenship comes after their tribal affiliation and their tribal loyalty. This loyalty has certain commitments on the tribe members and creates good benefits for them in return. A man in the Gulf countries or where tribal society is strong does not feel himself as a citizen in a modern state, but rather as a member of a wide tribal coalition, where he submits his loyalty to the leader and in return gets his share of the booty.[40] The leader of the tribe has an ultimate and appeasing authority over members that may count in some cases up to 2 million members. Every member respects the leader's opinion and obeys his decisions. In return, every member has a certain share from the benefits that the leader is having or gaining. Nevertheless, if the tribe is a social power and a control mechanism to maintain the social system and avoid chaos, then political tribalism is more about allegiance and loyalty to the regimes and royal families. Tribal loyalty stem from solidarity (Asabiya),[41] where Ibn Khaldoun considered it as the fundamental base for any reign. "Reign exists only through superiority, and superiority only through Asabiya."[42]

In the Arab monarchies such as Saudi Arabia, Jordan, United Arab Emirates, etc. the brutal security apparatus cannot be produced and then secure its function except through producing the tribal and privileged solidarity and be used as a cement to cohere these modern states' apparatus from inside. In such an apparatus, some key inner elements do exist to secure the unity of the authority, and the continuation of the state.[43] Presidents and kings in the Arab world can secure the loyalty of the whole tribe through appeasing its leaders and buying loyalty. A mutual

---

[40] Muhammad Ghabbash, *Over-Absolute Authority and Over-Incapable Society*, Aljazeera.net. 3 October 2004, viewed 12 November 2012. http://www.aljazeera.net/specialfiles/pages/480646bb-029c-43bb-bee6-d10db94abe22.

[41] Asabiya: a bond stemming from a blood relationship.

[42] Ibin Khaldoun, *The Introduction*, Dar Al-Arqam, Beirut, 2001, p.161.

[43] Ghaluion, op, cit, p.235–236.

relationship based on benefits in return for loyalty is a circle that could stay forever.

Moreover, the relationship between the tribe and the regime has developed from a mutual interest relationship into a partnership. In other words, tribal leaders and members did not only become loyal to the regime, but in fact they became part of it and have the interest to defend it to the last minute.

Overall, tribalism does not only guarantee loyalty and maintain it, but in fact it does freeze the society and foil any attempt toward any change or progress. The delicate overlapping tribal relationship between the leader and his adherents and its political commitments are very effective to satisfy both of them, and to keep opponents' voices unheard and to eliminate the gaps between social classes due to the tribal loyalty. This will lead to preserving underdevelopment and preventing progress, and make the country unable to confront foreign challenges without a foreign help.[44]

In Syria, the tribal society is a major and influential society, particularly in Aljazeera province, a vital province for Syria's food and water security, and for its rich oil fields as well. Tribes in Syria extend beyond borders and have family connections in Iraq and the Arab Peninsula. Therefore, winning their loyalty is very essential for the regime's stability and its persistence. The Baath Party, in an attempt to be a dominant common ideological framework for the society and the state in Syria, disregarded tribalism and sectarianism as mentioned in its theoretical principles. Article (15) in the Baath Party Constitution states: "The Arab Nationalism is the only bond between the people in the Arab countries, which ensures harmony between all of them, and overcome sectarianism, tribalism, racism, and regionalism".[45] Nevertheless, Hafiz Assad did not ignore the influential role of tribal loyalty to stabilize and sustain his regime. He created an excellent balanced relationship between the regime and the tribal leaders based on mutual interests. Many tribal leaders

[44] Khaldoun al-Naqeeb, *The Struggle between Democracy and Tribalism*, Dar Al-Saqee, Beirut. 1996, p.22.

[45] http://www.baathparty.org/index.php?option=com_content&view=article&id=3:3&catid=7&Itemid=102&lang=ar.

were backed by the regime to gain the membership of the People's Assembly. A membership gives a more prestigious position and secures more interests. Hafiz Assad granted great privileges to the tribes and sects leaders in Syria.[46] The regime tried to invest in this strong mutual relationship to suppress the revolution in 2011. He achieved some success in some tribes, but failed with some others. Most tribes were divided in between the regime and the revolution. This division has diluted the strong weight of tribes in Syria in supporting the regime or the revolution.

Religion (Islam). The link between Islam and authoritarianism has always been an important issue for many scholars. Marsha Posusney claims, "The broader, and prevailing culture theory for authoritarianism in the Middle East links it to the Islamic religion that dominates the region".[47] Moreover, both Bernard Lewis and Samuel Huntington believe that Islam and democracy are incompatible with each other, since democracy is a Western value. Although the Arab-Muslim culture is unharmonious with democracy, as Bernard Lewis always argues, it does not mean it endorses or justifies authoritarianism. Sheikh Youssef al-Qaradawi has passionately welcomed the Arab Spring. In an interview with Al-Nahar TV, he stated, "I supported all Arab Spring revolutions; in Syria, Yemen, Libya, Tunisia, and Egypt."[48] In another statement he said: "We oppose all kinds of dictators, in fact, we antagonize them whether they are religious, military, or having a Western style."[49] In order to reach a conclusion about

---

[46] Alaa al-Deen al-Khatib, "The Day when Hafiz Assad Passed Away", http://www.ahewar.org/m/s.asp?aid=407097&r=25&cid=0&u=&i=0&q=, viewed on 15 May 2014.

[47] Marsha Posusney, "The Middle East's Democracy Deficit", in *Authoritarianism in the Middle East*, Posusney & Angrist (ed), Lynne Rienner Publishers, London, 2005, p.5.

[48] Meeting with al-Qaradawi, television program, Al-Nahar TV, 26 January 2012.

[49] Yousef al-Qaradawi, Y. "*We Oppose the Dictator",* 24 November 2011, viewed on 15 December 2011. http://www.qaradawi.net/news/5364–2011–11–24–10–23–16.html.

these concerns, it is very important to examine the three main Islamic schools prevailing in the Middle East and North Africa: Sufism, Salafism, and Shiism.

Sufism has two divisions or schools of thought within it, and they are commonly referred to as traditional Sufism and moderate Sufism.

The traditional followers believe that politics are almost abandoned, but when there is involvement, the views and observation of the sheikh are to be followed and implemented by his followers without question. In the event of election, for instance, the sheikh and his followers have one decision, which is the sheikh's decision. They vote according to the sheikh's opinion, but not to their opinions individually. Therefore, this school presents a hotbed for authoritarianism; it is a "simple instrument of state domination"[50] as Jean Luizard put it, since the authority is able to guarantee the loyalty of prominent Sufi sheikhs in the country. This school is more about a personality cult, so the sheikh is obeyed in his views and his judgments in social and political affairs. It is very similar to the tribal system, but the loyalty here is to the sheikh, but not to the tribe's leader, and there are no rewards or benefits. The rewards are in the hereafter, as they believe. Muntaser al-Oqsury explains: The sheikh is obeyed, leaning on his affiliation to the Prophet House or to the Awlyaa.[51] He inherits the position from his family, and he represents the head of an organization consisting of a mixture of different groups of people in terms of gender and age. The sheikh is the main symbol, so the whole organization centered around him as an inspired and inspiring leadership.[52]

Meanwhile, the moderate followers of Sufism concentrate on the spiritual aspect of Islam in their lives more than on the personal cult. In fact, cult of personality is less observable in this school than

[50] Pierre-Jean Luizard "Le Role des Confreries Soufies dans le Systeme Politique Egyptien", in Monde Arabe Maghreb, Machrek 131 (jan/mars 1991): 26–53.

[51] Awlyaa: Individuals that are not prophets, but very close to Allah.

[52] Muntaser al-Oqsury, "Sufism: from Belief to Politics", Al-Ahram.org, 28 July 2013. http://digital.ahram.org.eg/articles.aspx?Serial=1361371&eid=6888.

the traditional Sufism school. Therefore, authoritarianism has no strong base in such an environment. They are involved in politics, in the government and in violent struggle against the rulers and against occupying forces. Sheikh Hasan al-Banna, the founder of the Muslim Brotherhood, is a great example of this school. Although he used to belong to Al-Hasafia *Tariqa* (school or order), he established a political movement and had political aspirations. Moreover, he participated in war against Israel. In Syria, the involvement of some Sufi sheikhs and their followers in the armed uprising in the 1980s motivated the regime to target them and murder their leaders, as it was in the case of murdering *Sheikh al-Mashaykh of the Rifa'iyya*[53] in Aleppo,[54] as Fred De Jong explained. Moreover, Marwan Hadid, who established and led the Fighting Vanguard in the mid-1970s fighting Hafiz Assad's regime was belonging to the Sufi school. It is very important to note here that both traditional and moderate schools of Sufism hold antagonistic positions toward all schools of Salafism.

Salafisim is the mainstream faction of Islam prevailing in the Arab Peninsula and some parts of North Africa. In the past few years, the Salafi faction in Egypt has grown to a level that can compete with Sufism and the Muslim Brotherhood too. "The Salafis call for a return to the example of the forefathers amounted to a discrediting of latter-day tradition, which described as cherishing mystical superstition as well as scholarly stagnation and political quietism,"[55] as Itzchack Wiseman stated. Salafism school is divided into three main schools: traditional Salafis, reformist Salafis and Jihadists Salafis.

Traditional Salafis are more concerned with the return to the example of the forefathers (the Prophet and his companions), so

---

[53] Rifa'iyya is one of many *tariqas* (schools or orders) in Sufism.

[54] Fred De Jong, "Les Confreries Mystiques Musulmanes au Machreq Arabe: Centres de Gravite, Signes de Declin et de Renaissance." In Les Ordres Mystiques dans l'Islam: Cheminements et Situation Actuelle. Popovic, A. and Veinstein, G. (eds.). Paris: EHESS, 1986.

[55] Tizchack Wiseman, "The Politics Of Popular Religion: Sufis, Salafis, and Muslim Brothers In 20th Century Hama", International Journal of Middle East Studies, Volume 37, Issue 01 February 2005, pp.39–58.

politics is an alien concept for them. They support the rulers as long as these rulers permit and allow people to perform the prayer. Until recently, they opposed calls for political change whether it was by peaceful means or violent means. Violent movements against the rulers are called Al-Khawarej by them, in reference to the people who rebelled against the Imam Ali, the fourth caliph after the Prophet Muhammad; he was his cousin and son of law. Non-violent movements are called liberal Westernized movements. This trend of Salafism has a big role in legitimizing authoritarianism and encouraging it to the point where rulers begin to subjugate the people. The Syrian regime never welcomed or tolerated traditional Salafism despite of its full submission to the ruler. In fact, many traditional Salafis were sentenced to three years in jail. The regime's concern about traditional Salafis is due to three reasons: 1) The fear of traditional Salafis to develop into Jihadists Salafis; 2) Salafism views Alawis as non-Muslims; 3) Salafism is an enemy of Sufism, which the formal religious institution in the country belongs to.

Reformist Salafis believe in gradual and peaceful change and reform, so violence or public mobilization is not acceptable due to the consequent dangers. They participate in elections and call for a relaxation in law concerning women's rights, for instance. The reformist Salafism is a community-engaging movement, which works for reform and change through participating in the civil society institutions.[56]

Concerning Jihadists Salafis (Jihadists), their ideology constituted the seeds for Al-Qaeda and ISIS. They perceive violence (Jihad) as the only means to overthrow regimes, liberate the occupied lands, challenge the dominating international order and to establish the Islamic State. Their main concept is loyalty and disownment (*Al-Walaa Wa- Al-Albaraa*). They do not recognize current regimes, so, for example, they were behind the assassination of Anwar al-Sadat, the former president of Egypt. They fought the Saudi regime

[56] Bassam Naser, "Reading in the ideology of Reformist Salafism", Al-Ghad, 30 June 2005, viewed on 2 November 2012.http://alghad.com/index.php/article/33186.html.

as well as the regimes in Algeria, in Mali, Somalia and now in Iraq and Syria. Most factions of this trend act now in the name of Al-Qaeda or the Islamic State (IS). They are less popular than the traditional Salafis, but they are working globally and cross-nations in an attempt to transfer themselves into a counter-globalization front.[57] It presents itself as the greatest challenge for the ruling regimes as well as the international system. In Syria, Jihadists were eradicated during the regime campaign in Hama and elsewhere in the country in 1982 and after. The events of 1982 contributed heavily to empowering the security services to eliminate Jihadists from Syria and to strengthen the regime's control over the country as never before. However, during Bashar Assad's era, some Jihadist activities occurred suddenly in the country, such as the attempt to blow up the American embassy in Damascus in 2006.

Regarding *Shiism*, there is no great difference whether Shias do follow *Velayat-el Faqih,* the rule and judgment of the cleric, or not, as long as all of them follow and obey their Ayatollahs. Therefore, having an agreement with the Ayatollahs will guarantee the submission of their followers. This is the experience of Paul Bremer, the American governor in Iraq in the first year of the occupation. He always preferred to deal with Shias rather than dealing with Sunnis, because Shias have an address, which is their Ayatollahs, while Sunnis have no address[58] Cherif Bassiouni argues: "The Shia religious hierarchy plays a determining role in interpreting the Qur'an. This role reinforces their spiritual and temporal influence in Shia society."[59] Many Salafis regard Shiism as a sect out of Islam.

Overall, religion and tribalism were the most important social forces that leaders in the Arab world have greatly manipulated in order to establish and sustain their authoritarian rule. Arabs can be mobilized or demobilized through the unique awareness to

---

[57] Abed al-Jabri, "From Wahabisim to Reformist Salafism then to Jihadisim", viewed on 10 November 2012.http://www.aljabriabed.net/terrorism17.html.

[58] L. Paul Bremer III, *My year in Iraq: The Struggle to Build a Future of Hope,* Threshold Editions, New York, 2006, p.380.

[59] Cherif Bassiouni, "Schools of Thoughts in Islam", The Middle East Institute, 24 January 2012. http://www.mei.edu/content/schools-thought-islam

their national identity in tribal and religious loyalty frameworks.[60] Religion can give the ruler double legitimacy, legal legitimacy and religious legitimacy, so authoritarian regimes always had vital interests to support traditional Sufism or traditional Salafism depending on the country. In Syria, the regime supported traditional Sufism, but in Saudi Arabia the House of Saud has allied with traditional Salafism since the formation of the kingdom.

Force and Fear

The politics of force and fear is dominant and common and still is in the republics as well as in the monarchies. Inhumane means are used by the regimes in order to suppress the opposition and horrify the populace. Almost in every country in the Arab world, one or more massacres have been committed by the regimes against their opposition. The Massacres of Palmyra Prison in 1980 and the Massacre of Hama in 1982[61] in Syria had a great impact on the people psychologically, socially and politically. In his novel *The Cochlea*, Mr. Mustapha Khalifa[62] recorded the images of massacres and tortures that he witnessed inside Palmyra Prison for thirteen years. Hafiz Assad has always proved throughout his long years in power that he belongs to this school when dealing with his opponents and opposition, starting from the coup of 1966 until his death in 2000. Torture to death, imprisonment, rape and all kinds of abuses were the way to deal with the opposition. All the opposition, Islamists, communists or Baathists have endured such treatment. He established a very strong security system spying on the people, the society and the state, creating an atmosphere of intimidation and fear among all Syrians and an environment of distrust among every family in

---

[60] Al-Naqeeb, op, cit, p.19.

[61] Kathrin Nina Wiedl, "The Hama Massacre – reasons, supporters of the rebellion, consequences", A seminar paper at Ben-Gurion University of the Negev, 25 September 2006.

[62] Mustapha Khalifa is a Christian Syrian films producer, he was imprisoned in the Palmira prison for 13 years.

Syria, causing great social problems. The lessons of Palmyra Prison and the city of Hama stayed present in the mind of every Syrian for decades and have been taught to the younger generations, making Syrians people intimidated to talk about politics privately as well as publicly. During his era, not a single peaceful demonstration was allowed or seen in the streets of any city in Syria, where demonstrations used to be a part of the Syrian's daily life during the French occupation and in the era after the independence. Moreover, Hafiz Assad reinforced his authority through a cult of personality. His image has been transformed from a president to god or half-god, copying the same policy of Mummer Gadhafi in Libya. He wanted to be more than a symbol for the nation and forever *lil-abad*, making Syrians believe that no existence or future for Syria was possible without Assad. Lisa Wedeen observed this phenomenon, she stated: "Political cults work to generate compliance by producing, through symbolic display, the potential for coercive power while economizing on its actual use."[63] Hafiz Assad succeeded to build a barrier or a wall of fear among Syrian people stronger than the Berlin Wall reflected to be part of their culture for almost forty years. Arabs used to speak about Syrians as the most suppressed and fearful people in the region, as they could not attend a single demonstration for decades and have accepted the humiliating inheritance of power from Hafiz to Bashar without any kind of resentment or a sign of opposition. Brutality was the direct and effective means to impose authoritarianism in Syria. Security services have penetrated all aspects of the society and the state constituting a tight control over the people. This made observers rule out any possibility for a popular uprising in Syria, even after the Tunisian and Egyptian revolutions in 2011. Therefore, breaking the barrier of fear was the beginning of eliminating authoritarianism and the starting point for change in the Arab world, and in Syria in particular. I think hopelessness and the unprecedented bravery among young people was a major factor contributing to breaking the barrier of fear. It was such a miracle.

[63] Lisa Wedeen, *Ambiguities of Domination*, University of Chicago Press, Chicago, 1999, p.156.

Arab Nationalism

The seeds of Arab nationalism, which were sown in the Arab word in the mid-19th century by two Lebanese Christian pioneers, Butrus al-Bustani and Nasif al-Yazeji, paid off in the 1940s, when Arab people were looking forward to their independence from the foreign powers. It had its peak in the late 1950s and early 1960s during Jamal Abdel Nasser's rule and after the Suez War in 1956.

The unity between Syria and Egypt in 1958 was one of its greatest results. However, the break up of that union did not undermine its strength and prevalence in the Arab world. In fact, Arabism stayed to dominate politics and public aspirations in the Arab counties, especially in Syria where the Baath Party trinity (Unity, Freedom, Socialism) was glorified ever day in the country. Syria was the beating heart of Arabism that was not only the Baath slogan, but a public belief too.

After the death of Jamal Abdel Nasser, no one was qualified to champion Arab nationalism more than Hafiz Assad, so he exploited the overwhelming public trend among the Syrian people toward Arabism and their aspiration toward unity with other Arab countries. He engineered foreign policy on the Arabism foundation. Even when he allied with Iran against Iraq during the war in the 1980s, he rationalized his decision with the claim that the Iranian Revolution was an asset to the Arab nation, where both were struggling against global imperialism and had a great common goal, which was liberating Palestine from Israeli occupation. But in 1991, when Syria allied with the United States and its partners in the war against Iraq, Syrian people started doubting the authenticity of Arabism in Hafiz Assad's discourse, and thus in his foreign policy. His ever-unjustifiable stance to join an international coalition led by the United States to strike Iraq was a flagrant contradiction to the notion of Arabism and a blatant breach to the basic ideology of the Baath Party, which conceived of the West as the imperialist enemy.

Adopting Arabism accompanied suppressing Islamism, because Islamism is an alternative political framework for the state and the society. Adopting Arabism meant also marginalizing and persecuting the non-Arab population in the country, such as

Kurds, Turkmans and Assyrians, who constitute more than 18% of the population. Hundreds of thousands of Kurds were denied Syrian nationality until 2011, when Bashar Assad tried to appease them by providing an attractive package of concessions in order to stop them joining the uprising.

The Struggle with Israel

The Palestinian issue has been the central issue for the Arab people since 1948, and the core of their daily life and politics, and where their foreign policy starts and ends. Many Syrian officers have participated in the Salvation Army in Palestine such as Adnan al-Malki, Adib al-Shishakly and Amin al-Hafiz. Moreover, Abed al-Karim al-Nehlawi (the officer who led the coup against the union with Egypt) stated, "The liberation of Palestine was the only motivation for me to join the army and go against my wishes to study medicine."[64] The defeat of the Arabs in 1948 was humiliating and disastrous, and had its implications on the whole Arab world. Internal instability such as coups, political turmoil and wars occurred.

In Syria, the imposition of the emergency law in the aftermath of the Eighth of March Revolution was justified on the basis of the conflict with Israel. However, the defeat of 1948 was followed by a shattering and calamitous defeat in 1967, where Israel occupied the eastern side of Jerusalem and territories in Egypt, Syria and Jordan. Hafiz Assad manipulated the war with Israel to sustain his legitimacy and his authoritarian rule. Perthes observed this degree of legitimacy;

> Not surprisingly, militarization and the pervasive reminders of the state of war and the country's frontline status have had an important legitimating function for the Syrian regime. As noted, the demands of the battle have done more than serve to justify heavy-handed rule and limitations of personal freedom.[65]

[64] Witness, television program, Aljazeera, 24 January 2010.

[65] Volkers Perthes, in Steven Heydemann(ed), *War, Institutions, and Social Change in the Middle East*, University of California Press, Berkeley, 2000, p.79–112.

Hafez Assad understood the overlapping relationship between sovereignty and identity, or between the state and Arabism. He sustained Syrian sovereignty, but legitimized his leadership through trans-state identity and ideological foreign policy.

In November 1970, Hafiz Assad gained victory over the radical Jedid Baathists as claimed in a coup called the Corrective Movement justified as needing to put aside social revolution to pursue national liberation, and in October 1973 he claimed victory over Israel. "The October War of Liberation (*Harb Tishrin al-Tahririyya*) was seen as the crowning achievement of Assad's regime. This war reflected a new phase in the process of maturation of the Syrian regime and President Assad himself,"[66] according to Eyal Zisser. After the 1973 war, he was nominated from the Baath Party as the hero of both months, October and November (*Batal Al-Tishrinayyn*). He staged an unprecedented platform nationally and regionally, enabling him to present himself and his regime as a Castle of Steadfastness and Confrontation against Israel and its clients in the Arab world, especially after the Camp David Agreement between Egypt and Israel in 1979. But his struggle with Israel concentrated on its clients (according to the regime discourse) such as Yasser Arafat and the Lebanese Forces, rather than on Israel itself. He crushed Yasser Arafat's foothold in Lebanon to an extent that Yasser Arafat himself was quoted as saying: "Sharon of Arab (meaning Hafiz Assad) has besieged us from the land and Sharon of Jews (Ariel Sharon) has besieged us from the sea."[67] Despite his behavior in Lebanon, Hafiz Assad won the hearts and minds of most Syrian and Arab people for being a bitter enemy for Israel and the only remaining leader refusing shameful peace with Israel and challenging the West's will in the region. Mr. Fadi, a

[66] Eyal Zisser, *Assad's Legacy*, C. Hurt & CO, 2001, p.9.

[67] Ahamad Haifawi, "The crimes of Assad Regime Against the Palestinians" Alrased.net, 27 May 2012, viewed 1 December 2012. Article, http://alrased.net/main/articles.aspx?selected_article_no=5685.

worker at *Al-Hariqa* Market in the center of Damascus, stated in May 1997:

> Yes we are not happy economically and struggling a lot in our daily life from the president's policy on economics, but we do appreciate his political heroic stances, he refused to receive Warren Christopher after *Qana* massacre (committed by Israel in Lebanon in May 1997), he is a brave man.[68]

There are three main factors in relation to the struggle with Israel, which have sustained the legitimacy of the Syrian regime and consolidated its authoritarian nature effectively during Hafiz Assad's era and his son Bashar Assad's alike:

1. Concentrating on the Palestinian issue as the center issue for the Arabs. Denouncing the peace agreements between the other Arab countries (Egypt, Jordan and the Palestinian Liberation Authority) and Israel from the Camp David Agreement with Egypt in 1979 to the Oslo Accord with the Palestinian Liberation Authority in 1993, and to the Araba Valley (*Wadi Araba*) Treaty with Jordan in 1994. All of them lacked public support across the Arab countries. Syria criticized these agreements as humiliating, and refused peace with Israel unless it agreed on a comprehensive peace in the region, and agreed on peace for land, but not peace for peace.
2. Supporting the resistance movements in the region such as Hamas, Hezbollah and Al-Jihad Al-Islami is congruent with the public in Syria and across the Arab countries. In return, the resistance movements never gave up praising the Syrian regime for its heroic position against Israel. In the July War in 2006, when Israel launched an offensive attack on Hezbollah and Lebanon, Bashar Assad stood firm, relying on his great alliance with Iran and to some extent with Qatar, criticizing most Arab rulers and describing

---

[68] Interview with the author on 30 May 1997.

them as half men.[69] It was a very great moment for Bashar Assad. In late 2008 and early 2009, when Israel launched an offensive attack on Gaza, the same scenario was repeated. Syria rallied behind Hamas and Al-Jihad Al-Islami, which are Sunnis movements. The regime wanted to send a message that supporting the resistance did not have any connection with identity or ideology, as Hamas does belong to the Muslim Brotherhood while Hezbollah is a Shia sect. This policy boosted the regime legitimacy among the people of the Muslim world and more importantly inside Syria too. Images of Bashar Assad and the Hezbollah leader flooded the shops and streets in Syria after the July War in 2006.

3. American and Israeli support to unpopular opposition such as the Reform Party of Syria led by Farid al-Ghadry has provided the Syrian regime with more public legitimacy. Mr. al-Ghadry visited Israel in 2007, and in May 2011 just after three months of the revolution, he stated that the Israeli flag will fly in the center of Damascus and he pledged to kick out Hamas and the Palestinian factions from Syria.[70] This discourse never enjoys publicity among the Syrian people. Mr. al-Ghadry gained no noticeable support from the Syrian people inside and outside the country. Not just Mr. al-Ghadry, but all the opposition figures who visited Israel after the uprising did not enjoy any kind of public support in Syria, but in fact, met with wide public denunciation.

The struggle with Israel was always the ready pretext for Syria's economic and political failure and to justify internal repression since 1963 and until the present day. Therefore, the regime always considers any activity from the opposition inside or outside Syria as a conspiracy from abroad, especially Israel and the United

[69] Oroubamedia, Bashar Assad describes the kings of Gulf as half men, posted on 29 November 2012, https://www.youtube.com/watch?v=JF7858iCEI8

[70] http://www.factjo.com/pages/fullnews.aspx?id=26805, 06May 2011, viewed on 03 April 2014.

States, as trying to undermine his strong and unbendable stance in defying and resisting the regional ambitions of Israel. Hinnebusch explains, "Syria's relatively great success in the struggle with Israel under Assad goes a long way toward explaining the greater stability of his regime."[71]

It was the well-built legitimacy that boosted the authoritarian rule in Syria that made Bashar Assad so confident of not expecting an uprising in the country following the Tunisian and the Egyptian Revolutions in 2011. In an interview with *Wall Street Journal*, he stated, "The people do not go into an uprising. So it is not only about the needs and not only about the reform. It is about the ideology, the beliefs and the cause that you have,"[72] but he was wrong and stupid.

AUTHORITARIAN UPGRADING

Many emergent internal and external factors have challenged authoritarianism, making the needs for adaptation and change urgent in order to guarantee the survival of the authoritarian regimes. Heydemann explains the concept more soundly:

> Authoritarian upgrading involves reconfiguring authoritarian governance to accommodate and manage changing political, economic, and social conditions. It originated in no small part as a defensive response to challenges confronting Arab autocrats during the past two decades.[73]

[71] Raymond Hinnebusch, *Syria: Revolution from Above*, Routledge, New York, 2001, p.13.

[72] Interview with Syrian President Bashar Assad, the Wall Street Journal, 31 January 2011, viewed on 31 January 2011. http://online.wsj.com/article/SB10001424052748703833204576114712441122894.html

[73] Steven Heydemann,."Upgrading Authoritarianism in the Arab World", Saban Center for Middle East Policy at Brooking Institute, Analyses Paper Number13, October 2007, Washington DC, viewed on 15 December 2012. http://www.brookings.edu/~/media/research/files/papers/2007/10/arabworld/10arabworld.pdf.

Authoritarian upgrading is not an ideology or a form of governance, but in fact a process of gradual limited and in some cases dramatic changes in the policies and rules of administrating the economy, society, the governance systems and including foreign policy. Its aim is to appease the public through contained and controlled policies addressing their grievances. Such policies would strengthen the regime's grip over the country and eventfully sustain it, and secure its survival and continuation. On the other hand, every country introduced different measures in accordance with its demands to escape the risk of internal challenges first, and external challenges second, so they introduce what they are obligated to introduce. The more the regimes feel the threat, the more they should move toward upgrading authoritarianism and offering concessions in order to survive.

Exhausted Authoritarianism

After almost three decades of radical socialist governmental policies in the economy and society (land reform, capitals nationalization, public spending, state subsidies, etc.), the Arab regimes found themselves facing a barrage of problems embodied in great economic and social grievances, with political decay posing a big challenge from within. In the economy, disguised unemployment drained the state economy, inflation rate was rising, the currency lost its value dramatically and there were many more crises. In the society, the rate of unemployment was on the rise, social injustice prevailed, poverty increased, the gap between the rich and poor widened, young people were unable to afford to buy property and get married, and thus marriage age got older, creating extra social problems. The education system was declining due to the lack of funding. Innovations were almost neglected. Scholars had little if any governmental attention or care.[74] The judicial system has lost

[74] Professor Muhyy Al-Deen al-Dasouki was a scholar in mechanics at the University of Damascus, and one of the greatest scholars in the Arab world. He was the first scientist in the Arab world to run engines by electricity, and had a proposal to use water rather than electricity for the same purpose, but could not

its high stature; corruption, nepotism and patronage prevailed. The governmental system became less institutionalized and more personalized. Adopted ideologies were twisted in front of personal interests. However, ideologies showed incapability facing the new challenges. In fact, there was a coup against the long-adopted ideologies. Moreover, ideology reached a stage of bankruptcy; no solutions were offered for the rising economic and social problems. Communism and socialism lost its base among intellectuals in favor of liberalism or Islamism.

In Syria, the remaining base of the Baath Party started to erode after getting confused between the regime discourse of socialism and its neo-liberal policies, which invaded almost every sector in the state. They found themselves alienated in front of the new hegemonic power of capitalism in the county. The Baath Party has lost its status in the county as Phil Sands claimed.[75] Additionally, the state recourses got very low and its ability to fulfill the people's demands became very limited. That was associated with the booming population growth, which propelled the state to open the country for private investments that would shoulder some of the state's duties such as education, health, construction services, etc. In other words, Syria by the beginning of the 1990s reached a point of ideological bankruptcy and ill-functionality putting the state under immense pressure to start a new phase toward neo-liberalism by introducing the Investment Law 10 in 1991.

External Challenges

In addition to the challenges from within, authoritarian regimes faced huge challenges from without and played a significant role in the state of anxiety that already prevailing in the Arab

achieve his project due to terrible financial circumstances and lack of governmental attention.

[75] Phil Sands, "Baath Party Reaches 64 Facing Unprecedented Challenge", The National, 07 April 2011, viewed 10 April 2011. http://www.thenational.ae/news/world/middle-east/baath-party-reaches-64-facing-unprecedented-challenge%20%20#page2.

monarchies as well as in the Arab republics. The forces of globalization, including free trade and free market forces, the penetration of state sovereignty and the cultural invasion were unavoidable. Furthermore, the information revolution after the 1990s transformed the whole world, making interactions between nations more common. The Arab countries were not capable of continuing to monopolize the information-feeding process for their citizens anymore. Moreover, their grip on controlling the society started to contract. Some countries tried to deter these forces and immunize their people, but they failed. Just a few years after the resounding fall of the Soviet Union, the Arab regimes started to move gradually from the immunity policy to the adaptation strategy in front of these new forces in order to contain them and to maintain the regimes' control over the people and on the land.

Upgrading Authoritarianism in the Arab World

It is very important to focus on authoritarian upgrading in the Arab world and its function, and its role to sustain the regimes in this region through varying the resources of power they needed to survive and continue. It was an adaptation policy in front of new challenges. Heydemann so comments:

> What is emerging in the Arab world, therefore, is a hybrid form of authoritarianism. It combines tired and-true strategies of the past-coercion, surveillance, patronage, corruption, and personalism-with innovations that reflect the determination of authoritarian élites to respond aggressively to the triple threat of globalization, markets, and democratization.[76]

Some Arab countries started this process as early as the 1970s, such as Egypt, where former president Anwar al-Sadat started different economic and political programs, opening the country to the market economy and privatization, and introducing some democratic measures in the governance system. In other Arab

[76] Steven Heydemann, Upgrading Authoritarianism in the Arab World, Saban Centre for Middle East Policy at Brooking Institute 13 October 2007.

countries such as Syria, authoritarian upgrading formally was born in 1991 with the introduction of Investment Law 10.

Heydemann identified five features as primary elements of authoritarian upgrading. All of these elements are evident in varying combinations in major Arab states, including Algeria, Egypt, Jordan, Morocco, Syria, Tunisia and Yemen. They are discussed below:[77]

Appropriating and Containing Civil Societies

As an indication of openness and a move toward democracy and freedom, the Arab regimes approved the activity of civil societies and non-governmental organizations (NGOs) in their countries such as human-rights organizations, the liberty of women programs, trade unions and some charitable religious organizations. They allowed the establishment and activities of new political parties, they approved more religious freedom and they applied some relaxation on media control. However, such organizations remained controlled and contained, and were closed off when their activities became a threat to the regimes. In Syria, civil society organizations proliferated significantly after 2000, after Bashar al-Asad ascended to power, but the reflection on domestic politics was minimal or nil.

Managing Political Contestation

As a move toward political participation, most of the Arab countries have undergone changes in the electoral system, including some Gulf monarchy states. Despite being very modest developments, it was noteworthy compared to what the system was before. However, these changes kept the regimes' control over the opposition and over the country as a whole as tight as before. Andreas Scheduler Explains:

> Today the most common form of political regime in the developing world is electoral authoritarianism. Electoral authoritarian regimes hold regular multiparty elections for

[77] Ibid.

> parliament and the chief executive. Yet they violate liberal-democratic minimum standards of freedom, fairness, and integrity in so systematic and profound ways as to render elections instruments of authoritarian rule, rather then instruments of democracy.[78]

In Egypt in 2005, for instance, the Muslim Brotherhood achieved their biggest gains ever in their political life before the revolution in 2011. They secured 88 seats in the People's Assembly. Mr. Ayman Noor from Al- Ghad Party had the opportunity to enter the race for presidency against Hosni Mubarak, but he was imprisoned after losing the race for perjury charges. The charges he had never encountered before entering the presidency race. This unprecedented political participation in Egypt did not make any tangible or real changes either in the Egyptian political life or on the public. The emergency law stayed in place, corruption increased, governmental policies of selling the public sector to the regime loyalists could not be halted. Police forces increased their control and brutality over the people. Khalid Said, a young man from Alexandria, had been tortured to death in the street in June 2010 by two policemen, an event that was considered by a lot of Egyptians as the spark for huge public anger that eventually led to the Egyptian revolution on 25 January 2011.

In 2003, during the local elections in Syria, the government lifted the Baath Party leadership privilege as a condition in the contest. To chair the local councils did not require Baathist membership any more. The regime distanced the Baathists, but supported and installed its independent clients. No candidate was allowed to run the election without an approval from the security authorities.

The Arab regimes had three aims from introducing political participation: first, responding to public anger and pressure for political reform; second, to elicit clashes and disputes in between the opposition parties and individuals over seats and the decision

[78] Andreas Schedler, Electoral Authoritarianism: The Dynamics of Unfree Competition, The Dynamics of Un-free Competition, Lynne Rienner Publishers, London, 2006, p.1.

of participation; and thirdly, the least important aim for such regimes, is improving its picture internationally. Some of these aims have been achieved in reality by the Syrian regime in the local elections of 2003, so the fermented electoral campaign led to some clashes in between the different candidates' supporters. Most of them were busy making reports against each other to the security authorities on false bases in order to harm each other, and to demonstrate their loyalty to the regime. The same scenario was repeated in 2007, but with more state control over the elections as the Baath leadership in the local elections was reinstated.

Capturing the Benefits of Selective Economic Reform

Since regimes reached ideological bankruptcy, the social base started to collapse. Therefore, finding a new socio-economic base to replace the old one was required to consolidate the regime and to secure it from any downfall. The regimes found a new base in their supporters by strengthening them through economic advantages. Heydemann explains: "Across the region selective processes of economic liberalization provide enhanced economic opportunities for regime supporters, reinforce the social base of authoritarian regimes, and mitigate pressures for comprehensive economic and social reforms."[79] Generally, as Weber argues, "as ideology inevitability declines, regimes must consolidate power through economic rewards to followers."[80] The regime loyalists in Syria have captured most benefits of the neo-liberalization process that Bashar Assad launched in the country. Business empires of some of the president's relatives and loyalists were very much noticeable in the country, especially after the second term of Bashar Assad in 2007.

---

[79] Steven Heydemann, Upgrading Authoritarianism in the Arab World, Saban Centre for Middle East Policy at Brooking Institute, 13 October 2007.

[80] Raymond Hinnebusch, *Syria: Revolution from Above*, Routledge, New York, 2001, p.7.

In Syria, the regime faced its ideological bankruptcy, and mounting public resentment after 20 years of brutal authoritarianism adopting socialism with a surprising move toward neo-liberalism. Hafiz Assad introduced Law 10 of investment in 1991 opening the door toward a new phase in the country. Neo-liberal policies started to invade the economy since the late years of Hafiz Assad until the uprising in 2011, the benefits of such a move were mainly captured by the regime's close loyalists, creating a new structure in the county.

Controlling New Communications Technologies

The Arab regimes were powerless in front of media penetration for their societies as satellite systems entered almost every home in the Middle East. Moreover, openness, and attracting business and investments, require an advanced telecommunications sector. It is the basic environment for the neo-liberalism process in the past two decades. Online banking and fast money transfer, fast internet and advanced communications are very essential for business and investments, small as well as large. Moreover, IT, media and telecommunications were regarded as an aspect of modernization, the dream for people in the Arab world. The Arab regimes tried to benefit from the new development of telecommunications for economic purposes, but they spent a lot of money on introducing monitoring measures. Information access represents the utmost anxiety for the Arab regimes. The role of cassette tapes recording Khomeini speeches and lectures cannot be forgotten in the Iranian Revolution. These regimes proved to be very weak when fighting information access in the age of the information revolution. They had fallen into a major dilemma; the combination between openness and their security, a real challenge that led to a policy of controlling communications technologies. In Syria, communications technologies are still behind compared to some neighboring countries such as Lebanon and Jordan, due to the state's control and relatively strict surveillance over this sector. Only days prior to the Syrian Revolution in 2011, the authorities in Syria lifted the ban on some internet sites such as Facebook.

Diversifying International Linkage

There was no doubt that diversifying international linkage would mitigate the international pressure that might be applied on the regimes from certain countries for certain issues. However, it is difficult to agree with Heydemann when he argued that the Arab authoritarian regimes started thinking Far East in order to escape the Western pressure for more political reform. In fact, such pressure has never been genuine in the first place as the most powerful Western powers have the responsibly for backing many authoritarian regimes in the Middle East and North Africa. Moreover, American and Western military presences or assistance to many regimes in the Arab world make them captive to their will and their interests. The hesitation of the United States to support the public uprising in the Middle East, particularly in Iran in 2009, and in the Arab world in 2011, against the most brutal regimes on earth can back my argument. Mr. Obama welcomed many dictators from the Middle East in the White House, but he never welcomed Mr. Muhammad Morsi or showed great support to him as the first elected president in Egypt and in the Arab world for decades. Muhammad Morsi was deposed by the military in July 2013 with American endorsement.

No doubt the Arab regimes have improved their relationships with Far East countries, especially on the economic level. However, the expanding economies of the Far East countries, their great achievement in the higher education sector and the relatively cheap products and services were the major reasons for countries in the Middle East to diverse their international linkage and turn slightly toward the south east.

After the collapse of the Soviet Union, the populist regimes in the Middle East turned their attention significantly to the West. The relationship between Syria and France, for instance, reached its peak in between 1997 to 2003. Moreover, Bashar Assad visited Britain in 2002, when the drums of war were beating against Iraq by Britain and the United States. It was a strange visit to a country that always was described by the Syrian official media as an imperialists, colonial and pro-Zionist country. "Syrian-French relations began to take a turn of partnership and strategic alliance, and it appeared clearly during the visit of President Chirac to Damascus in1997, and the great hospitality extended to him. Syrian-French relationship has continued at the same pace throughout the subsequent years, where Chirac received Bashar Assad in Paris in 1999 before Bashar came to power."[81]

Moreover, Syria has undergone an international isolation following the assassination of Raffiq al-Hariri, the former Lebanese prime minister, in 2005. However, that isolation was breached on the Western level by the invitation of President Sarkozy of France to President Assad to attend the Union of Mediterranean Submit in Paris in 2008. In 2008 Bashar Assad came back on the international scene with the project of Union for the Mediterranean launched by Nicolas Sarkozy. He was invited to the Union of Mediterranean on July 13, 2008, despite the cooling of Franco–Syrian relations imposed by President Chirac.

The West also reconciled with Qaddafi over the Lockerbie disaster and other problematic issues such as the bombings of a Berlin discotheque. Jack Straw, the British justice secretary at the time, did not distance a business deal involved in the release of Mr. Abdel Basset al-Megrahi, the suspect of the Lockerbie bombing in 2009.

When asked in the interview if trade and BP were factors, Mr. Straw admits: "Yes, [it was] a very big part of that. I'm unapologetic about that… Libya was a rogue state. We wanted to bring it back into the fold. And yes, that included trade because trade is an essential part of it and subsequently there was the BP deal."[82] Ironically Tony Blair, the former British prime minister, became one of his senior personal advisers afterward. Bringing

[81] Hussian Abd al-Aziz, "Is the Syrian-French Relationship Going to Change", VoltairNet.org, 11 June 2007. http://www.voltairenet.org/article149025.html, viewed on 25April 2014.

[82] "Jack Straw admits Lockerbie Bomber's release was Linked to Oil", The Telegraph, 4 September 2009, viewed on 12 November 2012. http://www.telegraph.co.uk/news/politics/6140801/Jack-Straw-admits-Lockerbie-bombers-release-was-linked-to-oil.html.

these authoritarian regimes back into the fold gave them nothing but more international legitimacy and less ethical responsibility over their subjects.

Overall, since the late 1990s until 2011, prior to the uprising, the Syrian regime showed great adaptation toward the forces of globalization and markets, and had manipulated their benefits and features to sustain its authoritarian original nature. Meanwhile, the democratization forces were mainly confronted, but not contained apart from some civil society organizations dealing with human rights, development and charities. According to Hinnebusch, "He [Bashar Assad] started to insist that democratization had to follow economic modernization rather than precede it—on the model of China, rather than that of the Soviet Union where it had unleashed instability."[83] However, was Bashar Assad genuine in his strategy of putting democratization after economic modernization or he was not entirely planning for political reform? Syria in 2010 had met the condition required for revolution according to Samuel Huntington's theory. He argued that revolution is "most likely to occur in societies which have experienced some social and economic development and where the process of political modernization and political development have lagged behind the process of social and economic change."[84]

THEORIZING REVOLUTION

Revolutions are not phenomena confined to certain societies in the West or in the East. In fact, they are global social phenomena that could strike several different types of societies. They are not only a phenomenon of the past, but in fact are just as likely to be the phenomena of the future, predominantly in the Middle East and North Africa, where authoritarianism is still the prevailing system

[83] Raymond Hinnebusch, "Syria: from Authoritarian Upgrading 'to Revolution, International Affairs" (Royal Institute of International Affairs 1944-), Vol. 88, No. 1 (January 2012), pp.95–113.

[84] Samuel Huntington, "Revolution and Political Order", in Revolutions, Jack Goldstone(ed), Wandsworth, USA, 2003), pp.37–45.

of governance. "For the great majority of the 169 states in the world, the conditions under which revolutions can occur still prevail,"[85] Halliday observed.

What is Revolution?

There are many definitions of revolution, Brinton for instance, the French revolution historian, stated "that revolution has come in common usage to be hardly more than an emphatic synonym for change perhaps with a suggestion of sudden or striking change. Even such emphasis is not always implied."[86] But if revolution is a change, then what is it a change of? Johnson defined revolution as a "change in, affected the use of violence, in government, and/or regime, and/or society."[87] All revolutions start from an inspired bravery breaking the barrier of fear to rebel against the rules, and to challenge the rulers in order to bring about a political, economical and social change. Pettee explains: "A revolution is a change in the constitution by illegal means."[88] Huntington defines revolution as "a rapid, fundamental, and violent domestic change in the dominant values and myths of a society, in its political institutions, social structure, leadership, and government activity and policies. Revolutions are thus to be distinguished from insurrections, rebellions, revolt, coups, and wars of independence."[89] Consequently, revolution is a collective action that begins with a public mobilization, but ends with shaking the prevailing stalemate in the political, social and economic system in the country or destroying the whole system, so no revolution is based

---

[85] Fred Halliday, "Revolution in the third world: 1945 and After", in E.E.Rice (ed.), *Revolution and Counter-Revolution*, Oxford: Basil Blackwell, pp.129–152.

[86] Crane Brinton, "*The Anatomy of Revolution*', Vintage Books, New York, 1965, p.3.

[87] Chalmers Johnson, *Revolution and the Social System*, Calif, Stanford, 1964, pp.6–7.

[88] Geotge Pettee, "The process of Revolution", in *Why Revolution*, Paynton & Balckey, Schenkman Publishing Co, Cambridge, 1971, pp.31–56.

[89] Samuel Huntington, "Revolution and Political Order in *Revolutions*", Jack Goldstone(ed), Thomson, 2003, pp.37–45.

on an individual action, but on a collective action. Additionally, revolution is associated with anarchy, mayhem and disorder destroying the country and costing lots of lives. Pettee pointed out, "It is not surprising that revolutions should be disorderly, wasteful, violent, and should require time to work out, and should consume energies and men. It would be astonishing if they were less so."[90] The revolution toll was very high in Syria, a million casualties, ten million displaced and towns and villages destroyed.

Why Revolution?

Two parties are involved in the revolution, the regime and the masses, so when the relationship between these two parties starts to deteriorate, the revolution is on the way. Many scholars have provided several explanations for revolution, so the concentration here is on those that are linked closely to the Arab Spring revolutions. Pettee laid the common ground for the causes of revolutions generally in all societies. He stated, "No revolution can actually occur unless the state has become a barrier to change, and the state cannot become a barrier to change unless its own form is in some way out of adjustment to the society it is supposed to serve."[91] James Davis also explained the roots of revolution. He suggests, "What provokes a group to attack a government is not simply deprivation or misery, but an intolerable gap between what people want and what they get."[92] Goodwin also explains the reasons for revolutions: "Revolutions, in sum, will undoubtedly continue to occur in those societies characterized by a combination of gross economic injustice and extreme political exclusion and repression by weak or suddenly weakened states."[93] Huntington also provides a valuable explanation for revolution. He argued:

[90] Pettee, op, cit, p.56.

[91] Pettee, op, cit, pp.31–56.

[92] James Davies, "Toward a Theory of Revolution", American Sociological Review, Vol.27, No.1, February 1962, pp.5–19.

[93] Jeff Goodwin, "The Renewal of Socialism and the Decline of Revolution" in *The Future of Revolution*, John Foran(ed), Zed Books, London, 2003, pp.59–72.

> Urbanization increases in literacy, education, and media exposure all give rise to enhanced aspirations and expectations which, if unsatisfied, galvanize individuals and groups into politics. In the absence of strong and adaptable political institutions, such increases in participations mean instability and violence.[94]

Camus draws a line under the causes of all revolutions by saying, "Freedom is the motivating principle of all revolutions."[95] The Arab regimes have been a barrier for a real change in the region for decades. They are responsible for obstructing the public aspirations toward democracy, liberty and development in the region, so people had no other option but revolution. Abdul Halim Khaddam, the former vice president of Syria, stated once: "The Syrian regime is unalterable, for being a security regime, you either take as a whole or rejected as a whole."[96] The political, economic and social situations in the Arab world make revolutions more justifiable. There is no real political participation in most of the Arab world. Moreover, destitution is well entrenched in the Arab countries (apart from the Gulf region); poverty, deprivations and inequality are the common prevailing phenomena across the Arab world. Many Arab countries have witnessed bread riots almost three decades ago or more. They were called the bread uprisings in Egypt, Jordan and Tunisia. Those revolutions were economically motivated and have economic demands. People in Egypt in January 1977 went for demonstrations to protest against the lack of wheat and the high price of bread. However, the Arab Spring revolutions are different from those uprisings. In addition to the prolonged deprivation in the most Arab countries, the Arab Spring revolutions came after unfulfilled promises of political reform accompanied with radical neo-liberalism policies. There was limited political participation, which was associated with great economic openness. The move

[94] Samuel Huntington, *Political Order in Changing Societies*, Yale University Press, New Haven, 1968.

[95] Albert Camus, *The Rebel*, Penguin Books, London, 1962, p.76.

[96] The Political Memory, television program, Al-Arabiya, 12 November 2011.

toward economic openness through adopting neo-liberal policies such as privatization and cuts in state subsidies have increased inequality in society, which constituted a fruitful ground for political volatility. Most Arab countries have a bleak record of political freedom, free press and freedom of expression. According to the Freedom House, "The Arab Spring of 2011 launched an era of sweeping political changes in the countries of the Middle East and North Africa, which has historically been the least free region in the world."[97] Indeed, freedom was the first demand of the Arab Spring revolutions. *Allah Akbar, Hurria* (Allah is Great, Freedom), that was the first slogan of the Syrian Revolution in 2011.[98]

In general, I think two reasons can explain the Arab Spring revolutions:

1. The Arab regimes in the past few years were embarking on neo-liberal economic policies in most sectors, but accompanied with more restrictions on political freedom and more restriction on political participation.
2. The Arab countries had witnessed (pre-the Arab Spring) a retreat from upgrading authoritarianism to authoritarianism mainly in relation to political contestations, which led to more public outrage.

The parliamentary elections in Egypt in 2005 were more transparent and fair compared to the parliamentary elections of 2010. Similarly, in Syria, the local council elections in 2003 endured less Baathist domination compared to the local council elections in 2007. Crackdowns on opposition and activists were getting more brutal both in Syria and Egypt.

[97] FreedomHouse, The Middle East and North Africa, viewed on 12 August 2013. http://www.freedomhouse.org/regions/middle-east-and-north-africa.
[98] Interview with the author over Skype on 12 April 2013.

Peaceful and Violent Political Change

After the collapse of the Soviet Union, communism lost its privileged status as an inspiring doctrine for challenge and revolt in the minds of young intellectuals and young people in the Arab world. Additionally, the experiences of Eastern European people in the aftermath of the fall of the Berlin Wall in 1989 did not occupy an important part in the minds of the Arab people. The revolutions in Eastern Europe in 1989 did not mean to them more than the collapse of the bi-polar system in the world and the failure of communism. It has never been an example to follow in their countries; most of them turned to the Islamic approaches and Islamic schools, but were divided between promoting peaceful and gradual change or violent and instant change.

Peaceful and Gradual Change

After many failing violent attempts to overthrow the regimes in the Arab countries in the last few decades, many voices have been on the surface prompting non-violent means for change. Such voices were raised by well-respected religious and intellectuals figures such as Khaless al-Jalabi, Jawdat Sa'id, and the leaders of many Islamic movements such as the Muslim Brotherhood in Egypt, Syria and Tunisia. These voices have enjoyed a good acceptance among young people. The lesson of Hama and Palmyra Prison in Syria is still present in the mind and heart of every Syrian, and the lesson of Algeria in the 1990s cannot be forgotten, where hundreds of thousands of people were killed and slaughtered as a result of mutual clashes between the Islamists and the military, when the Islamic Salvation Front was denied ruling the country after winning in the elections in 1991. Therefore, a trend of denouncing violence and adopting non-violent approach in order to make political change can be recognized in most of the opposition discourse. They believed that change is to be achieved gradually and within the system, but not through attacking it from the outside. In his controversial book, *The Doctrine of the*

First Son of Adam,[99] Sa'id argues that Muslims should follow the examples of the first killed man on earth (Abel), not to react violently against oppression and suppression, not to treat violence with counter violence and not to use violence when tackling the regimes. He stated, "Muslims should not involve in the guilt of committing killing or assassination, or calling people for such acts or behaviors."[100] Sa'id tried in his book to distance Muslims who work for Islamic societies from resorting to any sort of violence when trying to change the current society. He wrote: "When Muslims contemplate the facts and got aware that conditions cannot be changed through violence, this will shift their minds from adopting force and violence as a means to grab power."[101] It is not necessary to kill the evil, but only to practice legitimate disobedience. If the Algerian opposition resorted to this option, the whole society would have escaped the ordeal with minimum casualties,[102] as Khaless Jalabi argued. Gandhi also never allowed violence, even for the country's sake:

> There is no room for organized assassinations, and there is no room for murders even openly committed, and there is

[99] His argument stemmed from the story of the sons of Adam mentioned in the Quran; "But recite unto them with truth the tale of the two sons of Adam, how they offered each a sacrifice, and it was accepted from the one of them and it was not accepted from the other. (The one) said: I will surely kill thou. (The other) answered: Allah accepted only from those who ward off (evil). (27) Even if thou stretch out thy hand against me to kill me, I shall not stretch out my hand against thee to kill thee, lo! I fear Allah, the Lord of the Worlds. (28) Lo! I would rather thou shouldst bear the punishment of the sin against me and thine own sin and become one of the owners of the fire. That is the reward of evildoers. (29) But (the other's) mind imposed on him the killing of his brother, so he slew him and became one of the losers. Other saying by the prophet Muhammad also supports their argument strongly. The prophet says: the master of martyrs is Hamzah bin Abdul-Muttalib (his uncle killed and tortured in the Battle of Ehud), and a man who stood to an oppressor ruler where he ordered him and forbade him so he (the ruler) killed him." Quran, Surratt Al-Maeda.

[100] Jawdat Sa'id. "Madhab Ibn Adam al-Awal", Dar al-Fikr al Muaser, Beirut, 1993, p.95.

[101] Ibid, p.101.

[102] Jalabi, op, cit, p.254.

> no room for any violence even for the sake of your country, and even for guarding the honor of precious ones that may be under your charge. After all, that would be a poor defense of the honor. We can only win over the opponent by love.[103]

Violent and Instant Change

Choosing violence and turning to it for political change or civil strife is either to be solely learned or an innate response activated by frustrations.[104] Al-Kawakibi points out that the motivation for the populace to revolt violently against an authoritarian ruler is its ruthless and outrageous policies against the people,[105] so it is a reaction or response activated by frustration. On the other hand, most leading religious figures adopting the violent way for change belong to the Jihadists schools, which consider fighting the rulers who do not apply Sharia law in the country to be the greatest Jihad of our time. They do not believe in accommodating with them, or being part of their system, so they do not believe in reform through elections or through opposition pressure, because they do not recognize the system. Political violence in this context is solely learned. Johaiman, who rebelled against the Saudi family in Mecca in 1979, considered working in the government posts such as the security service *Haram* and not allowed.[106] No conciliation is possible between good and evil, so collision is inevitable, as they believe. The relationship between righteousness and evil, between good and bad, between the magic and the rule of Allah and between the light and the darkness is a relationship of struggle. The existence of one of them cannot be possible

---

[103] Gandi, *The Law of Love*, http://sfr-21.org/sources/lawoflove.html.

[104] Ted Robert Gurr, *Why Men Rebel*, Princeton University Press, Princeton, 1970, p.31.

[105] Abd –al-Rhaman al-Kawakibi, *The Natures of Despotism*, Dar al-Nafa's, Beirut, 2006, p.179.

[106] Fahed al-Qahtani, "The Earthquake of Johaiman in Mecca", The Organization of Islamic revolution in the Arab Peninsula. London, 1981, p.62.

without the annihilation of the other. None of them will be accepting the existence of the other.[107] The objectives of the Jihadists is also to uproot the secular social order that has been imposed on Muslims, and to create a unified system based on Islamic allegiance and a *Caliphate*.[108] Moreover, the clash of civilizations is very relevant in this context as evil for Jihadists is not limited to rulers that oppose the application of Allah's rule, but also encompasses all enemies of Islam: individuals, states or coalitions, and mainly the West, which are responsible for supporting Israel and the rulers in the region as they claim. Osama Bin Laden formed in late 1990s what he called the *World Islamic Front for Combating Jews and Crusaders*. It was a declared war on the West.

Nevertheless, violence as Arendt explains, "is by nature instrumental; like all means, it always stands in needs of guidance and justification through the end it pursues."[109] It is a vehicle, but not the destination. Similarly, Jihad was not imposed for itself, but as a means to attain different purposes and invaluable aims in this life and in the hereafter as they believe. Violence as a means of change was endorsed by Marx when he said, "Violence is the midwife of every old society pregnant with a new one."[110] Lenin also believed that "you cannot make omelets without breaking eggs."[111] Mao-Tse-Tung also stated, "Political power grows out of the barrel of a gun."[112] Both Huntington and Johnson emphasized violence as a means of revolution. Georges Sorel glorified violence and encouraged social movements to use it as a means of change. According to Keane, "George Sorel's *Réflexions sur la violence* (1908), the classic revolutionary syndicalist recipe

[107] Omar Abu Omar, (Abu Qatada), Dar al-rek: Beirut, 1999, p.15.

[108] Mohammad Hafez, *Why Muslims Rebel*, Lynne Rienner Publishers, London, 2003, p.186.

[109] Hannah Arendt, *On Violence*, Harcourt, London, 1969, p.51.

[110] John Keane, J. *Violence And Democracy*, Cambridge University Press, Cambridge, 2004, p.3.

[111] Ibid. p.3.

[112] Ibid. p.3.

for dramatically toppling the state by means of a mass social movement from below, is a striking example of this modern fetish of violence."[113]

Resorting to violence as a means for political change in the Arab or Islamic world has the danger of a brutal reaction from the regimes on one hand, and of regionalizing or probably globalizing the conflict on the other hand, especially when such regimes have enemies or ideological opponents behind borders. The situation will become more complicated when violent political change is transferred into a global Jihad, where cross-national Jihadists fight the regime among the revolutionaries. At that point, the regime will turn into a sub-state actor fighting a cross-national actor holding transnational ideologies and aiming for totally different ends. Changing the regimes will turn to be one step in the way for their final aim, which is establishing across borders an Islamic State (Khilafa).

The aims of the revolutionaries also have a great role to determine whether it will be a peaceful or violent revolution. If the revolutionaries' aim was reform, but not regime change, the possibility of mutual violence has less chance to occur. However, "Where the constituted authority is challenged by illegal acts of revolutionaries. In such instances, the routine response of any authority is to have resources to force, police or military,"[114] as Brinton argued. Therefore, violence is very much expected when incumbent regimes tackle anti-regime movements or public mobilization. A violent struggle for survival will take place between the regimes and the revolutionaries, as "there is no alternative to victory" for both parties. Therefore, once the violence begins threatening the structure of power, the elites are in a position either to "defect or protect"[115] the existing order.

[113] Ibid. p.147.

[114] Crane Brinton, "*The Anatomy of Revolution*", Vintage Books, New York, 1965, p.25.

[115] Val Bunce's phrase mentioned by Chip Gagnon in the *Myth of Ethnic War.*

Revolution in the Age of Globalization

There are two contrary views regarding globalization and revolutions, the first, which some scholars such as Foran and Lane believe, that revolution as a movement for social change is over in the era of globalization. The other view that scholars such as Selbin believe is that in the era of globalization, people's grievances will increase due to the social implications of radical neo-liberalism policies, making revolution inevitable.

Debating the future of the revolution in the age of globalization starts from debating the future of the nation-state under the hegemony of globalization, as social movements are largely confined to the nation-state both in their public mobilization or struggle, and indeed in their outcomes. Globalization entails openness, interference of some supra-state economic and political forces such as pro-democracy and human-rights organizations in national affairs, undermining the nation-state and threatening its sovereignty, making it weak. In such countries, where globalization plagued the state and the society, the potential possibility for social movements and revolutions is very low. In other words, revolutions as a means for taking power are irrelevant in the globalization age, where its forces control the international system, but not a certain state or states. The world is now very different from 1789 (the French Revolution) and 1917 (the Russian Revolution). The world in the age of globalization is more interconnected than ever and more interdependent than ever. This means "that however local the action—and all action must have local origin—it must conceive of itself in global terms"[116] as Kumar argues. Moreover, as globalization is the final stage of capitalism, this means that capitalism is fighting with its toughest weapons to abort any upcoming revolution, not necessary a world revolution, but any kind of movement that might disrupt its interests, shake its structure and risk its future, such as an Islamic revolution in the Arab world, or

[116] Krishan Kumar, "The Future of Revolution", in *Revolution in the Making of the Modern World,* Foran, Lane, and Zinvkovic (eds), Routledge, USA, 2008, pp.222–235.

political turmoil in the Arab Gulf threatening the collapse of the Western-backed ruling families.

On the contrary, globalization increases the chances of social movements in the future due to its harsh discontents economically and thus socially. Increasing the people's grievances may eventually lead to revolutions, as Selbin suggested, "as the global gap between the haves and the have-nots increase and neo-liberalism fails to deliver on its promise, revolution will be more likely."[117]

Selbin has outlined fourteen points on future revolutions, but they can be summarized in the following, where relevant to the Arab Spring:[118]

1. There is a global or transnational role played by the ideas, myths and conceptions which people share with one another. Stories established obligations between past, present and future generations in which each generation is called to defend the struggles of previous ancestors and to fulfill a historic duty to the future. The spread of the Arab Spring revolutions from one country to another can be explained under this context as Arab people have a lot to share with each other.
2. Despite the talk of globalization and its attendant glories, the immense majority of humanity remains profoundly immiserated by any reasonable measure. Whether revolution will be an option they choose remains to be seen. The rich get richer and the poor get poorer. In addition to political suppression, the social impacts of neo-social policies that have been undertaken in Arab countries have provided more possibilities for revolutions to occur.
3. People do not fight, do not risk their lives and those of their families, do not put their hopes and dreams on the line

[117] Eric Selbin, Eric, "Same as it Ever, The Future of Revolution at the End of the Century", paper presented at the meetings of the international Studies Association, Minneapolis (1998).

[118] Selbin, Eric. Theses on the Future of Revolution in the Future of Revolution, John Foran(ed), Zed Books, London, 2003, pp.83–94

> lightly; certainly do not do so for dry, distant, theoretical concepts. Revolutions are about passionate commitment and, as much, more cultural than social or economic in their origins. There is a great need for metaphoric elements, which moves people's hearts as much as their heads. The revolutionaries in Syria, when they turned to Jihadists, started naming their brigades and battalions after Islamic heroes during the time of the prophet (PBUH) and after: Khalid Bin Al-Walid, who conquered Persia and the Levant (*Bilad Asham*); Al-Hussein, the prophet's grandson, who was killed while rebelling against Yazid; and Saladin al-Ayubi, who defeated the crusaders in Jerusalem.

It is very important also to cast light on information and communication technology and network development in the past two decades and how these dramatic and unprecedented developments have changed the trajectories of many social movements and revolutions. Information and communication technology has transferred the world into a small village, making any event happening in any part of the world not a secret anymore. Local authorities are totally powerless in front of information access and the infiltration of information to the state's boundaries as opposed to a few decades ago. The events of Hama in 1982 took a couple of months to be heard of or talked about in the international media. Such a situation is not applicable any more in the age of information and communication technology. Moreover, information communication technology will help social movements, or rebels building their own realm, using an independent way of communication, so they can liaise and cooperate together without the need for the government's monitored facilities. In the words of Zivkovic and Hogan:

> Flows of information are now much harder to retain within the institutional boundaries, while the distribution of points of entry into the force field of communication allows for unsanctioned and official communicative pathways to be

opened, where organizational performance may be observed and indexed.[119]

Obstacles in Front of the Revolution

There are many elements which can be regarded as real barriers in front of a revolution. Deep social division in the country is the strongest social force which can impede the revolution's trajectory, and contributes heavily to its complexity. While homogeneous society would help mass mobilization, religiously and ethnically fragmented society would undermine mass mobilization. The ruling elite and their cross-society loyalists also constitute another big force undermining the revolution through resorting to policies and tactics countering the forces of revolution. Most of the Arab Spring revolutions have occurred in countries where the ruling elites are students of previous revolutions, making the revolutions not against the ruler only, but in fact against the system. Another large factor of countering the revolution is the foreign actor. This includes foreign states or sub-state actors whose interests would be at risk if the revolution was succeeded in the country. Some social movements have great regional and international outcomes, threatening the national interests of certain regional and international powers. In such cases, these powers will exert their utmost influence to abort the revolution or alter its objectives, and may lead if necessary to international intervention. Moreover, the regimes may resort to force and violence to suppress the revolution with the support of some international and regional powers, or it may use fraud through initiatives of reform and changes in laws and government in order to deceive the public and convince them to retreat from their revolution. According to Aristotle:

> Revolution is effected in two ways, by force and by fraud. Force may be applied either at the time of making the

[119] Andreja Zivkovic& John Hogan, "Virtual Revolution?" in *Revolution in the Making of the Modern World,* Foran, Lane, and Zinvkovic (eds), Routledge, USA, 2008, pp.182–198.

> revolution or afterward. Fraud, is of two kinds; for 1) sometimes the citizens are deceived into a change of government, and afterward they are held in subjection against their will; 2) in other cases, the people are persuaded at first, and afterward, by a repletion of the persuasion, their goodwill and allegiance are retained.[120]

The International Dimensions of Revolution

Revolution is a change within the state, but its effects may shake up regional and international politics. States are members of the international arena, so any changes in one state could create weaves of changes regionally and maybe internationally. Mark Katz explains this: "Revolution does not just change things inside one country. It can disrupt international relationships throughout an entire region or even the world."[121] The international dimension of revolution can be seen from two angles: How would international relations affect the revolution? And how would the revolution affect international relations? Revolution can upset the existing alliance patterns of a state, and create fears among others states derived from the revolutionary regime attempting to export their revolution,[122] as Katz pointed out. The French Revolution and the Russian Revolution, for instance, had great effects regionally and internationally. The French Revolution was the spearhead for the republic revolutions in Europe in the 18th century. Similarly, countries of Eastern Europe were under direct effects from the communist revolution in Russia in the early 21st century. Moreover, the USSR assisted Marxist movements and

[120] Aristotle, "Man and Revolution", in *Why Revolution*, Paynton & Balckey, Schenkman Publishing Co, Cambridge, 1971, pp.9–15.

[121] Mark Katz, "The International Relations of the Arab Spring", The Middle East Policy Council, Summer 2014, Volume XXI, Number 2.

[122] Mark Katz, The International Dimension of Revolution, in *Revolution: The International Dimension,* Mark Katz(ed) CQ Press, Washington, 2001, p.1.

revolutions around the world, posing a great threat to the United States and its allies. The Arab Spring started in Tunisia and spread, reaching the other edge of the Arab world, threatening the Arab regimes and the Western interests in the region.

However, revolution needs the assistance of the dominant powers for success. Without such support, the revolution would fail or struggle. In the age of globalization and unipolar system revolutions cannot succeed if they do not gain the support of Western powers and in particular the United States. Hamid argues that Western support to the Colored Revolutions in Eastern Europe was crucial for their success. "During the Colored Revolutions, the West had played an altogether different role, offering critical support not just for change but regime change."[123] Moreover, the role of the West welcoming the revolutions in Eastern Europe in 1989 was a very important factor for their great success. Such support was nil for the Arab Spring revolutions. In fact, Western support was concentrated toward supporting the counter-revolution forces in most of the Arab Spring countries in order to reinstate the old regimes.

CONCLUSION

In this chapter, a selection of theories and events were presented to help evaluate the elements of authoritarianism and authoritarian upgrading in the Arab world in general and Syria in particular. Such elements have been of great importance for the autocrats of the Arab world and Syria to hold power for many years and even many decades. External and internal challenges forced the authoritarian regimes in the Arab world and in Syria to engage in a discourse of rhetoric and adopt some limited, controlled and contained flexible policies in order to sustain power, and avoid

[123] Shadi Hamid, "The Struggle for Middle East Democracy", The Cairo Review of Global Affairs, unknown date, viewed on 22 August 2014. http://www.aucegypt.edu/gapp/cairoreview/Pages/default.aspx,

public resentments from growing. Ironically, authoritarian upgrading led to revolutions from below in some Arab countries, initiating the Arab Spring. Theories and literature reviews of revolution, its causes, its obstacles and dimensions were also presented here in order to evaluate the reasons behind the Arab Spring revolutions, and in particular the Syrian Revolution in March 2011, and explain its high cost and prolonged complicated trajectory.

Chapter Two

SYRIA UNDER BASHAR ASSAD'S 2000–2011

INTRODUCTION

It is very important to outline the situation in Syria during Bashar Assad's era since 2000, when he inherited power from his father Hafiz Assad, until March 2011, when the uprising erupted. However, this is not a comprehensive study of Bashar Assad's era before the revolution. It is more to cast light on the very important aspects that contributed to the people's grievances before the revolution on one hand, and those which contributed to the revolution's complex trajectory afterward on the other hand. Also concentrating on some aspects of authoritarianism, and upgrading authoritarianism in his era,[124] I will discuss inheriting power in Syria, military loyalty, the changing demographic structure in Damascus, domestic politics including the opposition's status, and in addition some economic and social policies that increased the people's grievances and constituted a platform for the revolution of March 2011. Moreover, the foreign policy of Syria during Bashar Assad's era occupies particular attention in this chapter in order to understand the international relations of the 2011 revolution in Chapter Six.

[124] Authoritarian upgrading involves as Steven Heydemann pointed out reconfiguring authoritarian governance to accommodate and manage changing political, economic and social conditions. It originated in no small part as a defensive response to challenges confronting Arab autocrats during the past two decades.

INHERITING POWER

After the Gulf War in 1991, when Syria was part of the international coalition led by the United States against Iraq to drive Saddam Hussein out of Kuwait, a succession plan in Syria began to be articulated on the ground and in the streets. The plan started by changing the common and public names of President Hafiz Assad, featured in national informal songs, from the hitherto always known Abu Suleiman (father of Suleiman) to Abu Basil (father of Basil). Everyone in Syria noticed this change and understood the message behind it. It was the succession plan. It was an attempt to shed light on Basil Assad (the president's eldest son) and draw public attention to his good behavior, his great sporting activities and, more importantly, to his progressive thinking on reform, fighting corruption and modernizing the country. For example, he was an early proponent for and chairman of the Syrian Computer Society. He was presented as a modernizer and a great advocate for openness in the country.

The discourse of modernization and openness was the most effective means to lay the groundwork for the succession of power in Syria. Upgrading authoritarianism started its discourse in the country as a prior condition for inheriting power. Therefore, there is little wonder why the succession plan was accompanied by two major developments in Syria: 1) the launching of the peace process between Syria and Israel after the Madrid Conference in 1991; 2) starting a period of economic openness (*Infitah*) in Syria with the initiation of Investment Law 10 in 1991.

The process was proceeding carefully and smoothly until it suddenly came to an abrupt stop. On 21 January 1994, Basil Assad was killed near Damascus International Airport in a car accident. It was, in many ways, like an earthquake in Syria, and a big blow for the hope of peaceful succession in the country, as Fisk stated then.[125] Basil was a strong man, and respected or maybe

[125] Robert Fisk, "Syria Mourns Death of a Golden Son" The Independent, on 21 January 1994, viewed on 12 January 2013. http://www.independent.co.uk/news/world/syria-mourns-death-of-a-golden-son-basil-assads-fatal-car-crash-throws-

feared by most of the top regime's officers and principals. The former deceased prime minister Mahmoud al-Zubi used to refrain from smoking in his presence as a sign of respect.[126]

Bashar Assad was then recalled to Syria, his unclear mission in London was terminated.[127] The same scenario of Basil's rapid accession was repeated for Bashar. Much concentration was given by the state media on his supposedly gifted and talented personality and his exceptional capabilities—including the fact that he held additional merits by virtue of being a Western-educated person. Indeed, he was portrayed as someone who had experienced democratic life in the West and who may have the enthusiasm to apply such democracy, or some of its principles, in his own country. His loyalists called him the "Hope of Syria" and the "Torchbearer". He was portrayed as very tough on corruption and on tackling corrupt officials in the government. The public scapegoat for this was the former prime minister Mahmoud al-Zubi, who was sent to court, along with his deputy Salim Yaseen and the minister of transport Mufeed Abed al-Kareem over a suspicious deal involving the purchasing of old aircraft that were then registered and paid for as new. Mr. al-Zubi allegedly committed suicide (or, more likely, was killed) after being sentenced to house arrest. Such a move nevertheless impressed the public, but did not prevent them from asking: What about the corrupt Alawi officers among the old guard?

George wrote:

> Bashar like his late brother Basil when he was being prepared to take over from his father was fully identified with the new mood, bringing forward younger, more dynamic individuals and spearheading an (admittedly somewhat

---

open-the-question-of-who-will-succeed-the-president-writes-robert-fisk-in-beirut-1408555.html.

[126] In Syrian culture refraining from smoking in front some people is a sign of respect towards them.

[127] Many reports said that Bashar Assad was in London actually for some medical treatment, but not as an ophthalmologist in some of London hospitals.

> cynical) anti-corruption campaign, again as Basil had done. Modernization and technology became his buzz-words.[128]

The discourse of modernization and openness was more noticeable, and actually more trustworthy in the country from a young man who was educated and had experienced democracy in the West. Therefore, Bashar Assad was more eligible to lead upgrading authoritarianism in the country despite his relatively weak charisma. Meanwhile, the regime launched a huge crackdown campaign on reviving Islamic cells, such as activists from the Islamic Liberation Party (Hizb Al-Tharir). As a case in point, Dr. Basil, a dentist who was an activist calling for a pan-Islamic state (Khilafa), was jailed from 1999 until 2004 for such activities. He stated: "The regime had us under close observation for a few months, [leading] eventfully to our capture in order to secure the plan of succession."[129] Moreover, Hafiz Assad destroyed all his younger brother (Rifat's) bases in Latakia to eliminate all kinds of possible threat that his son Bashar might face.

The introduction of Bashar Assad as his father's successor after the succession plan of Basil was aborted by his death, demonstrating that the matter was not about installing an unparalleled and matchless person with unique capabilities, nor about being a Western-educated leader. In fact, the matter was about keeping the power in Syria in the hands of the Alawis, and particularly in the Assad family, by any means. Therefore, upgrading authoritarianism was the most appropriate means alongside military loyalty.

The inheritance of power in Syria is an old-new phenomenon after 1970. It was raised to the surface first in 1983, when Rifaat Assad (a younger brother of Hafiz) tried to seize power when President Assad was extremely ill and apparently close to death; Rifaat was the second most powerful man in the country at the time. He was the commander of the so-called Saraya al-Difaa, a

[128] Alan George, *Syria: neither Bread nor Freedom*, Zed Books, London, 2003, p.31.

[129] Interview with the author in October 2006 in Homs.

very powerful armed elite division that was very loyal to him and who had a mission directive to protect the regime.

The question posed here is: If Hafiz Assad had died in 1983, would Syria have undergone a bloody struggle for power similar to what Syria has faced in the aftermath of the 2011 Arab Spring? In other words, would Rifaat Assad have resorted to similar tactics in 1983 in order to retain the family and the sect's rule, as Bashar Assad has used to maintain his power over Syria after the uprisings in March 2011? I presume the answer to be yes after observing the regime's violent response toward the peaceful protests in 2011, and the international will and support to keep Assad in power as an Alawi president.

The events since the 1970s have demonstrated that inheriting the country and the state of Syria rather than just ruling the state's power mechanisms were the long-term aims for Hafiz Assad and for the international community in general. Therefore, the widely spread slogan Lil-abad, 'Forever', was not empty rhetoric, but was in fact accompanied with strategies and tactics to achieve its realization on the ground.

MILITARY LOYALTY

Focusing on military loyalty is important not only to understand the smooth transition of power from Hafiz Assad to his son Bashar in 2000, but also and to a very large extent to understand the cohesion and the solidity of the very inner core of the regime, which constitutes one of the biggest actors for its survival after the revolution in 2011, making the revolution last much longer and incurring huge costs.

The concentration of Alawi power inside the Syrian army was radically and rapidly achieved after the abortive coup of Salim Hatum,[130] a Druze officer, in 1966. "After Salim Hatum's abortive coup, purges on an extensive scale were held in the Syrian Army

[130] Salim Hatum is an army officer and a veteran Baath Party member from the Druze community. He has joined the Eighth March Revolution, and participated in the coup against the former Syrian president Amin al-Hafiz in February1966.

and the Baath Party. Command of the purged military units was subsequently entrusted to Alawi officers in many cases,"[131] as observed by Van Dam. However, the Arab defeat against Israel in June 1967 triggered a conflict and a struggle for power between the two Alawi poles in the military and in the Baath Party too: Salah Jadid[132] and Hafiz Assad. The struggle in this phase was developed from inter-sectarian struggle after 1963 to intra-sectarian struggle after the 1967 defeat. Hafiz Assad was the defense minister when the humiliating defeat happened. Jadid held Assad responsible and tried to isolate him. However, Hafiz Assad, in return, started to tighten his control and grip over the military, so he replaced Jadid loyalists in the key military posts with ones he trusted most. For instance, he appointed his longtime friend, Mustafa Tlas, chief of staff in place of Jadid supporters. Such tactics guaranteed a successful coup in November 1970 by him against his opponents. After 1970, Hafiz Assad embarked on building a regime of two parts, private and public. As Patterson put it:

> The public part is the government itself, which is the formal structure of political and economic affairs that keeps the country running on a day-to-day basis. The private part is the army, police, and the security services. This is the security core Assad relies on to protect himself and his government.[133]

He then planned a coup against Salah Jadid and Hafiz Assad in September 1966, but he failed and later was executed.

[131] Nikolaas Van Dam, *The Struggle for Power in Syria*, Croom Helm Ltd, London, 1979, p.77.

[132] Salah Jadid is an Alawi army officer from Al-Haddadun Alawi Tribe, and a radical Baath Party leader. He was a member of the Secret Military Committee, which was established during the union with Egypt in 1959. He participated in the Revolution of 8 March in 1963, and in the coup against Amin al-Hafiz in February 1966. After the coup of 1970 by Hafiz Assad. He was imprisoned till he died in 1993.

[133] Ibid, p.61.

The public part was a cross-sects arena, while the private part was more like family, and tribal parts inside the Alawi community or the so-called inner solid core of the regime. The inner core consists of Assad's relatives as the regime has a personal and familial character,[134] as Zisser wrote. Hafiz Assad relied on Asabiya to guarantee full loyalty in order to consolidate his power among the Alawi community, and hence his rule in the country. Assad increased reliance on people with whom he had a close relationship, such as members of his own family, tribe or village and its surroundings in order to secure his position. His five brothers were all active party members and occupied eminent positions in the army, the party organizations and government. Rifa'at Assad was the most important and influential one. After the November 1970 coup he was in command of Saraya Al-Difa', elite army units of political and strategic importance which were stationed around Damascus and with which he was able to protect his elder brother's regime.[135] It was the solidarity or Asabiya that Ibn Khaldoun has regarded as the foundation for ruling, and considered by Hinnebusch as a means to consolidate power in the populist regimes in the Middle East. Such tactics have guaranteed the survival of Hafiz Assad's regime for thirty years in power. He was able to defeat and overcome many great challenges in the 1970s and 1980s. The plan of inheriting power made Hafiz Assad even more selective because some people and members among his family, tribe and sect who proved loyal to him during his time in power were not guaranteed to do the same toward his successor (his son), or may have rejected the plan in principle. Therefore, he made great changes in the army and the security leadership in the late 1990s, and eliminated possible dangers that might disturb the smooth transition of power in the country. Hafiz Assad was able to make the changes that he wanted in the regime that he built. According to Zisser: "The Syrian regime was a personal one that surrounded President

[134] Eyal Zisser, *Assad's Legacy*, C. Hurt & CO, London, 2001, p.31.

[135] Van Dam, op. cit., and p.90.

Assad, and to a significant extent was the work of his hands. At the same time, it was also a family and even a tribal regime."[136]

Zisser explains that three significant steps were followed to ensure a smooth transition of power from Hafiz Assad to his son Bashar Assad:[137] First, Hafiz Assad ousted three other potential candidates from Syrian political life: 1) dismissing Rifat Assad as a vice president in February 1998 and dismantling all his bases in Latakia by force; 2) pensioning off the chief of general staff Hikmat Shihabi in July 1998, a man who was long believed to hold a real interest in succeeding Hafiz Assad; 3) marginalizing the vice president Abd al-Halim Khaddam in national and regional affairs, mainly in the Lebanese sphere since it was a country he had dealt with most of his political life. Second, Hafiz Assad promoted young Alawi officers very loyal to Basher Assad to key military posts. These included Asif Shawkat, husband of Bushra (the older sister of Bashar), Bahjat Suleiman and Hasan Khalil. "It seems that most of the young [Alawi] officers are close associates of Bashar Assad or owe their promotion to him, and are thus ready to give him their full support."[138]

On 10 June 2000, Hafiz Assad died. The then vice president Khaddam announced the promotion of Bashar Assad from colonel to the rank of lieutenant general and appointed him the commander-in-chief of the Syrian Armed Forces. Problematically, however, Bashar Assad was 34 years old at the time, which was contrary to the constitutional clause stipulating that the president must be at least 40 years old. Consequently, the People's Assembly met and agreed almost unanimously to amend the constitution to reduce the president's minimum age from 40 to 34 years. Third, there was a decision to convene the Baath Congress on 17 June 2000, after an interlude of fifteen years, in order to appoint Bashar Assad as a member of the party's regional command and to approve his nomination to the presidency. According to

---

[136] Zisser, op, cit., p.19.

[137] Ibid, p.166.

[138] Ibid, p.171.

Mr. Khaddam, Hafiz Assad made the necessary arrangements in the army, but consulted no one in the party nor in the government about his plan of conferring power to his son.[139]

On 10 July 2000, a referendum on his succession to the presidency was held "in which almost the entire electorate participated in and voted for Bashar; 97.29% of the electorate voted for him."[140] On 17 July 2000, Bashar Assad took the oath of office and made his inaugural speech[141] as the new president of Syria. He continued relying on Asabiya to consolidate his rule, so he established a close circuit from within the close family. His brother Maher Assad, leader of the 4th division,[142] became the second most powerful man in the country. Moreover, he planted his Makhlouf[143] relatives in key and influential posts for controlling the whole state. "Muhammad Makhlouf in the oil sector, Hafiz Makhlouf to control the security and Republican Guards, and Ehab, and Rami Makhlouf to dominant the businesses, communications, investments, and tourism sectors"[144] as Bashir Zein al-Abdin observed.

Overall, military loyalty and the discourse of authoritarian upgrading such as reform and modernization secured the transition of power in Syria. Military loyalty, on the one hand, guaranteed a smooth nature of this transition, and the public, on the other hand, were looking forward to the young Western-educated new president for modernization, democratization, and real political reform in the country.

[139] The Political Memory, television program, Al-Arabiya, 5 November 2011.

[140] Alan George, "Syria. Neither Bread Nor Freedom", ZED Books, London, 2003, p.1.

[141] Full of Bashar Assad inaugural speech can be found on the following link: http://www.al-bab.com/arab/countries/syria/bashar00a.htm

[142] It is an elite army unit consisting of overwhelmingly loyal Alawis stationed in the mountains surrounding the presidential place in Damascus, and responsible to protect the regime.

[143] Makhlouf family is the family of Bashar Assad's mother Anisa Makhlouf, her brothers and nephews.

[144] Bashir Zein Al-abdin, "Can the Syrian Regime Maintain its Solidity?", Almokhtasr.Com, 13 April 2011, http://www.almokhtsar.com/node/11219, viewed on 10 April 2014.

THE CHANGING DEMOGRAPHIC AND SOCIAL STRUCTURE

During the period in between the independence and the Eighth of March Revolution (1963), Syria underwent a fundamental social restructuring through the creation of a new middle class "with only modest property, dependent on salaried state employment, modernizing in orientation and with an interest in state-sponsored development."[145] Creating a new elite in society transformed later to be the ruling elite through party mobilization, army recruitment and educational developments. They were mainly from worker and peasant backgrounds from urban and rural areas, and from all over the country. The new elite backed the Eighth of March Revolution, which has diminished the traditional oligarchical rule that prevailed for centuries. However, the problem with this new elite was its different ideological affiliations and different identities. They were divided into Baathist, communists and Nasserists from all ethnic and religious groups. After a huge campaign of land reform and nationalization of private capitals, Syria was transformed from a semi-feudal system of rule into a populist regime, where peasants and workers constituted the core of the political and social policies in the government.

Radical Baathists came into power in 1966 through a bloody coup, and the sectarian struggle was won by the Alawis. Hafiz Assad after the Corrective Movements was more selective, so he concentrated on the loyal Alawis to occupy positions in the party and the state institutions, constituting a neo-patrimonial rule. The appointment of Alawis was not limited to military and security positions, but in key ministries too, as well as in the regional command and the central committee in the Baath Party.[146] Concentrating on Alawi manpower has changed the social demographic structure of the major cities such as Damascus,

[145] Raymond Hinnebusch, *Syria: Revolution from Above,* Routledge, New York, 2002, p.13.

[146] Bashir Zein al-Abdin, *The Army and Politics in Syria*, Dar-Al-Jabeih, Amman, 2008, p.514.

Aleppo, Homs and Deir ez-Zur. The Alawi presence in Damascus and its suburbs constituted an Alawi belt surrounding the city. The following map shows the areas of Alawis in Damascus and its suburbs, which are inhabited overwhelmingly, and in some cases purely by Alawis.[147]

The presence of Alawis in Damascus and its suburbs took three forms: 1) owning properties in the rich neighborhoods of Damascus; 2) segregated Alawis in licensed and unlicensed cantons such as Mazeh Jabal 86, Assad's suburb in Hararsta, and the hills around Qudssaya; 3) renting properties in Damascus and its suburbs, thus mingling with the local people.[148] Mr. Ayham, a British Syrian from the town of Qudssaya in the west Damascus, stated:

> Many people of my area including my family had their land expropriated in the 1970s and 1980s, then it has been transformed gradually into a segregated Alawi area occupied by the Republican Guards and their families. They do not pay any sort of utility bills. In fact, most of the houses have no water or electricity meters' we call them the Alawis Settlements echoing the Israeli Settlements in the occupied land of Palestine.[149]

Great numbers of Sunni bourgeoisies from all over the country were coping with the new political and social development in the country. In fact, they constituted a great supporter to the regime, which guaranteed its survival and robustness because, as Jill Crystal stated, "its members [Sunni bourgeoisies] want money even more than they want political participation. If they find non-democratic ways to protect economic interests, they can live with

[147] "The Alawi Belt in Damascus: Information and Maps", The End of Terror, 24 June 2013. http://arab-worlds.blogspot.co.uk/2013/06/blog-post_24.html, viewed on 20 April 2014.

[148] "The Alawi Settlements in Damascus", 05 September 2012, http://syriahourra.blogspot.co.uk/2012/09/blog-post.html, viewed on 20April 2014.

[149] Interview with the author by telephone on 20 April 2014.

that."[150] The regime also supported a loyal urban merchant class in Damascus and Aleppo, and gave it prestigious status and great economic advantages constituting a great and robust alliance between Sunni business and Alawis military. It was a socio-economic base for the regime standing on the mutual interests between the regime and all groups of the society. Mutual interests mean mutual survival. In other words, Hafiz Assad built a system of overlapping interests between all groups in the society, making any attempt of rebellion or revolt from any group a big risk for that group itself first, so he linked their survival and their interests with the survival of the regime. In the year 2000, when Bashar Assad took control of the country, none of these groups showed a sign of resentment or rebellion. Mr. Eid, a small businessman who deals with properties and furniture from Zamalka, a suburb of Damascus, expressed his views on Bashar Assad ascending to power in Syria. He said: "If Bashar Assad wants to be the president, let him be. We need our life and business to continue in peace and safety, and as usual."[151] However, such statements of support or neutrality faded away when small businesses were affected severely by the free trade agreement with Turkey after 2007.

[150] Jill Crystal, "Authoritarianism and Its Adversaries in the Arab World", World Politics, Vol. 46, No. 2, Jan. 994, pp.262–289

[151] Interview with the author on 15 July 2000.

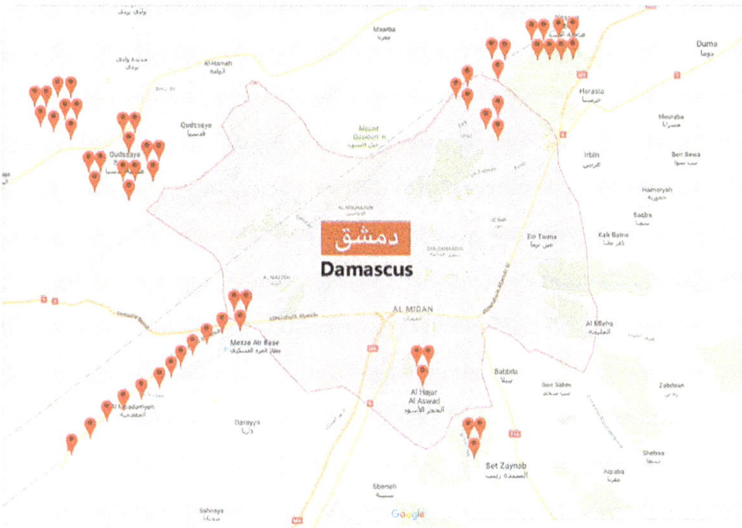

This map demonstrates the Alawi settlements in Damascus.

DOMESTIC POLITICS

Political reform was the most important public priority for the Syrian people, but Bashar Assad in his inaugural speech limited himself to few words about democracy, administrative reform and transparency. He did not have a clear roadmap toward political reform in the country. However, some civil society activists and intellectuals were very enthusiastic to take the lead and act to revive civil society institutions, such as human rights and pro-democracy organizations. Nevertheless, most opposition parties and prominent civil society figures had expressed their satisfaction with the idea of Bashar Assad assuming power in Syria; analytically, this was largely because of his success in selling himself as a reformer and a modernizer. Dr. Abdul Razzaq Eid, a prominent figure in the opposition, said: "We had to accept him, he had promising views to convince us with."[152] On the other hand Mr. Ali Sader al-Deen al-Bayanouni, the former general guide of the Syrian Muslim

[152] An interview with the author on 22 February 2013.

Brotherhood in exile, implied his acceptance for power succession in the country.[153]

This seemed to be an assurance from the major opposition factions in Syria that they held no preconception of Bashar Assad, and therefore they did not hold him responsible for any contentious events in the past. It was like an implicit acceptance of the power inheritance plan in the country. Such statements and assurances gave Bashar Assad a golden opportunity to start a pure new era in Syria, and to break off with his father's era, but he destroyed this opportunity with arrogance and ignorance.

Damascus Spring

The Damascus Spring refers to a period of almost two years which began immediately after Bashar Assad's inauguration in year 2000, where intellectuals, actors, public figures and university students were involved in informal political mobilization such as the establishment of civil society movements and forums like the National Dialogue Forum in Damascus and Al-Kawakibi Forum in Aleppo.[154] The activities of these forums were mainly limited to meetings and having regular seminars covering topics of political reform, democratization and domestic affairs. Their main and prime demand was political reform in the country. It was a time of reviving civil society movements.

On 27 September 2000, almost two months after Bashar Assad took control, 99 people, overwhelmingly comprised of secular intellectuals, actors and other public figures, signed what was called the Statement of 99. This statement called for an end

[153] No Limits, television program, Aljazeera, 07 July 1999. Mr. al-Bayanouni stated: When we oppose we do not oppose the person of Hafiz Assad or the person of Bashar Assad, but rather we oppose policies and do not hold any leader responsible for what has happened in the past. We will have our judgment on him through his programs, through his approaches, and through his policies [quoting two Quranic verses].

[154] "Attempts to Close the Forum of Al-Kawakibi Forum", Al-Hewar.org, 04, October 2002, http://www.ahewar.org/debat/show.art.asp?aid=3259, viewed on 22 April 2014.

for the state of emergency that had been declared in the country since 1964, also called for amnesty for political prisoners and moreover, called for freedom of expression and the rule of law. Such statement was a political maneuver against the regime, but not a political confrontation with it. Their demands were so basic and modest and did not contain ideological flavor or attack on the manner in which Bashar Assad reached power in the country.[155]

In January 2001, the creation of a committee to revive the civil society movement was announced in a statement, later to be called the Statement of 1000. This committee was more radical and explicitly called for an end to the state of emergency, for more political and media freedoms, the enacting of democratic election laws, the calling for an independent judiciary, the granting of economic rights to its citizens, and to stop legal discrimination against women.[156]

Despite having a secular orientation, Damascus Spring activists have been labeled by some top figures in the regime as being Western agents and as having foreign funding and hidden agendas; a label used by the regime, coincidentally, for Islamists, and in particular in a derogatory way against the Muslim Brotherhood. It is, however, very important to note that four Alawis were among the 1000 signatories: Aref Dalilah (the well-known economics professor), Mohammad Kamel al-Khatib, Adel Mahmoud al-Shaer and Hassan Abbas. Three of them decided to withdraw their signatures "for unclear reasons, could be due to some pressures from the regime,"[157] as Dr. Abdul Razzq Eid, a main participant in the statement wording, has claimed, leaving Aref Dalilah as the only Alawi signatory on the statement. Having few Alawis among the 1000 signatories indicates that some Alawis do want reform. However, the withdrawal of most of them due to regime pressure can indicate the extreme pressure of the regime on such activists from within and outside of the Alawi sect. Aref Dalilah suffered the

155 George, op, cit, p.40.

156 Ibid. p.45.

157 Interview with the author with the author on 22 February 2013.

longest period in prison compared to his fellows in the Damascus Spring.[158]

On 8 February 2001, Bashar Assad gave his first interview as president; he talked to the Asharq Al-Awsat newspaper in great detail about international and regional affairs, but too little about internal affairs. He stated:

> Those who allege that the last four decades were responsible for all appalling aspects of the present and for its problems they may prefer the coups period and the era of Western occupation to the era of stability, an era that began in 1963 and has reinforced in 1970 till our present day. They may want to say this, but were embarrassed to express their intentions bluntly.[159]

The signatories of Statement 99 and Statement 1000 failed to mention, along with their demands, issues like the struggle against Israel, the liberation of the Golan Heights and the Palestinian issue. Such issues were, and still are, very central in the concerns and considerations of the regime and the public alike in Syria. The defense minister at the time, Mustafa Tlas, accused the signatories as being a tool in the hands of the enemy. He asserted that the "absence of any mention of the Arab–Israeli conflict in the petition [the statement of 1000] proves that its signatories are in the pay of the enemy."[160] Abdul Razzaq Eid explained why the statement did not contain any hint toward the struggle with Israel:

> We did not want to deal with those issues of that kind, and we wanted to concentrate on local social and political

[158] "Damascus Spring", Carnegie Middle East, unknown date, viewed on 20 July 2014. http://carnegie-mec.org/syriaincrisis/?fa=48518&reloadFlag=1.

[159] "President Assad speaks about his vision", Asharq Al-Awsat, 08 February 2001, viewed on 8 February 2001. http://www.aawsat.com/details.asp?section=4&article=25244&issueno=8108

[160] "Tlas Hints for Evidence of the Statement 1000 Signatories Deal with CIA" AL-Quds Al-Arabi, in17 April 2001, viewed 8 February 2013. http://81.144.208.20:9090/pdf/2001/04Apr/12%20Apr%20Thu/Quds01.pdf.

> demands about freedom and democracy. On other hand, we were activists, not a proper opposition yet, and the other side is a regime, and not a state. Therefore, we did not have the ability to form a proper and complete program dealing with all the concerning issues of the country and the people.[161]

The Muslim Brotherhood entered this arena from exile on 03 May 2001: They issued a Draft of National Honor Pact for Political Activity. It contained three goals:[162] 1) building the modern state; 2) meeting and addressing the challenges facing the general construction to the state; 3) confronting the Zionist project. However, few days earlier, on 01 May 2011, Bashar Assad gave an interview with the Spanish newspaper El-Pais describing the Damascus Spring as an unrealistic term, claiming that not all people love spring; some people do prefer winter or summer. His challenging words can be best described as a declaration of the complete success of the process of inheriting power in the country. He consolidated his base of rule, and all threats were contained making him able to challenge, disdain and even insult the activists who were aiming for genuine reform in the country. A campaign of arrests launched by the security forces against the activists, starting with the arrests of two MPs, Riyad Saif in August 2001 and Ma'moon al-Homsy in September 2001,[163] breached their political immunity. By mid-2002, most activists were jailed and the Damascus Spring was buried completely.

I think the regime conceived Damascus Spring activists and their activities, after the inheritance of power was completed, as great threat to Bashar Assad's new rule, a threat at a time when he was making great efforts to consolidate his power after the inheritance of power was successful, so any concessions toward such activities would strengthen them, and undermine his endeavors to consolidate his power in the country. A strong and

---

[161] An interview with the author on 22 February 2013.

[162] "Draft of National Honor Pact for Political Activity", 03 May 2001, viewed on 22 January 2012. http://www.mokarabat.com/mo2–14.html.

[163] George, op, cit, p.56.

independent civil society would undermine the regime's power, so authoritarian regimes do not accept political or social opposition and never tolerate the development of an independent civil society that could form a counterweight to state powers.[164] Therefore, it was hardly surprising when Adnan Omran, the then information minister, labeled the civil society activists as a form of new colonization.[165] It was not more than a pretext to suppress this phenomenon in the country, and to imprison most of the activists, so the regime chose confrontation with them, but not containment.

Too many accusations were charged to the regime old guard that they were the real obstacle for Bashar Assad's reform plans. However, such views were dismissed as merely myths by many observers inside and outside the country. A Syrian businessman interviewed by a Western NGO indicated that they perceived this perspective to be a cover for Bashar Assad, which was wholeheartedly believed by European officials who were only too willing to believe in the new Syrian leader.[166] I believe the real powerful and influential old guard inside the regime were pensioned off or removed by Hafiz before the inheritance of power, such as Hikmat al-Shihabi, the chief of staff from 1974 till 1998, and Ali Duba, the chief of military security division.

Containing Civil Society and Managing Political Contestations

Political civil society organizations such as Al-Atasi Forum were like a new form of colonization, as Adnan Omran has stated, so the regime confronted them, restricted their activities and persecuted. However, the regime tried to contain and control civil society organizations of different natures as an aspect of upgrading

[164] Ignacio Alvarez-Ossorio, Syria's Struggling Civil Society, Middle East Quarterly Spring 2012, pp.23–32.

[165] Muhammad al-Zoubi, Damascus: The Mother of Both Springs, Ahewar.org, 26/August 2013, viewed on 23 April 2014 http://www.ahewar.org/debat/show.art.asp?aid=374980.

[166] International Crisis Group, Syria Under Bashar (II): Domestic Policy Challenges, 11 February 2004.

authoritarianism during Bashar Assad's era. Between 2000 and 2010, civil society organizations have proliferated remarkably, and were engaged in different areas such as human rights, women rights, cultural, developmental, environmental and charitable organizations. The number of organizations registered with the Ministry of Social Affairs and Labour (MoSAL) went up from 513 in 2000 to 1580 in 2010, as records of the Central Bureau of Statistics shows.[167] However, they had no effective role in the domestic politics, and in the Syrian uprising of 2011 too. Many organizations have offered significant services to the public, and in particular the charities. Wael Sawah confirmed that the law in Syria places limitations on civil society organizations and gives the Ministry of Social Affairs and Labour (MoSAL) exclusive and great power to deal with such organizations.[168] Government control over such organizations was actually strengthening through establishing GO-NGOs, which eventually led to weakening the independent NGOs, especially developmental and environmental organizations. Laura Ruiz de Elvira wrote:

> GO-NGOs have had a privileged access to the state's resources and to foreign actors, an access they have tried to monopolize. They have participated in most of the workshops and projects managed by foreign institutions. By doing so, they have prevented independent associations from participating in these kind of activities. Hence, the tactic of creating GO-NGOs has been an effective method to perpetuate the regime's power and to control the associative sector.[169]

[167] Central Bureau of Statistics (CBS), http://www.cbssyr.org.

[168] Wael Sawah, "Syrian Civil Society Scene Prior to Syria Revolution", Humanist Institute for Co-operation with Developing Countries, The Netherlands, 2012, February 2014. http://www.hivos.net/Hivos-Knowledge-Programme/Themes/Civil-Society-in-West-Asia/News/Syrian-Civil-Society-Scene-Prior-to-Syrian-Revolution.

[169] Ibid.

Despite their role in alleviating suffering and filling the shortfall of the state in its duties toward the people in society, charities were under great surveillance. New measures of restrictions were frequently issued by the authorities against them whenever their activities could not be controlled, or the implication of their activities were hardly contained. However, the regime always had a great interest in the continuation of these organizations because such controlled and contained activities would strengthen its rule, extend its life, and boost its reputation. They concentrated on treating problems in society rather than the causes of these problems.

In 2003, the government lifted the Baath Party membership privilege as a condition for leadership in local elections. It was a modest, but meaningful step, and undermined the status of the Baath Party as the leader of the state and society, so to chair the local councils did not require Baathist membership any more, and there was no electoral Front List.[170] The government adopted an open lists system, where Baathists and independents were equals. It was an attempt to ease the Baath grip over society and the state, and to demonstrate political reform in the country. However, no candidate was allowed to run in the elections without approval from the security authorities,[171] as stated by Waleed, an independent member of council in Damascus between 2003 and 2007. Adnan al-Sheghri, the head of Baniyas Council in 2011 and a member since 2003, stated that the head of council of any village needed the approval of the mayor in that province, but for the city needed the approval of the president himself. It was called *republican palace approval.*[172] Many concessions ceased to exist since 2007, when the regime started feeling relaxed toward international pressures and in front of the opposition. In the local

[170] National Progressive Front (NPF). It is composed of the Baath Party, the Communist Party of Syria (HSS), the Arab Socialist Union (IIA), the Socialist Unity Party (HTI), the Arab Socialist Movement (HA), and the Socialist Unionist Democratic Party (HDTI).

[171] Interview with the author on 01 August 2014.

[172] Interview with the author on 03 August 2014.

elections of 2007, for instance, the government reintroduced the Front List in the local elections, which was scraped in 2003. Moreover, the People's Assembly elections in 2007 witnessed an increase in the Front candidates. The Front MPs increased from 167 to 172 at the expense of independent MPs.[173] Also, charities run by religious figures faced evident restrictions too. Laura Ruiz de Elvira observed two restrictions that were imposed by the regime on the charitable activities of the clergies in 2008. First, forbidding charities and mosques to hold the *mawa'id al-rahman*[174] during Ramadan. The second was applied to anyone working in a clerical role—such as imams or prayer leaders at mosques and teachers at religious institutions—compelling them to step down from any official post held in a charitable institution.[175]

Damascus Declaration

The Damascus Declaration for Democratic National Change was first established on 16 October 2005 in the Damascene office of Hasan Abdul Azzem. It was a brave and unprecedented move that came as a result of cumulative efforts starting from the Damascus Spring interactions.[176] It was similar to a coalition of opposition parties containing senior opposition figures. To this end, the coalition was founded by the following parties:[177] 1) the Social Democratic Union; 2) the Muslim Brotherhood; 3) the Communist

---

[173] http://www.electionguide.org/elections/?inst=Assembly&cont=Syria&yr=2007.

[174] *mawa'id al-rahman* (Tables of the Most Merciful (Allah)), are charitable events aiming to provide food for poor people in some certain mosques during Ramadan.

[175] Laura Ruiz de Elvira "State-Charities Relations in Syria: between Reinforcement, Control and Coercion", in *Civil Society and the State in Syria*, Laura Ruiz de Elvira& Tina Zentil, St- Andrews University Papers, 2012, pp.5–30.

[176] Abdul Razzaq Eid, "And They Ask You about Damascus Declaration", Akhbar Alarab, 23 August 2011, viewed on 23 August 2011. http://www.akhbaralarab.net/index.php/araa2/40799-q-q-

[177] Damascus Declaration, Carnegie-mec.org, July 2012, viewed on 25 April 2014. http://carnegie-mec.org/publications/?fa=48515

Labor Party; 4) the Future Kurdish Party, and other assorted Kurdish parties; 5) the Movement for Justice and Development; 6) public figures such as Riyad Saif, Mrs. Feda'a al-Horany (the daughter of Akram al-Horany, one of the prominent politicians after the independence), Michel Kilo, Jawdat Sa'id, Haithm al-Maleh and Nawaf al- Basheer, a leader of the al-Baqqara Tribe. The latter is from the city of Deir ez-Zur. The Muslim Brotherhood joined the Damascus Declaration, in fact, and as a spokesman for the Muslim Brotherhood, Mr. Zuhair Salem stated: "The Muslim Brotherhood was a founding member in the Damascus Declaration, but for the safety of other founding members, the Muslim Brotherhood preferred to be invited to the this coalition."[178]

In December 2007, a few months into Bashar Assad's second term in office, those who signed the Damascus Declaration held their first National Council meeting, but disputes prevailed within the leadership between the Arab nationalists, some leftists, the Islamists and the new liberal Syrian nationalists.[179] This discord eventually led to the withdrawal of the Arab nationalists from the coalition. In the aftermath of that meeting, most prominent leaders were arrested, but some, such as Dr. Abdul Razzaq Eid, escaped abroad and formed the National Council for Damascus Declaration in Exile.[180]

The Damascus Declaration group was a more organized and more challenging opposition framework, but it came at a time where the regime was facing a critical international threat after the American invasion of Iraq in 2003, and after the assassination of Rafiq al-Harir; the former Lebanese prime minister in February 2005. The regime and its loyalists conceived this coalition as to be a tool or a part of the international threats against Syria,[181] so the regime cracked down on the activists, making the coalition very

[178] Interview over the telephone with the author on 26 January 2013.

[179] Damascus Declaration, Carnegie-mec.org, July 2012, viewed on 25 April 2014. http://carnegie-mec.org/publications/?fa=48515

[180] Interview with the author on 22 February 2014.

[181] Faisal Jaloul, "Window on Damascus Declaration", Mukarabat.com, June 2008, http://www.mokarabat.com/mo13–50.htm, viewed on 22 April 2014.

weak. Therefore, external challenges (regime brutality), and internal crises (leadership disputes) deprived the Damascus Declaration of the opportunity to play any role in political life or among the public. "The public used to respect these activists, but feel sorry for them,"[182] as Mr. Maher al-Isaa, an independent member of the Damascus Declaration, commented. Regardless, the Damascus Declaration was more about veteran personalities such as Riyad al-Turk, and some intellectuals. It was not about programs or strategies; they did not have the ability to establish a road map for political, economic and social reform in the country. They had no ability to take the lead on any certain issues. In addition, their discourse overlooked great issues such as the conflict with Israel, the Palestinian problem and Arab nationalism. Moreover, inconsistent ideologies played a leading role in making this coalition an ill-fated body.

The National Salvation Front

Before talking about the National Salvation Front, I think it is very important to indicate the invitation that was made by the American Foreign Ministry to some opposition figures in the United States in 2005 to discuss the regime change in Syria. After this meeting, most of the people invited decided to form the Syrian Nation Council in the United States. It was a registered body in Colombia District, Washington DC. This body was later dissolved automatically due to the lack of support from the United States, so some of its members decided to join the Front of National Salvation

In December 2005, Vice President Abdul Halim Khaddam defected from the regime following the assassination of the former Lebanese prime minister Rafiq al-Hariri on 14 February 2005. It was a very difficult time for the regime, where international threats and international isolation were mounting against it. Soon after his defection, alongside the Muslim Brotherhood, he formed

[182] Interview with the author on 28 January 2013.

in Brussels the Front for National Salvation on 17 March 2006. It was very difficult for the Muslim Brotherhood to justify their move in front of the public, and in front of their partners in the Damascus Declaration. Mr. Zuhair Salem, meanwhile, justified their alliance with Khaddam, as it "was to encourage other figures in the regime to defect and make sure that their place is vacant in the opposition. On the other hand, Mr. Khaddam was a top politician and had a lot of information about the regime."[183] However, such a move was a damaging blow to the Damascus Declaration, so most of its members criticized the Muslim Brotherhood for not consulting with them before taking that decision. Mr. Salem explained:

> We did not have to take permission from anyone, however, we did send many indications to some of our partners in the declaration informing them of our plan about the Front, and moreover we have invited the declaration to join the Front believing that a carriage can be led by two horses, but they refused. We wanted to be the spring that links between the two carriages.[184]

The Front had annual meetings in London, Brussels and Berlin. No democratic election took place to elect the general secretariat in the Berlin Conference in September 2007. When Mr. Khaddam listed the names appointed for the general secretariat, Dr. Mahmoud al-Sayed al-Doghem, an independent dissident who was at the conference, expressed his dissatisfaction and called the general secretariat as the general treachery.[185]

The Salvation Front had a different agenda compared to the Damascus Spring and Damascus Declaration. It was based on regime change, and introduced itself as the real alternative to the regime for the people in Syria and for the whole world.[186]

---

[183] Interview with the author over the telephone on 01 February 2013.

[184] Ibid.

[185] Interview with the author on 11 October 2009.

[186] http://www.alghoraba.com/wthaeq/17_jabhat_alkhalas.htm, viewed 20 April 2014.

However, its influence inside Syria remained ineffectual as most of its activities were outside the country. The Front tried to build bridges with people inside the country at a time when the regime in Syria was under a real threat from the United States. They established a newsletter system through a Hotmail domain to provide the Syrian people with regular information, news and articles about the regime and the need for change.[187] The Syrian regime, as another aspect of authoritarian upgrading, was controlling communications, and responded to the Front by monitoring the users of all Hotmail domains in Syria. And, indeed, eventually they took the decision to block all access, which in turn compelled people to use proxies in order to seek a means around the blockade and maintain access to the Front's feeds.[188]

In April 2009, the Muslim Brotherhood decided to withdraw from the Front, after an inflamed dispute between them and other members: mainly with Khaddam following the Muslim Brotherhood's unilateral decision to hold its opposition activities against the regime during the Israeli offensive on Gaza in January 2009. Mr. Salem justified holding their activities for three reasons:[189]

1. It was a message to the Arab and the Islamic world that we appreciate the stance of the Syrian regime for its support to the Palestinians.
2. It was a message to the regime that if President Assad is sincere about wishing to support the Palestinians and resisting Israel, then they too have the same aims and objectives.
3. It was a message to Israel not to take advantage of the dispute between the regime and members of the Syrian opposition.

[187] Interview with the author over the phone on 29 January 2013.

[188] "2006 has the biggest block campaign since the Internet was Introduced in the country", Syria News.com, 19 November 2006. http://www.syria-news.com/readnews.php?sy_seq=42783, viewed on 20 April 2014.

[189] Interview with the author over the telephone on 26 January 2013.

In return, Mr. Khaddam stated: "I cannot confirm this reason as the real reason for their withdrawal, but I was surprised by their move."[190] An NSF independent member, had a different view about the Muslim Brotherhood's withdrawal: It was not about Gaza, but in fact, it was about a deal between them and the regime mediated by Iran and Turkey, so withdrawing from the Front was a precondition to convincing the regime of their goodwill, but the regime as usual betrayed them.[191]

After the withdrawal of the Muslim Brotherhood, the Front became very weak and gradually died. The hopes of changing the regime faded away, especially after the regime was able, through extensive diplomatic efforts spurred on by leadership changes in important external countries (most notably in France and the US), to mitigate against international challenges, break its international isolation and restore its strength.

Overall, domestic politics (political reform and human rights) and the struggle between civil society and the regime were the pivotal issues for all the opposition bodies. There was no broad program concerning the identity of the state, the struggle with Israel, the notion of Arabism, the Palestinian issue, or the role of resistance movements such as Hamas. They failed to offer the public an attractive alternative to the regime; they could not build legitimacy, as there was no clear road map to rule the country. Most strikingly, they proved to be undemocratic and lacking in structural and administrative transparency. Moreover, their differences and fragmentation were far more evident than was their harmonization. Such a situation can explain to a large extent the feeble and divided Syrian opposition after the revolution in 2011. Still, there was no doubt that the regime's brutality had undermined their public outreach and communication strategy, and hence undermined their activities. However, the internal problems among the opposition were more damaging.

---

[190] The Political Memory, television program, Al-Arabiya, 05 November 2011.

[191] Interview with the author on 28 January 2013.

Human Rights

The human rights record during Bashar Assad's era before the uprising was not as ruthless as during Hafiz Assad's time, but it remained bleak and depressing especially after Bashar Assad consolidated his power over the country. The state of emergency remained in force allowing the security agencies unrestricted power such as making arrests without warrants and torturing with impunity.[192]

In February 2011, the Syrian Human Rights Committee reported that during 2010, Syria had witnessed many sizable human rights violations. Random and arbitrary arrests remained a societal menace, and the Syrian security authorities continued to demean Syrians' integrity by abusing and physically torturing them to the extent that many lost their lives. The fate of dozens who disappeared in the Sednaya Prison Massacre[193] is still unknown in light of the state's persistence on maintaining a total blackout of information pertaining to it, as well as taking all measures to prevent the leaking of the massacre outside the prison walls. In addition to this, there have been unprecedented arrests of women and young women, an issue that has its sensitivity among Syrian society. As a case in point, people were concerned about the arrest of two female students, Tal al-Mallouhi and Ayat Ahmad, and female writers Raghad al Hasan, Tohama Ma'rouf, Hadia Youssef and Fatimah Ahmad.[194] Tal al-Mallouhi and Ayat Ahmad's arrests put the country on edge prior to March 2011.

Overall, the regime in Syria after Bashar Assad took control in 2000 offered very few concessions in the realm of domestic politics and human rights in the country, and most of these

---

[192] "Ian Black, Human Rights Record Unchanged Under Assad, Report says", The Guardian, 16 July 2010, viewed on 22 April 2014. http://www.theguardian.com/world/2010/jul/16/syrian-human-rights-unchanged-assad.

[193] Sednaya Prison is mainly for political prisoners. Sednaya Prison Massacre happened in December 2008 after a tension occurred between the prisoners and the prison security forces.

[194] Syrian Human Rights Committee, Report 01 February 2011, viewed on 2 March 2011. http://www.shrc.org/data/aspx/d13/4303.aspx.

concessions were recalled when Bashar Assad consolidated his power and escaped the international threats following the American invasion of Iraq in 2003, and the assassination of the Lebanese prime minister Rafiq al-Hariri in 2005. Consequently, the regime reproduced itself as a completely robust authoritarian and brutal regime in 2007 and thereafter. In fact, those political concessions were not more than a political maneuver aimed to buy time and consolidate the rule of the new weak president.

THE ECONOMIC DEVELOPMENTS

At the Baath Party Congress in 2005, the Social Market Economy Approach was adopted in an attempt to imitate the Chinese style of reform. However, economic reform was constrained by two sets of contradictions:[195] 1) technical contradictions due to different viewpoints between experts and government departments over the most efficient means of stimulating socio-economic development; 2) contradictions due to conflicting interests between classes, groups and persons. These conflicts of interests were focused on the market economy sphere. Noticeably, the policy of economic reform was a great reflection of authoritarian upgrading in the country, so the regime and its close loyalists could capture the benefits of selective economic reform. Ehab, and Rami Makhlouf were in the position to dominate the businesses, communications, investments and tourism sector.[196] Neo-liberal policies generated benefits, but were mainly captured by the regime's close loyalists creating a new phenomenon in the country such as the emergence of Rami Makhlouf's business empire. In November 2006, Cham Holding Company was established, and chaired by Rami Makhlouf.[197] This company was the prime beneficiary from the government's plans of privatization and neo-liberalism in the

---

[195] Samir Seifan, *Syria on the Path to Economic Reform*, University of St-Andrews, UK, 2010, p.8.

[196] Bashir Zein Al-abdin, "Can the Syrian Regime Maintain its Solidity?" Almokhtasr.Com, 13 April 2011.

[197] http://uk.aliqtisadi.com, viewed on 15 April 2014.

country. The then prime minister in Syria, Naji Otri, issued a decree giving Cham Holding Company the priority in establishing independent financial and administrative projects in Syria.[198]

During this period of Bashar Assad' s era we can realize that the regime in Syria has changed from an obsolete populist authoritarian regime into a flexible authoritarian regime, where the new businessmen constitute its wagon toward the economic growth. This new regime did not eliminate the authoritative nature of the Baath Party organizations, but in fact weakened it.[199]

It is very important to examine the economic policies in some sectors in order to have a clear view about wider economic developments in Syria during Bashar Assad's era, which resulted in the implications that led to a revolution.

Trade and Investment

After signing the multilateral Great Arab Free Trade Area (GAFTA) in 1997, Syria also signed bilateral free trade agreements with some Arab countries, such as the UAE, Saudi Arabia and Jordan, shortly after Bashar Assad ascended to power in 2000. Syria also entered into negotiations with the European Union between 2004 and 2008 to sign its EU Association Agreement (known as the SEAA). In 2007, the free trade agreement between Syria and Turkey came into effect.[200] Moreover, Syria won WTO observer status after its first request had been refused in 2001 because of US opposition, as Jennifer Freedman claimed.[201]

It was a very radical openness and maybe a reckless policy, such as free trade agreements, and especially the SEAA, that

---

198 "Otri enhanced the duties of Cham Holding Company", 05April, 2007. http://syria-court.com/readnews.php?sy_seq=12236, viewed on 15 April 2014.

199 Muhammad Jamal Barout, *Syria in the Last Decade*, Arab Centre for Research and Policy Studies, Doha, 2012, p.147.

200 http://www.syrecon.org/trade/agreements.html, viewed on 23 April 2014.

201 Jennifer Freedman, "Syria Wins WTO Observer Status as U.S. Drops Opposition to Membership", Bloomberg, 04 May 2010, viewed on 12 June 2010. http://www.bloomberg.com/news/2010–05–04/syria-wins-wto-observer-status-as-u-s-drops-opposition-to-membership.html.

would in all likelihood cause far more harm than good to the Syrian economy—at least in the short term. This led Hinnebusch to argue it was good for Syria that the EU declined to ratify the agreement.[202] The competitiveness of Syrian goods and services in the national and foreign markets was very low. Thus, its growing industry was to face tremendous pressures and challenges, and maybe eventually collapse. People, academics and experts loyal to the regime were arguing that by seeking to secure these agreements, Bashar Assad had done something of great benefit for Syria and the Syrian people. Mr. Naser, a student of law at the University of Damascus, was particularly excited about Syria's EU Association Agreement. He argued, "The state is doing a great job. If this agreement is ratified, we will start buying German cars for cheap prices."[203] The Syrian–Turkey free trade agreement is a very important trade agreement that Syria signed after Bashar Assad came to power. The agreement was signed in 2004, but came into force in 2007. The background for this agreement is mainly economic and political for both countries. For Turkey:

> Turkey has to align her preferential trade regime applied toward third countries in accordance to the rules and regulations of Turkey–EU Council Decision of 1995. According to that, Turkey will take the necessary measures and negotiate agreements on a mutually advantageous basis with the third countries in order to harmonize her commercial policy further with the EU's.[204]

Moreover, Turkey enjoys greater economic abilities, enabling it to win the Syrian market on many levels, and achieving economic

---

[202] Raymond Hinnebusch, forwarding Jorg Dostal &Anja Zorob, *Syria and Euro-Mediterranean Relationship*, Univesity of St-Andrews, UK, 2009, p.2

[203] Interview with the author on 3 May 2007.

[204] Yontem Sonmez Scott McDonald, and Jonathan Perraton, "Turkey and Its Preferential Trade Agreements (PTAs)", Paper prepared for the 10th Global Economic Analysis Conference, "Assessing the Foundations of Global Economic Analysis", Purdue University, West Lafayette, IN, USA, 2007. https://www.gtap.agecon.purdue.edu/resources/download/3298.pdf.

gains. Meanwhile, the political reasons can be divided into pragmatism and ideology. Since the Justice and Development Party (AKP), which possesses an Islamic background, came to power in 2002, a new approach of relationship was adopted between Turkey and the Islamic countries, and in particular the Arab countries. On the other hand, Turkey has adopted a pragmatic approach, relying on the Strategic Depth Doctrine,[205] a doctrine which aims to enhance its regional position economically and politically.

For Syria, Mr. Ghassan Habash, the then economic minister assistant, predicted benefits for the Syrian economy from this agreement: the Syrian–Turkish free trade agreement was to open a market of seventy million people in front of Syrian products, and the entry of Turkish products to the Syrian market would improve the competitiveness of Syrian products, which would be in the interest of consumers. Moreover, Turkish investment in the country would increase due to cheap labor in comparison to Turkey.[206] The trade volume increased between the two countries from $1,174,246 in 2007 to $2,272,415 in 2010. See Table 1.

However, the real implications of this agreement on the Syrian economy was rather different after more than four years of its implementation, causing the Syrian authority to suspend the agreement in December 2011, after which the relationship with Turkey deteriorated, especially following the uprising in March 2011. Nedal al-Shaar, the economy minister, stated the trade balance between Syria and Turkey was unfair, where Syria's exports to Turkey were almost a third of its imports from that

[205] Strategic Depth Doctrine, it is a doctrine introduced by Ahmed Davutoglu, the Turkish foreign minister, the doctrine sees that Turkey needs to employ its historical and geographical hereditary in its foreign policy in the best way possible.

[206] Rana Hajj Ibrahim, the Free Trade Agreement between Syria and Turkey, Tishreen, 26 May 2004. http://tishreen.news.sy/tishreen/public/read/2051, viewed on 27 April 2014.

country.[207] The trade balance between the two countries can back Mr. Al-Shaar's views. See Table 1.[208]

Year	Export ($)	Import ($)	Trade Volume ($)	Balance of Trade ($)
2007	797,312	376,958	1,174,270	410,354
2008	1,113,026	639,3121	1,752,239	473,813
2009	1,115,013	327,640	1,442,653	787,373
2010	1,641,805	630,610	2,272,415	1,011,195

Table 1. Recourses: Ministry of Foreign Affairs, the Turkish Republic.

In addition, Turkish investments in Syria reached an unprecedented level: "It was nearly 260 million dollars in 2010, and Turkish companies took the first place in the ranking of foreign investment with respect to project numbers."[209] According to an independent study assessing the implications of the agreement on the Syrian economy, the agreement led to growth in the tourism sector and in foreign investment in the country. Meanwhile, the agreement has led to negative implications on many growing national industries such as the textile, fashion, furniture and grain industries. More than 20% of furniture enterprises, between 70–100 textile and fashion enterprises, and more than 40 factories in grain industries

[207] "The Free Trade Agreement with Turkey is not fair, and must be reviewed", Aksalser.com, 02 October 2011, viewed on 27 April 2014. http://www.aksalser.com/?page=view_news&id=53a496bb6f06541ec5d6aa9afc68b60.

[208] Turkey-Syria Economic and Trade Relations, http://www.mfa.gov.tr/turkey_s-commercial-and-economic-relations-with-syria.en.mfa, viewed on 13 February 2013.

[209] Ibid.

were closed down.[210] Such a situation had great further economic and social implications on the people that own or work in those enterprises. Mr. Hani, a textile enterprise owner from Homs, stated:

> The textile business was transferred from the hands of the middle-class businessmen into the hands of giant investors who rely mainly on the international market, while Turkey has won the national market, so we struggled to survive, but eventually we had to close our business off. Many friends in this business met the same fate.[211]

Sami, a furniture business owner from the town of Saqba, the most important place for the furniture industry in the country, referred to the decline in the furniture industry, stating:

> 1) The monopoly of Joud&Co, an oligarchic family close to the Assad family that works in the wood trade, controlled the prices of wood, so the price of wood went up sharply since 2008. 2) The lack of competitiveness of the furniture industry in comparison to the Turkish ones: we do not have the developed materials or the new machines. We still rely on machines that are 30 years old, and while some items rely on hand only, such as sculpture work, we still need modern tools. Therefore, we lost the national and regional markets. 3) We tried to host a number of national fairs for furniture in order to revive the industry, but the authorities granted us security clearance for one festival only.[212]

The investment sector has also grown significantly. After the Syrian withdrawal from Lebanon in 2005, most Syrian assets in

[210] An Economic Assessment to the Free Trade Agreement between Syria and Turkey, Aliqtisadi.com, 3 February 2012, http://uk.aliqtisadi.com, viewed on 27 April 2014.

[211] Interview with author on 07 February 2013.

[212] Interview with the author on 03 April 2013.

Lebanese banks moved into Syria in the shape of investments or bank deposits, causing a sudden boom in the property market in Syria. Therefore, the property sector was one of the main targeted sectors for investment. "The Syrian government has taken several steps to increase the role of the private sector in property development. A major part of this process involves the government divesting itself of some of its huge land holdings."[213] Legal and economic distinctions between national and foreign capital had been lifted in 2007, resulting in a huge flow of foreign capital into Syria. The Arab Gulf States also had a significant share in the investment sector in Syria, so while the UAE took the lead among the Gulf economies in the total value of foreign investment in Syria, Qatar took the lead in terms of investments in the financial sector specifically. Jasem Hussein wrote:

> The possession of Qatar National Bank reaches more than 50 per cent of the "Qatar National Bank–Syria" with a capital of $300 million. Additionally, "Qatar International Islamic Bank" owns 30 per cent of' Syria International Islamic Bank. On the other hand, Qatari investors are the main shareholders of "Cham Islamic Bank". This heavy Gulf investment in the Syrian economy was to help Syria to succeed in its new adopted economic policies.[214]

Agriculture

The agriculture sector has long been a pivotal sector within the wider Syrian economy, so any damage to it would lead to significant damage to national industry as well as export-led trade. On a related note, food security, which has always been one of Syria's most crucial strategic policies, fundamentally relies on the

---

[213] Robert Goulden, "Housing, inequality, and economic change in Syria", British Journal of Middle Eastern Studies 38: 2, 2011, pp.187–202.

[214] Jasem Hussein, "The Future of Gulf Investments in Syria", Aljazeera.net, 12 March 2012, viewed on 2 February 2013.http://studies.aljazeera.net/reports/2012/03/201231110171119 2912.html.

agriculture sector. In the mid-2000s it accounted for 25% of GDP, 20% of total exports and employed 20% of thenational workforce.[215] Agriculture is also very important for providing raw materials for food and various industries in the country.

Syria is a country suffering from water shortages, so continuous and sustained efforts to improve existing, and create additional, water resources are always urgently needed. "Total annual water resources in Syria are 16 billion m^3, while the total use is 19 billion m^3, resulting in the depletion of underground resources."[216] However, drought has never been the only problem for the agriculture sector. As the agriculture in Syria enters its third phase after independence, small and medium agriculture properties began to scatter and divide due to family disputes over inheritance. Pollution and desertification were also big factors in the agriculture crisis in Syria.[217]

There are two more national and natural factors that exaggerate the water shortage crisis in the country, population growth and drought. Regarding population growth, the annual growth in 2011 was 1.8%, according to the World Bank Report in 2012. And the problem of drought, which affects the country every few years, puts the agriculture sector at risk and poses more challenges for the government's strategic decision-making. The drought that hit the country, and Aljazeera province in particular, between 2007 and 2010 was met with no serious governmental policy remedies in terms of seeking proper solutions or viable alternatives. "As a result of four years of severe drought, farmers and herders have seen their livelihoods destroyed and their lifestyles transformed, becoming disillusioned with government promises of plenitude in rural areas,"[218] so stated one observer. Consequently, many agricultural laborers and landowners have

---

[215] Atieh El Hindi, in *Agriculture and Reform in Syria,* Hinnebusch, El Hindi, Khaddam, and Ababsa, St-Andrews Univesity, UK, 2011, p.15.

[216] Ibid, p.15.

[217] Muhammad Jamal Barout, p.124.

[218] Suzanne Saleeby "Sowing the Seeds Dissent" Jadaliyya.com, 16 February 2012, viewed on 11March 2012. http://www.jadaliyya.com/pages/index/4383/sowing-the-seeds-of-dissent_economic-grievances-an

had no other option but to leave their land and migrate into urban areas for jobs and a better standard of life. As a result, the agriculture sector has lost a great number of its workforce. In Horan Region, irrigation relies heavily on underground water, which is facing the danger of depletion. The local authorities in Daraa banned the digging of new wells and ordered the closure of unauthorized ones. However, exemptions used to be granted from the mayoral office for one million Syrian pounds,[219] as Mr. Al-Butain, an engineer in Daraa city council, reported. These selective exemptions created substantial economic and social problems in the city, where rich people who could afford to pay for the exemptions were able to farm their lands and sell their products, whilst land belonging to poorer people stayed dry and was eventually abandoned. Such a situation created a substantial problem in Horan, especially for the villages of Daraa, as the people there had no other source of income.

Business Networking in Syria

The alliance between the urban Sunni bourgeoisies and the ruling, mainly Alawi, elite was based on traditional rule, which is understood as the military for Alawis and business for urban Sunnis. This traditional rule was established by Hafiz Assad and has never existed before. Bassam Haddad observed this alliance:

> In Syria, the sociocultural divide between the regime elite and capitalists coincided with the socioeconomic divide: the regime elite were predominantly rural and minoritarian and belonged to the underprivileged classes (some even by rural standards), while members of the business community were predominantly urban and Sunni and belonged to the dominant class.[220]

---

[219] Interview with the author on 25 March 2013.

[220] Bassam Haddad, *Business Networks In Syria*, Stanford University Press, Stanford, 2012, p.41.

That was the situation until mid-1990s, when young Alawi men close to the Assad family, predominantly his cousin Rami Makhlouf, started to become heavily involved in business and commerce in the city of Latakia[221] as Saqer, an Alawi businessman from Latakia, pointed out. The structure of the relationship between the regime and business, or more accurately between urban Sunnis and rural Alawis, has changed since Bashar Assad came to power or only a few years before, when business was no longer a monopoly of the urban Sunnis. The ruling elite entered the realm of business as a kind of consolidation of their rule. Mr. Sobhi, a resident of Latakia city, stated, "the '*Shabbiha*'[222] have given up their anti-social behavior, which was very common during Hafiz Assad's rule, and turned to real business after Bashar Assad took over the country. They started wearing suits, owning companies, and doing business."[223] A member of the Commerce Chamber in Damascus, commented:

> The rules of the business game have changed 180 degrees during Bashar Assad's rule. We used to pay such as royalty to the regime's men such as the top officers in the military and security during Hafiz Assad's rule in order to keep our business running. These people now wanted to be our partners in the business. They set a certain percentage of the annual profits to their accounts.[224]

Bashar Assad has appointed members from his close relatives to dominate the business sector in the country, and to capture its benefits in order to consolidate his power further over the country. Ehab and Rami Makhlouf dominate the business, communications,

[221] Interview with the author on 12 April 2014.

[222] Shabbiha: An informal civilian militia recruited by the regime, and mainly from the Alawi minority.

[223] Interview with the author on 19 March 2013.

[224] Interview with the author on 17 March 2013.

investments and tourism sectors[225] as Bashir Zein Al-abdin observed. According to Mr. Husam, one of the top businessmen in Aleppo, "Everyone used to know that Rami Makhlouf was the shadow of Bashar Assad, he was not more than an administrative man in Bashar Assad's business empire."[226] Controlling politics and business means that authoritarianism has reached its worst level,[227] as al-Nufaisi argued.

A joke was circulating in Syria about Rami Maklouf, mocking the situation in the country; why do people complain about Rami, he only has two shops in the country, one in Damascus and other in Aleppo, but he decided to merge them physically together.

THE SERVICES SECTOR

The education and health services were the most important services in the country during Hafiz Assad's era, which advocated equality among the people, although the situation changed after a few years of Bashar Assad's ascendency to power. Inequality was certainly very noticeable in society, and the poor were feeling alienated as the effects of neo-liberalism segregated them from the rest of society.

The Education System

Free, quality education for every Syrian and Arab national was an important achievement for the Baath Party in the country. Equality was somehow achieved between rural and urban areas; education was no longer a monopoly of the rich urban families, so the gap between rural and urban areas, and between rich and poor, almost vanished in relation to education opportunities from 1963. By the

---

[225] Bashir Zein Al-abdin, "Can the Syrian Regime Maintain its Solidity?" Almokhtasr.Com, 13 April 2011, http://www.almokhtsar.com/node/11219, viewed on 10 April 2014.

[226] Interview with the author on 22 March 2013.

[227] M O H A M M E D, The Arabs before and after the war on Gaza 2009, Posted on 06 February 2011, https://www.youtube.com/watch?v=vP_nv5afmzs.

1990s, everyone recognized the birth of a new educated generation as it spread throughout the country. In Baseer, a village in Daraa with a population of 3000 people, for example, where illiteracy has not been recorded for a long time, its people are now highly educated, and over 130 people are doctors or engineers.[228]

In 2002, the General Assembly ratified Law 32, making education free and compulsory for the primary and intermediate levels. It was a good step forward to improve the education of the people in the country. Problems, however, started with upgrading the education curricula in 2004, where not enough qualified teachers could fill the requisite vacancies. For instance, they imposed two foreign languages at the intermediate level: English and French. But a lot of schools could not get enough French language teachers; such problems opened the need for private teachers and then private schools. The proliferation of private schools later absorbed the best teachers, leaving the public schools lacking in true quality, and creating a public trend toward private schools. The victims of these new challenges were the poor, who could not afford to pay for private schools or who could not afford private teachers.

The proliferation of private universities played a similar role in creating inequality in society. Wealthier people who could not study the subject they desired in the state universities could do so in private universities, but the ones who could not afford such private education would have to be limited to what their grades qualified them to study. Mr. Maher, a student of chemistry at the University of Damascus, said: "I could not afford to go to a private university to study medicine as my friend Husam did. He had lower marks compared to mine, but he is lucky enough as his father is very rich, so he can afford studying at a private university."[229] The fees of private universities were too high for normal people to afford. The cost of universities was prohibitive for the majority of the students.

---

[228] The village of Basser is in the northern city of Daraa, almost halfway to Damascus. http://www.fallouh.net/node/74.

[229] Interview with the author on 10 February 2010.

Fees of up to $12,000 per year—compared to as little as $20 in the public sector—rule out the majority of the population.[230]

Some others are blaming the government for such a seemingly unfair situation. Mr. Ali, a professor at the University of Damascus, stated: “The government policies are making it very difficult for the students to enter the state university. The regime wants to encourage them to go to private ones and benefit their owners, which are the regime’s loyalists.”[231] Consequently, rich people have more opportunities and choices in higher education than poor people, making inequality among the people in the country increase. Moreover, graduates of private schools and private universities have more job opportunities in the future due to the gap between private education and public education deepening the class division in the country.

The Health System

The health service was also a free service for every Syrian and Arab national in the country in the 1970s, 1980s and for most of the 1990s, when the state provided a free and generally satisfying health service. However, disguised privatization of the health system actually started in the late 1990s with the idea of transferring hospitals to General Independent Associations, where patients were obliged to pay some of their treatment costs. The hospitals in Syria either belong to the Ministry of Higher Education, such as the Children’s Hospital, or to the Ministry of Health, such as the Red Crescent. Dr. Wael al-Halqi, a former health minister, refuted allegations of privatization of the public hospitals, but did not provide reasons for why the hospital turned to being partly-free after being completely free for the public for decades. He confirmed that 65% of the hospital beds are still free and only 35% of them are hired at a rate, which is equal to half of the Ministry of Health’s

[230] Sarah Birke, “Syria’s education crisis”, GlobalPost, 5 August 2010, http://www.globalpost.com/dispatch/education/100713/syria-universities?page=0,1, viewed 01 August 2014.

[231] Interview with the author on 23 February 2010.

tariff, pointing out that the emergency service is still free around the clock.[232]

Likewise, Dr. Suleiman Mashqook, the general director of hospitals at the Ministry of Health, justified the new changes as transferring hospitals into General Associations is a step toward providing a much better medical and health service through securing additional financial resources for hospitals to spend on updating the medical equipment and for the necessary maintenance.[233] However, transforming hospitals into General Independent Associations cannot be isolated from the neo-liberalization policies in the country. Mr. Darwich, a long-serving doctor in private and public hospitals in Homs and Damascus, stated: "We were a few years away from total private health service in the country."[234] After 2000, the country witnessed a fast-growing private hospital industry across the country, for many reasons, the first that the rapidly growing population made state hospitals unable to absorb the needs of the people, whilst the state had concurrently almost stopped building any new hospitals. General governmental expenditure on health, as a share of total governmental expenditure, declined from 7.20% in 1999 to 6% in 2011,[235] according to the World Health Organization. Second, the private hospital business is very profitable, where huge profits are driving doctors to concentrate on the private healthcare sector to make more money. That led to a poor quality of work in the public hospital, while no legal responsibility deterred doctors from misconduct or negligence. Dr. Mutee' Karam, the general director of the Children's Hospital, expressed his unhappiness with the new measure of charging the patients, especially in his

---

[232] The Ministry of High Education precedes the Health Ministry in Selling the Cure to Syrians", Syrian Observatory for Human Rights, 12 February 2011, viewed on 3 March 2013. http://www.syriahro.org/12–2-2011-syrian%20observatory10.html.

[233] Ibid.

[234] Interview with the author on 9 February 2013.

[235] Country Statistical Profiles, World Health Organization. http://applications.emro.who.int/docs/RD_Annual_Report_2011_country_statistics_EN_14587.pdf.

hospital, which is the only hospital of its kind in the country and a destination mainly for poor and low-income people in the country.[236]

LEGISLATION

There have been many presidential directives, ministerial decisions and decrees issued and implemented during the years prior to the uprising that have caused public resentment and social problems. A selection of them are discussed below:

1. Law Number 26 was issued in 2007 for Daraa. This law has a national security background. Daraa borders Israel, and the fear of Israeli penetration into the country through this region is high, and any Israeli attempts therefore have to be preempted. Accordingly, Law 26 freezes the ownership of all kinds of properties, so people could not sell or buy, or transfer the ownership of any property. However, the local authorities in Daraa started to grant exceptions by applying for security consent. The ownership transformation required consent from the security services, which could cost up to one million Syrian pounds and could take a number of years. Mr. Al-Kafri, a businessman from Daraa, bought a property in Daraa from someone in 2007, and applied for security consent in order to transfer the ownership. He waited for the consent for more than three years and never received it. He argues: "The law was to protect the city from any Israeli penetration, taking into account that Daraa is on the borders with Israel, but in fact, the law was abused, aiming to drain more money from the people. It is a huge amount of money and it is corruption."[237]

[236] "Muwasah Hospital on its way to Privatization", 04 October 2010, http://www.jpnews-sy.com/ar/news.php?id=12545, viewed on 13 March 2013.

[237] Interview with the author on 17 March 2013.

2. Legislative Decree 49[238] was issued in September 2008. The Kurdish area in the northeast was the most affected area by this law, both economically and socially. Indeed, many letters of appeal were written by some representatives of the local people to President Bashar Assad himself, but the letters were ignored,[239] as Fatih, a Kurdish Syrian from Al Qamishli stated.
3. The 2008 decision of the late mayor of Homs, Iyad Ghazal, to transfer the old town of Homs to a huge residential and commercial complex called the Dream of Homs. This was designed to take advantage of the downtown of Homs, owned by the Endowment Ministry, so people would be renting their properties from the ministry itself, and yet the ministry refused to renew the rental contracts for the people. Many local protests took place outside the mayoral palace, but without reaching a solution.[240] The mayor, according to Mr. Zayn, a local businessman participating in the protests, said the following to a delegation of people who went to meet him in order to discuss the problem: "This project will be achieved under any circumstances and whether you like it or not." It was evident that Bashar Assad was backing the mayoral decision.[241] Mr. Zayn believes that the main aim behind such a project was to "reshape the demographic structure in the city between Alawis and Sunnis,"[242] as the

[238] Legislative Decree 49 stated: "The establishment, transfer, modification or acquisition of any right to a property in a border region or its use for rent or other commercial purpose for a period of more than three years in the name of or for the benefit of an individual or legal entity is prohibited, unless prior permission has been given, and regardless of whether or not the property has been developed, or whether or not it lies within the area designated for land use". Kurdish Watch Report 6, July 2010, http://www.kurdwatch.org/pdf/kurdwatch_dekret49_nivisar_en.pdf.

[239] Interview with the author on 21 April 2014.

[240] "New protest demanding halt of Dream of Homs", Zaman Al Wasl, 22 January 2008, viewed on 1 August 2014, https://www.zamanalwsl.net/news/3088.html,

[241] Interview with the author on 22 March 2013.

[242] Ibid.

downtown of Homs was dominated by Sunnis, and taking into consideration that Homs had great status in the Alawi religion.[243] Demographically, the city had been experiencing a significant growth of Alawis in the past twenty years.

4. The decision of the minister of education to dismiss 1200 fully covered (*Munaqaba*t) teachers from the Ministry of Education. This decision ignited great public resentment among some religious leaders. Sheikh al-Bouti[244] for instance was very critical of this decision.[245] There was another decision issued by of the Ministry of Higher Education to ban fully covered female students (*Munaqabat*) from university. Both decisions, in fact, created a massive public outrage.
5. The Expropriation Acts adopted by the government in the 1970s and 1980, regarding building new roads and new motorways (especially the North Circular and the South Circular in Damascus and its suburbs), have been in action since 2006. Hundreds of thousands of people had their homes destroyed and were displaced as a result, with very minimal levels of compensation. Such procedures and actions caused a pronounced degree of public ferocity against the regime. Mr. Samir, a local resident of Jobar in the east of Damascus, stated: "Our house was seized by the government in June 2006 to build a motorway in the area, it was a three story building, but what we got from the government as compensation was hardly enough to buy a flat in a remote area in the country."[246]

[243] There is a letter by some Alawi religious leader confirms the important status of Homs in the Alawi religion. This letter called Waheed Al-Ayn (The One Eyed).

[244] He was the most influential scholar on the Syria domestic scene; he had a strong relationship with Hafiz Assad. Al-Bouti has also had a weekly TV program since the mid-1990s, and two weekly lessons in al-Iman Mosque in Damascus, which are attended by thousands of people. He was killed in al-Iman mosque on 21 March 2013, while preaching, but no one has claimed the responsibility yet.

[245] "Bouti attributes the shortage of rain to the Mamalakat Iymanukm Series and to the dismissal of the Munaqabat", 13 December 2010 http://www.syria-news.com/var/articlem.php?id=12814, viewed 30 April 2014.

[246] Interview with the author on 31 July 2014.

CORRUPTION AND LAWLESSNESS

During Bashar Assad's rule, corruption has reached an unprecedented level, especially in the public sector, and in the public life too. People started to believe that issuing new decrees or laws concerning public life, such as banning smoking in public areas or introducing strict seatbelt laws, were good in principle but would be abused by the authorities eventually in order to drain more money from the public. A policeman, so it was assumed, could turn a blind eye to someone smoking in a restaurant or to someone not having his seatbelt fastened for a certain amount of money. Indeed, some restaurants had a deal with local policemen in order to allow their customers to continue to smoke. In January 2011, whilst having lunch in a restaurant in the al-Sha'lan area of Damascus, someone asked the waiter whether he could smoke in the restaurant. The waiter said yes, do not worry; we have sorted the policemen out. Such scenes were very common across the country during Bashar's era.

Corruption also reached the military sector in an unprecedented degree. Some barracks commanders used to publicly ask for money from young soldiers. Mr. Youssef, who served as a recruit soldier in the national army, stated:

> While I was serving in the military, the commander of my barrack called us for an unexpected meeting in the big square inside the barrack and asked us, who wants to go home today and stay with his family for three days as a legal absence for 5000 Syrian pounds? A few of the soldiers said yes and have gone home. On the next day the commander held a meeting for the rest of the soldiers and told us to pay only 1000 pounds and go home and enjoy a stay for 2 days with our families.[247]

Lawlessness was certainly felt in the country, whilst a lot of street fighting was occurring between citizens because of traffic congestion, car accidents, or related arguments. Most policemen, local

[247] Interview with the author on 22 January 2011.

authorities, and judges were always on the side of the person who would pay more; these aspects of statelessness could be seen in every corner of the country. In February 2005, Numir Assad, a cousin of President Bashar Assad, along with some armed men robbed Al-Harm, a money transfer company in the center of Damascus, stealing 43 million Syrian pounds: it was an unprecedented event in Damascus.

In another corner of Damascus, in December 2009, gangs (Shabbiha) attacked the vice chancellor of the International Syrian University, Professor Abdul Majeed al-Sadoon, an Iraqi national, in the streets of Damascus. That was the punishment for not allowing a female student, who was related to the president, to undertake her exams after failing to produce sufficient ID. Al-Sadoon was later jailed on baseless charges.

Another sign of lawlessness can be found in the coastal region, where some members of the Assad family used to rent out their IDs to some smugglers for a daily charge, to enable them to cross the borders between Syria and Lebanon, at Aarida and Adabusyyah villages, without being stopped or inspected.

In the University of Tishreen in Latakia, the PhD program was monopolized by Alawis, so "Sunni students from Latakia or Tartus who were willing to follow a PhD program had to go to other universities in the country or to seek a big Wasta,"[248] according to Dr. Hassan.

SOCIAL OUTCOMES

The neo-liberalization policies that were adopted in the name of reform since Bashar Assad ascended to power have increased public grievances. Inequality increased in the country. Poor people were more alienated and more isolated. Their lack of opportunities to access private schools and private universities meant that their children had limited opportunities in the future if they were able to carry on their education. This resulted in a severely segmented

[248] Interview with the author on 19 March 2013.

and atrophied society. The gap between rich and poor has noticeably widened during Bashar Assad's rule since 2000. Moreover, the middle class has been gradually diminishing, especially in the rural areas, where poverty has risen remarkably. Scenes of elderly men selling things in the roads of Damascus, Aleppo and other major cities were getting common, reflecting the harsh poverty hitting the people in the country. Syria had never witnessed such scenes before. Dignity became under attack.

The Millennium Development Goals (MDGs) report in 2010 indicated that:

> Poverty has a clear geographical dimension in Syria. Despite the slight decline of poverty ratios in general in Syria in the decade between 1997 and 2007, the improvement has been uneven at the subnational level, where the poverty ratio in the northeast region is still the highest (15.4% in 2007) nationally, accounting for 55.5% of the total number of poor in Syria.[249]

Moreover, the country was transformed from being a reasonable country in terms of living costs, into a relatively expensive country, and among the highest regarding cost of office locations as reported by Cushman & Wakefield, a global real estate company. They reported that Syria occupied number eight globally in the prices of office locations in 2009.[250] The sharp hike in prices caused tremendous social problems, such as no affordability for young men to get married, which has resulted in more unmarried men and women in society. This has also led to a lack of affordability to buy or rent properties in certain areas, which has

---

[249] Syrian Arab Republic, Third National MDGs Progress Report, 2010. http://www.undp.org/content/dam/undp/library/MDG/english/MDG%20Country%20Reports/Syrian%20Arab%20Republic/MDGR-2010-En.pdf.

[250] Hong Kong & Tokyo overtake London as world's most Expensive Office Locations 24 February 2009 London, viewed on 15 March 2013. http://www.cushwake.com/cwglobal/jsp/newsDetail.jsp?Language=EN&repId=c23200006p&Country=GLOBAL&Country=c37000238p&Language=EN.

increased the informal housing areas, and hence, a segregated society, where poor people have retreated to impoverished neighborhoods. Young people felt desperate and had no aspirations, with a rise in crime and divorce rates in the country, along with other consequences.

> The livelihood of most "informal housing" dwellers depends on informal (casual) employment and informal businesses, with insecure perspectives. This segment of the population may be seen as the most socially and economically vulnerable, and loaded with unemployed and frustrated youth.[251]

as observed by Dr. Mahmoud Abd al-Fadil, a lead author of a UNDP report on poverty in Syria.

Miss Randa, a lawyer in Damascus, monitored some social problems in Syria from 2005 to 2009 that had never been seen before in the country, and came mainly as a result of economic hardship. She stated that between 2005 and 2009 was the worst for Damascus and its suburbs in terms of burglary claims. Criminals used to break into houses, cars, shops and small business plants. Every year, there is a new record of divorce average in the country, and the deteriorating economic situation of the people was the main reason for most divorce cases.[252]

Indeed, it was a decade of destroyed chances of genuine political reform, rational economic openness and serious social welfare. The economic reforms were indispensable for the regime's survival, as Carsten Wieland argued.[253] However, the economic and social implications of such policies on the public were huge. Social inequality has increased, and the gap between rich and poor has widened greatly, making revolution inevitable, and only

---

[251] Mahmoud Abd al-Fadil, "Macroeconomic Policies for Poverty Reduction: The Case of Syria", United Nations Development Program, 2006.

[252] Interview with the author on 29 March 2013.

[253] Carsten Wieland, "Assad's Decade of lost Chances", in *The Syrian Uprising: Dynamics of an Insurgency*, Carsten Wieland, Adam Almqvist & Helena Nassif, St Andrews Papers, St Andrews University, Scotland, 2013, p.10.

waiting for a spark. Salamah Kilah, a prominent Arab socialist scholar, observed the economic changes in Syria from 2000 to 2011, he believes that liberalization has won ultimately in the country in 2006–2007. Complete openness was achieved, and the prices were global. The agriculture and industrial public sectors were on the verge of collapse. The state subsidies on the major commodities were terminated apart from bread. The wealth centered in the hands of few, while the majority became pooper. The economy was in the hands of new businessmen: the children or relatives of long-serving corrupt bureaucrats and army officers. That made the public uprising inevitable.[254]

THE RELIGIOUS INSTITUTION

The religious institution derives its importance from the influence of religious figures in Syrian society. Religious discourse is influential in the country, so it was contained, exploited and sometimes confronted when posing a threat to the regimes. The religious institution during Bashar Assad's presidency was the continuation of what his father had designed over three decades earlier. However, during Bashar Assad's time we can notice concessions and constraints toward the religious institution. Concessions were an aspect of authoritarian upgrading when international threats were culminating between 2003–2007, and constraints afterward when the international threat faded away, although constraints were even tighter following the rise of some Jihadist groups and individuals in Syria and Lebanon. Thomas Pierret observed the sudden changes that took place in 2008 toward the clergy in the country:

> In previous years, the regime's rapprochement with the clergy had been encouraged by the foreign policy crisis; this time it was the dramatic improvement of Syria's international position (the takeover of West Beirut by pro-Syrian militias

---

[254] Salamah Kilah, "The Fates of Totalitarianism in the Process of Revolution", Alhewar Almutamaden, 25/04/2012, viewed on 24/04/2012, http://www.ahewar.org/debat/show.art.asp?aid=295850.

in May 2008, Bashar Assad invitation to attend the 14 July ceremonies in Paris that same year) that allowed the regime to enact this reversal.[255]

Sheikh Abdul Rahman from Damascus experienced the changing regime's stance toward them: "The regime preserved a good relationship with the religious institution, so much relaxation was applied on our activities and our speeches, but once the American danger faded away, the old strict rules were put back in place, and even tighter."[256] In late 2010, months prior to the uprising in Syria, Kareem Fahmi wrote that Syria, "which had sought to show solidarity with Islamist groups and allow religious figures a greater role in public life, has recently reversed course moving forcefully to curb the influence of Muslim conservatives in its mosques, universities and charities."[257] Moreover, the regime's campaign against the Salafis (traditional Salafis) increased significantly in the few years prior to the uprising in 2011. The Syrian Human Rights Committee reported the imprisonment of dozens of Syrians after being convicted of following a Salafi orientation.[258] This campaign seemed to be a result of the increasing Shia influence in the country, which holds an intolerant approach toward Salafism.[259] The regime would never allow Salafism to build a strong base in the country, as Salafis regard Alawi as an out-of-Islam sect on one hand. On the other hand, traditional Salafism is the breeding ground for Jihadism. Moreover, the crackdown on Salafism was also in line with the interests of Sufism trend in the country. In fact, as Pierret wrote,

---

[255] Thomas Pierret, *Religion and State in Syria*, Cambridge University Press, Cambridge, 2013, p.212.

[256] Interview with the author on 7 March 2013.

[257] Kareem Fahmi, "Syria's Solidarity With Islamists Ends at Home", The New York Times, 3 September 2010, viewed on 1 May 2014. http://www.nytimes.com/2010/09/04/world/middleeast/04syria.html?r=0..

[258] Islamist Detainee, Syrian Human Rights Committee, 27 January 2011, http://www.shrc.org/en/?p=20569, viewed on 1 May 2014.

[259] Ahmad Zidan, "The Prison: to be a Salafist", Umahtoday.net, 4 April 2010 http://www.umahtoday.net/arabic/?Action=Details&ID=943, viewed on 1 May 2014.

"Some figures of religious establishment, and highly respected ones at that, openly encouraged state severity against the partisans of Ibn Taymiyyah"[260] (Salafists).

Al-Qubaysiat

A female activist group operates mainly in Damascus, targeting wealthy families. It was established by Munira al-Qubaisi in the 1970s; she was a student of the late Grand Mufti Kufftaro and very loyal to Sheikh al-Bouti. The group operated secretly, but was recognized by the regime in May 2006 and was allowed access to mosques, but this concession from such a regime must be for its benefit and for some services in return such as penetrating the group and securing their loyalty to the regime. Al-Qubaysiat are a non-political community, but focus on attracting Muslim women to practicing Islam and protecting them from the dangerous challenges around them, building a pious Muslim women. However, its trend is in the Sufi tradition, following the Naqshbandi way (*Tariqa*), so following the views of the leader is compulsory for all members.

Jihadists

Jihadists had seemingly been eradicated in Syria since 1982, but after the American invasion of Iraq in 2003, many Jihadists cells were revived in the region, so the instability and anarchy that prevailed in Iraq following the invasion constituted a back yard for the Jihadist groups to revive not just in Iraq, but in several other countries in the region too. The Jihadist groups regrouped again, exploiting the instability in Iraq for arming themselves and planning for different activities in the region. Such a situation constituted a great internal threat to the Syrian regime.[261] Indeed, Syria endured several attacks targeting state institutions and some

---

[260] Pierret, op, cit, p.108.

[261] "New Challenges face Damascus", Akhbarak.net, 12 September 2006, http://www.akhbarak.net/articles/5144022, viewed on 1 May 2014. http://www.akhbarak.net/articles/5144022, viewed on 1 May 2014.

foreign embassies. In 2006, for instance, two major attacks were launched in Damascus: targeting the Syrian TV Centre in June 2006, and another attack targeted the American embassy in September 2006.[262] In September 2008, a large attack targeted a security compound in the city of Damascus, killing 17 people.[263] Most of the people who were convicted of terrorism were imprisoned in Saydnaya Prison, but many of them were released just after the 2011 uprising, and later constituted a great part of the fighting groups in Syria.

SYRIAN FOREIGN POLICY UNDER BASHAR ASSAD

Syria had two fundamental reasons for diversifying its linkages, both regionally and internationally. The first reason was political, as Syria had lost its main global ally, the Soviet Union, in 1989, and then regional allies Egypt and Saudi Arabia after 2003. This forced Syria into finding different allies around the world and in the region upon whom the government could somehow rely in its alleged passive struggle against Israel. Moreover, Syria wanted new alignments not just to challenge international isolation, but also to sustain the regime domestically. Economics was behind the second reason, as Syria was moving toward a market economy, which required a sound and peaceful relationship with the rest of the world. Pertinent to this was that diversification of international linkages were an important aspect of authoritarian upgrading. This was, after all, the politics of most authoritarian regimes in the Arab world that sought to sustain their regimes.

In 2000, when Bashar Assad inherited the presidency from his deceased father amid a period of global stability, it was seemingly a good opportunity for Bashar Assad to develop his relationships with the outside world, both regionally and internationally. Then, however, a cascade of events began to unfurl that would challenge

---

262 "Terrorism hits the Heart of Damascus", Alriyadh.com, 13 September 2006, http://www.alriyadh.com/186338, viewed on 01 May 2014.

263 "Terrorism that bleed Syria since 1970s", Tishreen, 18 March 2012. http://tishreen.news.sy/tishreen/public/read/253682, viewed on 15 April 2014.

this harmony, and lead to a cacophony of noise for Syria: 9/11, the American invasion of Iraq in 2003, and the Lebanese crisis following the assassination of Rafiq al-Hariri, the former prime minister, in February 2005.

Between 2003 and 2007, the regime seemed to reach its nadir with the outside world and was quite probably under threat of American invasion, until Iraqi insurgent resistance saved Syria by miring the George W. Bush administration in a protracted struggle for Iraq, right next door to Syria. By mid-2007, all regional and international pressures seem to have been abated, leading the regime to start restructuring its relationship with the outside world, but this time with more confidence and more certainty, inaugurating a new phase in its history. Strikingly, this phase can be considered as the golden age for the Syrian regime, for the first time since 1963. The real external and internal threats were diminishing, and the regime reproduced itself as a strong authoritarian regime immune to internal threats. This phase lasted until early 2011, when the waves of the Arab Spring tsunami started to make landfall at the Syrian borders.

Relationship with Israel

Since the Middle East conference in Madrid in 1991, Syria was publicly committed to peace with Israel as part of a strategic plan; something which Hafiz Assad confirmed was in the interests of the nation. Indeed, it became a strategic option after the failure to achieve the strategic parity with Israel that was previously sought by the regime. Although Hafiz Assad could not achieve either of his strategic options (parity or peace) with Israel before his death, he always maintained that he had kept Syria safe and secure in front of any Israeli direct attacks. Specifically, the main Syrian demand for achieving peace with Israel is the return of all land that was Syria's before the 1967 war. Despite extensive (but biased) American mediation, conciliation was never reached, postponing the peace process between Syria and Israel, so the formal state between Israel and Syria remained a state of war.

During Bashar Assad's rule, Israel attacked Syria several times, three of them directly in the Syrian heartland. In April 2001, Israel attacked a Syrian radar center in Lebanon, killing three soldiers. In October 2003, Israel launched an attack against an alleged Palestinian camp, some 20 kilometers north of Damascus. In June 2006, four Israeli jets were observed above the presidential palace in Latakia. In September 2007, Israel also attacked an alleged nuclear plant near Deir ez-Zur.[264] These were all signs of weakness in the regime, and in Bashar Assad as leader, leading to huge public resentment. After every Israeli attack, a formal statement was released by the Foreign Ministry, reassuring people and pledging that Syria would respond, but at the right time and in the right place. Farouk all-star, the foreign minister at the time, released a formal statement following the attack in 2003:

> We behaved in a responsible way, we complained to the United Nations, and most of our people supported us and we have to achieve his will. The attack generated a huge public anger. Our people want retaliation, but we are committed to the peace process. We have many cards in our hands to use. Bearing in the mind there are many Israeli settlers in the Golan Heights.[265]

Syrian people considered such statements very humiliating. They used to mock al-Shar' pledges on the streets; people became more and more dissatisfied with Bashar Assad as a strong leader, able to protect them in front of Israeli aggression. The inability of the Syrian regime to respond against Israel was accompanied by a frustrated and humiliated feeling prevailing among the majority of

---

[264] Tarek Tarshishi, "The assassination of Mughnyah Emphasizes the Readiness of Israel for a War", Al-Akbar.com, 18 February 2008. https://www.al-akhbar.com/node/124323, viewed on 13 April 2014.

[265] "Syria to Retaliate", Alwatan.com, 10 October 2003, http://www.alwatan.com/graphics/2003/10oct/27.10/dailyhtml/news4.html

Syrians.[266] To this end, Bashar Assad could not maintain the heroic status that his father had long claimed as the hero of November and October (*Batal al-Tishreenain*), in reference to the Corrective Movement in November 1970 and to the October War with Israel in 1973. In relation to the Golan Heights, Bashar Assad also followed his father's strategy after the disengagement agreement in 1974, emphasizing its liberation either by war or by peace.

Overall, two major points can be made in this context: First, Syria under Bashar Assad is still a country at war with Israel as the offensive enemy on its borders, creating huge security concerns that seemingly legitimize the strict adopted measures that the regime has hitherto taken. Second, although the Syrian people were not satisfied with President Hafiz Assad's domestic politics, his foreign policy toward Israel made sense to them, and they were somehow satisfied with it. On the contrary, the response of Bashar Assad toward Israeli actions created great dissatisfaction among people in the country. However, supporting Hezbollah and Hamas was the main great foreign policy behavior that helped Bashar Assad sustain legitimacy, and hence consolidate his power because such behavior had great public base.

The Relationship with Hezbollah and Hamas

Syria under Hafiz Assad has always supported the liberation factions against Israel in the region regardless of their affiliations and their identities, as long as they adopted resistance against Israel and were in line with the Syrian regime's interests. Since day one, Bashar Assad maintained his father's strategy, so he too was committed to the resistance option; he provided Hezbollah, Hamas and other resistance factions such as Al-Jihad Al-Islami great political support. For instance, Khaled Mishal, the chief of Hamas' Political Bureau, used to reside in Syria from 1999 under

[266] Omar Koush,"Why the Syrian Regime does not Respond to the Israeli Attacks?", Aljazeera.net, 10 May 2013, viewed on 10 May 2013. http://aljazeera.net/opinions/pages/b6593c76–78c3–415d-8fef-7a89fec67065.

the protection of the Syrian regime.[267] It is an ideology and a defensive strategy at the same time for the Syrian regime against Israel. Moreover, allying with Iran in supporting Hamas and Hezbollah has reinforced the legitimacy of Bashar Assad at home. Such a foreign policy of supporting the resistance groups and defying Israel, forming the so-called Axis of Resistance and Refusal, was responding to the prevailing public opinion in Syria and in the Arab counties too.

Bashar Assad's support to Hezbollah in the War of July 2006 against Israeli attacks, and his support to Hamas against Israel's war on Gaza, December 2008–January 2009, replenished his regime's nationalist legitimacy[268] and made him the most popular Arab leader, according to a poll held in 2009.[269] However, Syrian support to Hezbollah in Lebanon was aiming for another main goal, which was maintaining Syrian influence in Lebanon after its withdrawal in 2005 through boosting the influence and role of Hezbollah in the country. Robert Rabil observed the importance of Hezbollah to Syria:

> Damascus needed Hezbollah should Syria wish to reclaim its "historical" role in Lebanon. And, while Syrian intelligence could activate its Palestinian allies inside Lebanon, these were not organic to Lebanon's society. Only Hezbollah could serve as the Trojan horse which could bring Syria back into Lebanon.[270]

---

267 Khaled Mishal, the chief of Hamas political bureau, was dismissed from Jordan in 1999, and welcomed in Syria since then. He left Syria in January 2012 after refusing to support the regime against the uprising http://mesi.org.uk/ViewNews.aspx?ArticleId=2461, viewed on 2 May 2014.

268 Raymond Hinnebusch, "Syria: from Authoritarian Upgrading to Revolution", International Affairs (Royal Institute of International Affairs 1944-), Vol. 88, No. 1 (January 2012), pp.95–113.

269 "Assad is the Most popular Arab Leader", MESI, 22/05/2009, http://mesi.org.uk/ViewNews.aspx?ArticleId=2461, viewed on 2 May 2014.

270 Robert G. Rabil, "Has Hezbollah's Rise Come at Syria's Expense?" Middle East Quarterly Fall 2007, pp.43–5.

The Syrian Relationship with Lebanon

A few years prior to the beginning of his presidency, Bashar Assad was heavily involved with Lebanese issues. "He built a cell of new influential loyalists in the country: Suleiman Feranjyeh,[271] Michel Semaha[272] and Emile Lahood (the former Lebanese president),"[273] as Mr. Khaddam has claimed. It was a backup to the Syrian influence over Hezbollah.

Bashar Assad's first problem in Lebanon was his support for President Emile Lahood to seek another presidential term. This problem cost Syria its very presence in Lebanon, leading them to withdraw their troops in humiliation, in response to Security Council Resolution 1905 that was adopted in the aftermath of Rafiq al-Hariri's assassination in February 2005. The killing of Mr. Rafiq al-Hariri certainly created more antagonism toward the Syrian regime in Lebanon, particularly from Rafiq al-Hariri's supporters, making them supporters for a regime change in Syria. Saad al-Hariri, the son of Rafiq, who inherited his father's political status, said in August 2006: "Let's get rid of Bashar. Kaddam and the Brotherhood are the alternative."[274]

The war of July 2006 boosted the legitimacy of Hezbollah in Lebanon, and its successful military campaign against his rivals in West Beirut in May 2008 shifted the balance of power in the country dramatically in its favor, making him the strongest single link in the country, dominating domestic affairs as well as Lebanese foreign affairs. After May 2008, Hezbollah became the

---

[271] Suleiman Feranjyeh is the grandson of Suleiman Feranjyeh, the late Lebanese president. He is the leader of Marada Party.

[272] Michel Semaha is an influential figure in Lebanon; he worked in the intelligence the government, and as an adviser to the former president Amin Jumail. *In 2013 Semaha was convicted of planning for terrorist attacks targeting mosques and churches in Lebanon, and targeting religious figures in the country. His plans were organized by some Syrian figures including Bashar Assad. Strangely, Semaha was released on bail in January 2016.*

[273] The Political Memory, television program, Al-Arabiya, 05 November 2011.

[274] Hasan Aliq, "Al-Hariri: let's get rid of Bashar", Al-Akhbar.com, 24 August 2006, http://www.al-akhbar.com/node/10044, viewed on 1 May 2014.

unquestioned single most powerful force in the country.[275] Certainty, such a situation was of core interest to the Syrian regime in Lebanon and in the region as a whole.

The Relationship with Egypt and Saudi Arabia

After the Gulf War against Iraq in 1991, Syria, Egypt and Saudi Arabia constituted a triangle of the most influential countries in the Arab world. This alliance helped Syria to strengthen its position in the region, and replace the demizing role of Iraq in Arab politics. However, after Bashar Assad ascended to power in 2000, tension between Syria, and both Egypt and Saudi Arabia, steadily increased, originally because of the Syrian stance against the American invasion of Iraq in 2003. However, the relationship became tense following the assassination of Rafiq al-Hariri, as Saudi Arabia blamed Syria for that incident. The continuation of Syrian support to Hezbollah and Hamas has also deepened the gap between Syria and both Saudi Arabia and Egypt, creating great division in the region. Two blocs or axes were formed in the region: 1) the Axis of Resistance and Refusal consists of Syria, Iran, Hezbollah, Hamas and Qatar to some extent; and 2) the Moderate Axis consists of Saudi Arabia, Egypt and Jordan. Therefore, Syria changed its traditional regional alignments, so Iran replaced both Egypt and Saudi Arabia in Syrian politics, and the influence of Iran in Syria was increasing significantly.

Relationship with Iran

The relationship between Tehran and Damascus has had sectarian ideological dimensions since the Iranian Revolution. Despite the enmity between Iraq and Syria, there was no explanation as to why Syria would ally with Iran against Iraq during the war in the

[275] Antony Shadid, "Hezbollah Emerges in Forefront of Power in Lebanon", The Washington Post, 18 May 2008. http://www.washingtonpost.com/wp-dyn/content/article/2008/05/17/AR2008051701292.html?sid=ST2008051702666. Viewed on 1 May 2014.

1980s, especially as this was a clear contradiction to Baath ideology on Arabism and liberating the whole occupied land for the Arabs. Iran is not an Arab country and, moreover, it is considered to be occupying Arab land (al-Ahwaz) since 1926. However, the Syrian regime has always claimed that Iran is an ally in the conflict against Israel.

After Bashar Assad came to power, the Iranians invested more heavily in the relationship with Syria, especially after the fall of Saddam Hussein in Iraq, and the collapse of the Arab influential triangle (Syria, Egypt and Saudi Arabia). Exploiting the strong alignment between Syria and Iran against Israel in the Axis of Resistance, Iran was increasing its influence inside Syria. After dominating Iraq, Iran has been using Syria as a strategic land hub for Iranian regional dominance from the Gulf to the Mediterranean Sea, so Syria became an Iranian lung in the Arab world, incubating and nursing all the Iranian roles and activities in the Arab region. Therefore, if the Syrian regime collapsed, it would be one of the greatest disasters for Iran.[276] Despite the importance of all aspects of the Iranian–Syrian relationship, political and cultural cooperation have remained the most important aspects, where Syria has always been the weakest link.

The Iranian Cultural Consultancy in Damascus was a very active institution, holding many seminars and lectures promoting Shiism, encouraging Iranians to make pilgrimages in Syria, and building Husaianiat (Shia schools) across the country. In between 2001 and 2006, 12 Husaianiat were built in the town of Saydeah Zainab in the south of Damascus, and three colleges for Shia education. In 2003, permission was granted to the first Shia university to operate in the country.[277] In Darayya, a western suburb of Damascus, Shias claimed ownership of an old shrine, claiming it belongs to Saydeah Sokaina, the daughter of Imam al-Hussein. It was the third shrine after Saydeah Zainab in the

[276] The Press Front, television program, Al-Arabiya, 17 June 2011.

[277] "A study warns of Shia Expansion" on 22/04/2008, viewed on 30 April 2008 http://www.aawsat.com/details.asp?issueno=10626&article=467879#.UVt0Uat4aDR.

south of Damascus and Saydeah Ruqayya in the center of Damascus. Such activities certainly made some Syrian people concerned about the Iranians' agenda in their country. Moreover, Shia activities such as religious celebrations (Latmyyat) have increased significantly since 2006, and became very noticeable, especially in Damascus. Shia pilgrims were on the streets of Damascus all year round. Mr. Amin, a shop owner in Al-Hamidiyeh Old Souq said:

> Every time these pilgrims come, we have to abandon our trade and just watch their ceremony. Their ceremony begins at the top of the market and ends in the Umayyad Mosque, and last for more than five hours. On other hand, we do not like their ceremony; it is very nasty scene. They bleed themselves including children. We do not want to see such scenes in our country.[278]

In Aleppo, the Iranian consulate was operating like an intelligence services center,[279] according to Mr. Naji, a businessman and member of the Chamber of Commerce from Aleppo. Aljazeera region also endured huge efforts and activities to promote Shiism among the people, taking advantage of the worsening economic situation in that region.[280] The aim was to create pockets of Shia communities in order to dilute the Sunnis' overwhelming dominance, which extends from Baghdad to Damascus, and from Aleppo to Mosul. Such a situation has created irredentist disputes among the tribes in Aljazeera province. Moreover, Iran offered thousands of education scholarships to Syrian students to study in Iranian universities. In one case, Mr. Asem, a student who was offered a place to study engineering in Iran, came back soon after he started his education program. He said: "I was under immense pressure, they wanted me

[278] Interview with the author in Damascus on 15 January 2011.

[279] Interview with the author on 15 May 2012.

[280] "Deir Ez-Zur, where poor people were left as an easy prey against Shiism", zamanalwsl, 11 November 2013. viewed on 15 May 2014, https://www.zamanalwsl.net/news/43019.html.

to embrace Shiism. I have refused, but got so afraid, so I decided to come back home and forget all about my studies."[281]

The Shia community in Syria and in the region was the weakest link for the Arab countries, but in contrast, an asset for Iran for its effort to export its revolution and expand its influence outside Iran. In fact, the Shia community in the region became a real Trojan horse for Iran. Therefore, there is a big motivating factor for Iran to increase the numbers of Shias in the Arab world.

Syrians were a bit concerned over the relationship with Iran for two reasons: 1) Iran is a Shia country that has played a big role in the sectarian divisions and violence across Iraq after the American invasion; 2) There has always been an ideological dimension behind the Iranian relationship with other countries in the region, so a very close relationship with Iran might destabilize countries through mobilizing the Shia minorities.[282]

Syria's Relationship with Iraq

Before the American invasion in 2003, a détente between the two countries prevailed. Syria was willing to break Iraq's international isolation, and trade between the two countries was revived. Syria also benefited from the oil for food program, a program adopted by the United Nations to help the Iraqis counter the severe implications of international sanctions against the Iraqi regime. However, during the American invasion in 2003, Syria remained against, but not due to ideological reasons. In fact, the Syrian regime knew that it was next after Saddam Hussein if America won in Iraq, so the regime helped some Syrian volunteer fighters reach Iraq to fight with Iraqis against the occupation.

Standing against the 2003 invasion, Bashar Assad gained more national legitimacy in the country. Moreover, the chaos in Iraq that followed the fall of Saddam's regime constituted a great

[281] Interview with the author on 21 January 2011.

[282] Abdul Salam Ismael "Welcoming the Relationship with Turkey and Denouncing the Relationship with Iran", 9 November 2009, viewed on 22 March 2013, http://www.3bdulsalam.com/?p=2043.

barrier of fear among Syrian people of the same scenario if the regime in Syria collapsed. Chaos was the alternative; this is what the regime in Syria tried to convince people. Such prevailing public concern strengthened the regime further. The relationship between Syria and the new rulers of Iraq had never been so close, and in fact it reached its worst level between 2009–2010. On 22 September 2009, Mr. Al-Maliki, the prime minister of Iraq, launched an unprecedented attack on the regime in Syria following an explosion in Baghdad that killed dozens. "We will continue in our adopted way to achieve the aims of our people who voted for us to eliminate the ruminants of Ba'athists and Al-Qaeda who launch their attacks from Syria."[283] The relationship between the two countries continued to deteriorate to a level that demanded Turkish intervention to mediate, in a bid to cool down the mounting tension between the two sides.

Relations with Qatar

After Amir Hamad assumed power in 1995, radical changes in its foreign policy toward the Arab world were taken. The establishment of the Aljazeera Broadcast Centre added far more weight to the country's soft power potential, regionally and internationally. Qatar also decided to adopt a friendly relationship with the resistance wing (Syria, Iran, Hamas and Hezbollah). Syria and Qatar were the only two Arab countries who formally supported Hezbollah and Hamas against Israel in June 2006 and January 2009, respectively. It was an asset to Bashar Assad's regime domestically and regionally to have Qatar on board the Axis of Resistance. However, Qatar's good relationship with Israel and the presence of the American military base on its soil do pose big questions of its role in the Axis of Resistance.

The political rapprochement with Qatar created great economic interests for Syria. Qatari investments in the country

[283] "Al-Maliki attack Syria Again", in Syria Light 22 September 2009, http://www.syrialight.com/?option=content&view=article&id=10062&mid=1, viewed on 15 March 2013.

increased heavily, mounting to $6 billion in early 2011.[284] The Syrian–Qatari relationship was an exceptional one, as "what made this relationship so special is its nature that overcame the traditional nature of the relationship between countries,"[285] according to an official Syrian source. Amir Sheikh Hamad himself expressed his delight at the great relationship between the two countries. He stated, "The mutual relationship between Qatar and Syria is a good example of a mutual Arab-Arab relationship."[286] Both Qatar and Syria had great interests for developing their mutual relationship. While the economic benefits for the Syrian regime meant survival and more consolidation of power, political benefits for Qatar were to strengthen its position and its weight in the region by siding with the Axis of Resistance. Such a position gave Qatar a great popular support in the Arab world.

The Relationship with Turkey

Since the Justice and Development Party came to power in 2002, the relationship between the two countries underwent dramatic improvements on all stages, politically, economically and culturally. The same stance that they both adopted toward the American invasion of Iraq in 2003 laid the groundwork for a strong relationship between the two countries. In addition, Turkey played a mediator role between Syria and Israel before the relationship between Turkey and Israel deteriorated in the aftermath of the Israeli attack in May 2010 on the Gaza Freedom Turkish Flotilla, which was heading to Gaza in an attempt to break the imposed Israeli sanctions on the isolation of Gaza. On the other hand,

[284] "Syria threatens Qatari investments", Al-Bawaba.com, 17 May 2011. http://www.albawaba.com/main-headlines/syria-threatens-qatari-investments, viewed 02 May 2014.

[285] "Syria & Qatar, Overcome the Traditional Structure of the Mutual Relationship between the Countics." 8 May 2008, http://sana.sy/ara/174/2008/05/31/176983.htm, viewed on 20 March 2013.

[286] "The Amir of Qatar: The Mutual Relationship Between Syria & Qatar is An Ideal Relationship Between the Arab Counties", 31May 2009, http://www.syria-news.com/readnews.php?sy_seq=96145, viewed on 20 March 2013.

Turkey has sought Syrian help in finding a solution with the Kurdish PKK (Kurdistan Workers' Party) fighters, benefiting from the Syrian influence over them.

Although the entire rapprochement between the two countries was very momentous, history was made when both countries held, for the first time ever, a common military exercise in April 2009, followed by the establishment of the Strategic Cooperation Council between the two countries in September 2009. Veysel Ayhan wrote:

> The September 16, 2009 treaty between Turkey and Syria, nations that were on the brink of war in 1957–58 and in 1998, is a historic and an important day for their neighboring countries, and for the Middle East in general.[287]

After the first meeting of the Ministerial Council of the high-level Strategic Cooperation Council, which was held in Aleppo and Gaziantep in October 2009, Mr. Ahmet Davutoglu, the Turkish foreign minister, stated: "I proclaim our common slogan to be a common fate, a common history, and a common future."[288] This official statement can demonstrate the very deep relation with Turkey. Moreover, after 2009, Syria started to introduce an official map of Syria without the Iskenderun region,[289] making many Syrian people concerned about a hidden agreement between Syria and Turkey regarding that region, so maybe the regime was preparing the public mood for such an agreement.

In sum, the relationship with Turkey was one of the most important radical achievements in Syrian foreign policy during Bashar Assad's rule. It served the authoritarian upgrading process in many ways: 1) It challenged international isolation through opening new links; 2) It responded to public opinion that was

---

[287] Veysel Ayhan, "Turkey-Syria High Level Strategic Cooperation Council Period", 8 December 2009. http://www.orsam.org.tr/en/showArticle.aspx?ID=107.

[288] Ibid.

[289] Hussein Khalifa,'Syria without Iskenderun", Alhewar.org, 04 December 2007, http://www.ahewar.org/debat/show.art.asp?aid=117253, viewed on 02 May 2014.

concerned about the strong relationship with Iran; 3) It established a great economic partnership, which generated many advantages to the regime's loyalists. Moreover, Syria regional's struggle against Israel was boosted after tension occurred between Turkey and Israel in 2010 following the Gaza Freedom Flotilla crisis.

Relationship with China

Despite the fact that both parties believe in the ideological bankruptcy of the other in the past two decades, the relationship has remained good between the Chinese Communist Party and the Baath Party in Syria. The Chinese president visited Syria in 2001 and the visit of Bashar Assad to China in 2004 had clear economic dimensions rather than just political goals.

China today is different from what it was during the Cold War. It does not have a clear political orientation, and cannot be described a Syrian ally or Arab ally. In fact, it seeks to preserve good relationships with both the Arabs and Israel. According to Mrs. Maryam, a former Syrian diplomat in China, "We always worked for a good mutual relationship, but China's relationship with most Arab counties is almost the same, and mainly concerning economic interests."[290]

Relations with Russia

The Soviet Union was a great ally for Syria during the Cold War: In 1971 Hafiz Assad gave the Soviets use of Tartus military facility, a large base on the Syrian coast, which is the only military fueling port for the Russian Navy in this area.[291] It is also for material support such as fueling and technical services such repairs and maintenance. Since the mid-1990s, the relationship between Syria and Russia was deteriorating due to the debt crisis in Syria, a crisis

[290] Interview with the author on 22 April 2012.

[291] Abul Karim Saleh al-Muhsen, "The Historic Status of the Syrian Russian Relationship and its Prospects" Alhewar.org, on 12 May 2012, http://www.ahewar.org/debat/show.art.asp?aid=307325, viewed on 30 May 2012.

that can be traced back to the Soviet era. However, Bashar Assad's first visit to Russia was in 2005 on a request of president Putin in order to reschedule the Syrian debts toward Russia. The visit pushed the relationship forward when the two sides agreed to write off 73% of Syrian debt. In return, the two sides agreed to a deal worth $3.6 billion in new arms deals and energy investment for Russian companies such as Tatneft.[292]

In 2008, Syria backed the Russian invasion into Georgia, when most countries in the world opposed it. Indeed, the Syrian–Russian relationship got even stronger with the Russian president's visit to Syria in 2010. A long-term contract was signed, but "while the overall value of Russian arms deals with Syria has more than doubled in three years from $2.1 billon in 2007 to $4.7 billion in 2010, Syria is a relatively small customer for Russia's arms industry. In 2011, Russia arms exports to Syria comprised only 5 percent of the total,"[293] as Daria Solovieva pointed out.

However, the cultural relationship cannot be underestimated, it is always great, and Russia still grants Syrian students scholarships every year. Almost two hundreds Syrian students go every year to study at Russian universities privately, and many Syrian officers and professors have Russian wives. Equally, Russian experts are much relied upon in the public sector in Syria.[294]

The relationship between the two countries is a relatively strong one, but perhaps not to the level that it used to be during the Cold War. Russia is not the godfather for such regimes any more. Russia under Putin is very different: It is not about anti-imperialism or combating aggressors any more. According to Mr. Samir Shishakli, an expert on Russia, "In the past twenty years,

---

[292] Richard Weitz, "Syria's Assad Sees Georgia War as Opening Moscow Options", World Politics Review, 03 September 2008, viewed on 13 February 2013. http://www.worldpoliticsreview.com/articles/2618/syrias-assad-sees-georgia-war-as-opening-moscow-options.

[293] Daria Solovieva, "Why Russia is backing Assad's Regime in Syria", International Business Times on 02 October 2012, viewed on 10 May 2013, http://www.ibtimes.com/why-russia-backing-assads-regime-syria-799087.

[294] "About the Russian-Syrian Relationship", RT, 07 August 2009, http://arabic.rt.com/info/18591, viewed on 10 December 2012.

the Zionist lobby in Russia has grown massively and is controlling the decision makers directly, which explains the close relationship with Israel."[295] Russia has a very good relationship with Israel, but maintaining a good relationship with Syria has a different purpose. It was mainly to strengthen the regime in front of Islamic fundamentalism to prevent the Islamists taking control of the country serving the national interests of Russia, the US, Israel[296] and the Arab regimes as well. For the Syrian regime, a strong relationship with Russia was very important for two main reasons: 1) Russia was still the prime country that Syria relied on for defensive weapons against Israel, 2) Syria needed to mitigate international isolation through building new, or restoring old, relationships with countries in the world.

Relations with Europe

Bashar Assad started a different foreign policy with Europe, and a radical one in some cases. Tony Blair was the first British prime minister to visit Syria in October 2001 in some thirty years. In return, Bashar Assad visited the United Kingdom in December 2002, just a few weeks before the invasion of Iraq; he was the first Syrian president to visit the United Kingdom and meet the queen. From the Syrians' perspective, this relationship was certainly very strange to fathom, as Britain had always been conceived by Baath ideologues as an old imperialist and colonialist country that supported Zionism and the formation of Israel.

France was a very important European friend to Syria too. It was the first non-Arab country that Bashar Assad visited after ascending to power; President Jacques Chirac was the only Western head of state to attend the funeral of the late Syrian president Hafiz Assad in 2000. He pledged to provide all sorts of

[295] An interview with the author on 29 March 2013.

[296] Mark Katz, "Mideast Watch: A Russian-Syrian Alliance?" 05 September 2005, http://www.upi.com/Business_News/Security-Industry/2005/09/05/Mideast-Watch-A-Russian-Syrian-Alliance/UPI-79891125934110/#ixzz2Kr496nM0, viewed 13 April 2013.

support to help the new Syrian leader—Bashar—to steer a radical reform.[297] And while the relationship deteriorated after the assassination of Rafiq al-Hariri, it was fully restored again when President Sarkozy invited Bashar Assad to attend the Mediterranean Summit in France in July 2008.

The relationship with Spain was also a fruitful one; as a case in point, Syria was fully cooperating with Spain in regard to the Madrid terrorist attack in 2004. Worryingly, many Spanish citizens with Syrian origins were detained, imprisoned by the Spanish government and then deported to Syria to face terrorism charges (and torture). Mr. Mohannad Al-Mallah, a Spanish Syrian, was detained in Spain over the Madrid bombing in 2004, but released without charges. He stated: "The Syrian authorities cooperated fully with their Spanish counterparts in my case, and some other Syrians were deported from Spain to Syria after the Madrid bombing, and faced torture."[298]

Overall, "Syria's relations with EU Member States gained momentum since 2008. A general consensus in favor of EU engagement with Syria emerged in 2009, recognizing Syria's key role in a number of critical issues in the region."[299] Such developments strengthened the regime domestically; enabling Bashar to gradually restore authoritarianism back into the country through invalidating many concessions he had to offer in the past few years, when international threat was looming.

The Relationship with the United States

The United States supported the inheritance of power in Syria in the year 2000. Secretary of State Madeline Albright from the

---

[297] Marwan Kabalan, "Syrian Foreign Policy: between Domestic Needs and the External Environment", in *Syrian foreign Policy and the United States*, Raymond Hinnubsuch, Marwan Kabalan, Bassma Kodmani & David Lesh, the University of St-Andrews, Center of Syrian Studies, Scotland, 2010, pp.27–42.

[298] Interview with the author on 6 March 2013.

[299] European Neighborhood and Partnership Instrument, Syrian Arab Republic National Indicative Program, 2011–2013, p.3.

Clinton administration endorsed the smooth and peaceful transition of power in the country from father to son. It was very supportive American stance toward a regime that had been described as a terrorist sponsor. Thereafter, Syria was a key ally of the United States and its allies in the war on terrorism. It provided significant intelligence and security service cooperation with the United States. Indeed, it was so much so that Syria was one of three centers in the Middle East for detaining and torturing Al-Qaeda suspects. Robert Bear, a former CIA officer, stated, "If you want an effective interrogation on a detainee, send him to Jordan, if you want him to be tortured to death then send him to Syria, but if you do not want to hear about him anymore, send him to Egypt, that was the custom."[300]

In 2003, Syria opposed the American invasion of Iraq, but played great tactical politics with both the United States and the Iraqi resistance, as the Syrian regime wished there not to be a winning party in the war, because if either party won they would be a threat to the regime. While George W. Bush and his neo-con team had a great intention to change the regime in Syria and to shape a new Middle East, the Islamic resistances and Jihadists were a great threat to the Syrian regime. The United States lost the war and Bush's mission in the Middle East collapsed, but resulted in creating another Al-Qaeda base in the world which bred thereafter the Islamic State in Iraq.

The assassination of Rafiq al-Harari in Lebanon increased tensions between Syria and the United States dramatically. Washington withdrew its ambassador from Damascus following the incident. Condoleezza Rice then stated: "The Syrian Government is not on the right track of improving the relationship with the United States, but on the track of deteriorating the relationship with Washington."[301] However, when Obama came to power in 2009, he had decided to send a US ambassador back to Syria. The then State Department spokesman Ian Kelly stated: "We continue

[300] "From Condi to Neo-Condi", a documentary film. Aljazeera. 11 May 2013.

[301] "Washington justifies its ambassador withdrawal from Damascus as the relationship is deteriorating", Aljazeera, 16 February 2005.

to have concerns about Syria's role in this region, and we think one way to address those concerns is to have an ambassador in Damascus."[302]

Overall, foreign relations were manipulated by Bashar Assad as a part of authoritarian upgrading and helped him stabilize his regime through diversifying his international links. He boosted his nationalist legitimacy from standing with the Resistance Axis to Israel on one hand, and he restored its great status in the world and in the region through skillfully playing on the international rapid changes on the other hand.

CONCLUSION

Before the uprising in 2011, two phases of Bashar Assad's era in Syria can be detected: 1) from 2000 to 2007, where the regime relied on offering some limited concessions domestically in order to consolidate its power through authoritarian upgrading, and to challenge the increasing international threats; and 2) after 2007, where the regime managed to survive in front of international threats. The regime reproduced itself as a strong authoritarian regime domestically. He also restored its position as a key regional player not to be ignored in the Middle East. In both phases, the radical neo-liberal economic policies strengthened the regime, but generated harsh social implications for the public, and were reflected in an unprecedented rate of social inequality since 1963, which constituted, along with political repression, the roots of the 2011 revolution.

---

[302] Elise Labott, "Obama to send U.S. ambassador back to Syria", CNN Politics, 24 June 2009, viewed on 12 May 2014. http://edition.cnn.com/2009/POLITICS/06/24/us.syria/index.html?iref=nextin.

Chapter Three

A REVOLUTION FROM BELOW

INTRODUCTION

Revolution was inevitable in Syria after having had a wretched and disappointing decade of Bashar Assad's rule, and after authoritarianism reproduced itself fully in the later years of his era before the 2011 uprising. The Arab Spring in Tunisia and Egypt offered Syrians the prototype of a long-awaited solution. However, fear was still dominant, and was still the overwhelming obstacle. In this chapter, I will cast light first on the Arab Spring revolutions in Tunisia, Egypt, Libya, Yemen and Bahrain, and their different circumstances. Then, I will try to observe and analyze the revolution in Syria during the peaceful phase, and how it started, and its developments step-by-step until it spread to many parts of the country. Also, I will discuss the role of social actors in Syria such as tribes and ethnic and religious groups, and their position toward the Syrian Revolution, which contributed heavily to its complexity.

WINDS OF CHANGE

Oliver Schlumberger once famously predicted that winds of change would one day "blow throughout the Arab world,"[303] but the revolutionary winds which blew in 2011 upon Tunisia took all observers of Middle Eastern politics by surprise. In fact, what

[303] Oliver Schlumberger, "Arab Authoritarianism: Debating the Dynamics and Durability of Non-Democratic Regimes" in *Debating Arab Authoritarianism*, Schlumberger (ed), Stanford University Press: Stanford, 2007, p.1–20.

happened in Tunisia constituted more than a mere change: It was a political tsunami that aimed to uproot the long-established regimes of the Arab world. The resilience and the strength of the authoritarian regimes in the Arab world reached a level that made them immune to changes that might have been brought about through reforms. In fact, the Arab regimes proved to be irredeemable, genuine reform was no more than rhetoric, and would lead to their collapse if applied. Therefore, reform rhetoric may have contained public resentment for some time, but once this rhetoric lost its influence and its magic, and the regimes instead consolidated their power more and reproduced themselves as strong and full authoritarian regimes, revolution was on hold. The Arab regimes have increased their level of suppression under the dominance of globalization through imposing neo-liberalism gradually upon the region and reducing what they used to offer to their people.[304]

THE ARAB SPRING

In their "Arab Spring Fever"[305] article in August 2007, Amr Hamzawy and Nathan Brown suggested there was little hope for the future of democracy in Arab countries as the move toward democracy in many Arab countries was aborted. This perception was derived from the events that followed the adoption of democratic elements in some Arab countries such as Egypt, Iraq and Lebanon in 2005. Great hopes were sought to achieve a political spring in the Arab world through gradual constitutional, economic and political reforms, but not through revolutions from above or revolutions from below.

[304] Muhammad Al-Attar, "Open Debate with Fawaz Trabulsi about the Syrian Revolution" Al-Jadaliyya, 04 March 2013, http://www.jadaliyya.com/pages/index/10447/, viewed on 10 March 2013.

[305] Amr Hamzawi & Nathan Brown, "Arab Spring Fever", in Carnegie Endowment for International Peace, 29August 2007. http://www.carnegieendowment.org/2007/08/29/arab-spring-fever/tqj.

The Arab regimes before the Arab Spring were different in their political categories, so "Arab regimes apart can be divided into three basic political categories; weak or failing [Lebanon, Iraq], strict authoritarian [Syria, Tunisia, Algeria and Libya] and semi-authoritarian states [Egypt, Jordan, Sudan, Mauritania and Morocco]."[306] However, the Syrian regime, in addition to being an authoritarian regime, was also considered a sectarian rule too. Ironically, the Arab Spring, which occurred through revolution from below, first cast its light upon one of the most authoritarian Arab regimes, Tunisia, then spread to a semi-authoritarian regime, Egypt, demonstrating that changing the political, economic and social systems in the Arab world have only one solution: revolution. The revolutions are the reaction to the predicament of all Arab authoritarian regimes, kingdoms or republics, because their external legitimacy is shaken and their internal legitimacy has been exhausted. They no longer provide the least necessary services and the social distribution patterns for their people as they used to do in the past. Furthermore, they lost their legitimacy, which was derived from their role in the national liberation and the Arab–Israeli conflict.[307] For some time, there have been ominous signs of revolutions on the horizon in the Arab world, but elements from within, such as authoritarian upgrading, and elements from without, such as the global war on terrorism, delayed revolutionary political and social movements.

Evidently, the war on terrorism also played some important role in the Arab Spring, but a double opposite role in delaying or advancing the Arab Spring. The regimes manipulated the war on terrorism to crack down more severely on the opposition, especially the Islamists, and so tightened their grips on the people. Such behavior may have been seen as a pushing element toward the uprisings, but in turn, could be considered as an additional obstacle in front of the people for uprising and have delayed the Arab Spring.

---

[306] Ibid.

[307] Al-Attar, opt, cit.

Tunisia

Tunisia, after being considered a marginal country in regard to Middle Eastern and North African politics, was an unlikely ignition point for the Arab Spring. On 14 January 2011, deposed President Bin Ali left the country after almost a month of public uprising that began as a reaction to a tragic event involving a man working as a street vendor on 17 December 2010. His name was Muhammad Bouazizi. Through setting himself on fire he sent a great and clear message to his generation that death is much better than living under such regimes. The Tunisian Revolution created a great sense of public awareness among all Arab people with regard to the power they held as individuals and how they could use it in order to topple their leaders and regimes. For instance, the power of peaceful demonstrations and the power of non-violent means both were highlighted by the Tunisian Revolution. In other words, "the power of non-partisan youth movements"[308] was clearly emphasized, according to Popovic and Djuri. Although public mobilization in Tunisia was peaceful, the regime reaction was violent. The security forces tried to suppress the uprising violently. However, the military refused to enter the struggle, posing an important question about military loyalty toward Ben Ali. The chief of staff Rasheed Ammar refused orders from Bin Ali to fire at the demonstrators,[309] empowering Tunisian people to win the battle against Ben Ali. The Tunisian Revolution began in Sidi Bouzid city, almost 200 miles south of the capital, Tunis, a day after the Bouazizi incident (17 December 2010). It reached Tunis on 9 January 2011 and continued for almost 28 days.[310]

---

[308] Srdja Popovic and Kristina Djuri, "People Power", in *Revolution and Political Transformation, in the Middle East*, Middle East Institute View Point, Volume I August 2011, pp.14–18.

[309] "Ben Ali Ordered the Army to Shell the Al-Qassrein (City)", Aljazeera.net, 12 April 2011, viewed on 25 May 2014.http://aljazeera.net/news/pages/efc55c85-210e-4075-a98a-96d37f40a0b8.

[310] Yasmine Ryan, "How Tunisia's revolution began", Aljazeera.com, 26 January 2011, http://www.aljazeera.com/indepth/features/2011/01/2011126121815985483.html, viewed on 23 May 2014.

It was not only the military impartiality that helped the uprising in Tunisia, but the relatively great social harmony in the country played a great role too. The Tunisian society is a harmonious society, free from ethnically driven conflicts.[311] Therefore, "Tunisia's 'spirit of solidarity' signaled the start of the revolution and the starting point for freedom of association and institutional reform for civil society activity."[312] Civil society organizations, and opposition parties and movements, were very restricted under the Bin Ali regime. Politics was dominated by the ruling Constitutional Democratic Rally Party, and the activities of genuine opposition parties were ruthlessly restrained. Before January 2011, only a handful of Tunisian civil society organizations were active and independent.[313] However, some civil society organizations such as the Tunisian General Labour Union (UGTT), and the grassroots of some political parties, as individual activists, have played a great role in organizing, and hence, spreading mass public mobilization in the country.[314] The day that Bouazizi burned himself was a normal day for Tunisians in Sidi Bouzid, but the Union turned it into an extraordinary day. Sit-ins began in Sidi Bouzid headquarters of the union, and all the subsequent days until 14 of January 2011. All the marches, sit-ins, and clashes with security forces used to go out from the UGTT's branch in Sidi Bouzid,[315] as Sami al-Tahiri, the general assistant of (UGTT) stated.

---

[311] Shelley Deane, "Tunisia The role of Civil society in Tunisia's Transition", International Alert, February 2013.

[312] Ibid.

[313] National Democratic Institute, Washington DC, unknown date https://www.ndi.org/tunisia, viewed on 25 May 2014.

[314] Ryan, op, cit.

[315] Al-Tahiri: "They want to wipe the role of the (UGTT) in the revolution", Al-Arabi Al-Jadid, 04 May 2014, viewed on 25 May 2014. http://www.alaraby.co.uk/politics/a4f190de-f1ad-4927–8748-a76c0c7c5e20.

Egypt[316]

Egypt was the first recipient country of the political shockwaves stemming from events in Tunisia. On 25 January 2011, which coincided with the Day of Police Force in the country, a national holiday, young Egyptians, great numbers of different civil societal institutions and grassroots opposition parties responded to many calls on social media networks such as Facebook to replicate the Tunisian uprising. Although the people of Egypt had reasons to revolt, they were certainly lacking ideas about how to do so. However, the Tunisian Revolution provided them with a prototype or a blueprint of how to implement their goals. Tens of thousands of Egyptians gathered on the streets of Cairo, and after a few days, millions were congregating in, and occupying Al-Tahrir Square in the center of the city. The peaceful demonstrations were countered by violence from the security forces and *Baltajïyya* (hooligans), who were hired by the regime, and the military was deployed into the streets in order to keep security at a premium, but not to interfere in the struggle. Eventually Mubarak stepped down and handed power to the Military Council. The formal military stance pushed the struggle in the people's favor against Mubarak. Therefore, the Egyptians' respect for and trust in the military institution, and their admiration of its formal role in the struggle, convinced them to return to their homes and to leave the revolution's fate in the hands of the military, an institution where power had been concentrated for decades, and Mubarak was one member of this institution. The spirit of solidarity among Egyptians toward their goal of removing the Mubarak regime played a key role in the revolution. Although the Christian participation in the uprising was minimal, the religious division in the country was not effectual.

---

[316] Most information and details about the Egyptian Revolution are derived from The Road to January 25, a documentary film. AljazeeraChannel, The Road to January 25, Posted 15 March 2011, http://www.youtube.com/watch?v=738_EReBFCs.

> Countless protesters' signs highlighted the crescent and cross next to each other. Perhaps the most moving of images was of the Coptic Church service held in Tahrir Square that Muslims helped facilitate; when the service came to an end, all jointly shouted, "Amen, amen." Similarly, Christians with hands clasped together encircled Muslims so they could pray without harassment. These amazing images were broadcast to the world.[317]

Moreover, civil society organizations, and many opposition parties such as the Muslim Brotherhood, participated effectively in the revolution of 25 January 2011, and contributed heavily to its success. The movement of *Kuluna Khalid Sa'id*[318] (All of us Khalid Sa'id) played an important role in fueling public resentment against the Mubarak regime since the Khalid Sa'id tragedy in July 2010, and constituted one of the main components of the public demonstrations that led to the revolution of 25 January.[319] Nadine Sika explains the participation of pro-democracy organizations in the revolution of 25 January:

> The roles pro-democracy organizations played, especially protest movements like Kifaya,[320] and the April 6th Movement,[321] were central to the January 25th revolution. With the onset of the Jasmine Revolution in Tunisia, these

[317] Paul Gordon Chandler, "Behind Egypt's Revolution", Christianity Today, 07 March 2011, viewed on 29 May 2013. http://www.christianitytoday.com/ct/2011/marchwebonly/behindegyptrevolution.html.

[318] Khalid Said Movement was established in 2010 after the tragic death of Khalid Said through torture by the police force in Alexandria city.

[319] Kuluna Khalid Sa'id (All of us Khalid Sa'id), Aljazzer.net, 07 February 2011, http://www.aljazeera.net/news/pages/6a39f4ee-e832–4615–80d2–5435909a2020, viewed on 28 May 2014.

[320] Kifaya: The Egyptian Movement for Change, established in 2004 as a coalition of Egyptian figures, belongs to different political orientations. Its main aim was ousting Mubarak, and aborting the power succession in the county.

[321] Sixth of April Movement: a group of independent Egyptian youth, established on 6 April 2008 calling for reform through peaceful means such as protests and strikes.

> movements were able to mobilize Egyptians through new framing techniques, which combined both economic rights with political rights such as "food, freedom, and human dignity".[322]

Another important factor cannot be underestimated in the Egyptian revolution, which is heavy engagement in the capital (Cairo) from the early hours of the revolution. Since day one, protesters occupied major roads and squares in the capital, and then later they managed the massive sit-in in Al-Tahrir Square in the center of Cairo. Such a situation embarrassed the regime, halted the country and crippled the authorities, and hence helped the revolution maintain until Mubarak stepped down on 11 February 2011.

People in Yemen, Libya, Bahrain and Syria tried to use the same ideas put into practice during the Tunisian as well as the Egyptian uprisings, and the same means of peaceful demonstrations, and sit-ins in order to topple their regimes, but this did not work due to the complicated circumstances that surrounded the political and social system in each of these countries.

Libya

Due to its geographic location between Tunisia and Egypt, Libya found it very problematic to immunize itself from the issues in the countries surrounding it. With this in mind, the events in Tunisia may have shaken Libya, but the events in Egypt erupted the uprising inside the country. Protests developed quickly into an armed struggle between the regime and the people, and that can be mainly attributed to the lack of civil society organizations and activities in the country under Gaddafi, and also to the excessive use of force by Gaddafi's forces against the protesters. "In Libya, political civil society is a novelty. Mostly banned under Muammar

[322] Nadine Sika, "Civil Society and Democratization in Egypt: The Road Not Yet Traveled", Muftah.org, 29 May 2012. http://muftah.org/civil-society-and-democratization-in-egypt-the-road-not-yet-traveled/#.U40SbJRdXdI, viewed on 29 May 2014.

Gaddafi, non-governmental organizations (NGOs) have mushroomed in post-2011 Libya, thanks to newly acquired freedoms."[323] That made the revolution a spontaneous movement, and lacking in sufficient coordination and organization that are so essential for non-violent campaigns.[324] Moreover, Libya is a multi-tribal society that lacks social harmony. It has a very strong tribal component.[325] In fact, Liu described it more closely:

> Libya's Gaddafi revoked the tribe as a legal unit and reorganized local administrative structures according to the interests of his regime. But tribes remained socially and politically influential both during and after the colonel's rule. Primarily a mix of Arabs and Berbers, with Touareg and Tebu minorities in the south, the tribal system often performed the functions of political parties and civil society organizations, which Gaddafi had abolished following the 1969 coup d'état.[326]

Therefore, when the key tribal leaders in the country refused to back him, Gaddafi's power started to fall. Unlike Tunisia and Egypt, Libya had no strong military institution it could have relied on from either the regime or the protesters to determine the winning side in the struggle, or at least to shift the balance of

[323] Barah Mikaïl, "Civil Society and Foreign Donors in Libya", European Institute for Research on Mediterranean and Euro-Arab Cooperation MEDEA, 23 July 2013. http://www.medea.be/2013/07/civil-society-and-foreign-donors-in-libya-part-1/. viewed on 29 May 2014.

[324] Erica Chenoweth, "Did the Libyan uprising have to be violent?" wagingnonviolence.org, 25 August, 2011. http://wagingnonviolence.org/feature/did-the-libyan-uprising-have-to-be-violent, viewed on 28 May 2014.

[325] Martin W. Lewis, "Libya's Tribal Divisions and the Nation-State", Geo Currents, February 27, 201, viewed 29 May 2014. http://geocurrents.info/geopolitics/libyas-tribal-divisions-and-the-nation-state.

[326] Ted Liu, "Ethnicity and Tribalism in Arab Transitions", FRIDE, October 2012, http://www.fride.org/descarga/PB_137_Ethnicity_and_Tribalism_in_Arab_Transitions.pdf, viewed on 29 May 2014.

power toward it. Saïd Haddadt pointed out the situation of the military institution under Gaddafi:

> The armed forces have been subjected to heavy pressure, and their foundational pillars have been weakened by the regime's efforts to set up a popular army founded on the participation of all citizens—through general conscription and their course to popular militias. To achieve this goal, the regime abolished traditional military ranks and promoted the creation of a quasi-military structure but only some divisions to protect Gaddafi.[327]

Hence, Gaddafi had no alternative for defending his regime against the wave of revolution but to hire mercenaries, mainly from Africa, to fight alongside his security forces,[328] and the struggle developed into a severe internal war. The revolutionaries in Libya eventually asked for Western military intervention under the United Nations umbrella after Gaddafi and his sons threatened the annihilation of Benghazi city.

The Arab League adopted a resolution calling for the Security Council to impose a no-fly zone on Libya and to set up a safe zone area in the eastern part of Libya in order to protect civilians.[329] As a result, the Security Council adopted resolution 1973[330] in March 2011, legalizing military intervention. NATO Secretary General

---

[327] Saïd Haddadt, "The role of the Libyan Army in the Revolt against Gaddafi Regime, Aljazeer, 16 March 2011, viewed on 10 May 2012. www.aljazeera.net/mritems/streams/2011/3/17/1_1048489_1_51.pdf.

[328] Anna Mahjar-Barducci, "Gaddafi's Mercenaries in Libya", Gatestone Institute, 30 March 2011, http://www.gatestoneinstitute.org/2000/gaddafi-mercenaries-in-libya, viewed on 30 May 2014.

[329] "Washington welcomes the Arab League call for No fly zone over Libya", Al-Arabiya.net, 12 March 2011, http://www.alarabiya.net/articles/2011/03/12/141180.html, viewed on 28 May 2014.

[330] Resolution 1973: „authorizes members that have notified the Secretary-General, acting nationally or through regional organizations or arrangements, and acting in cooperation with the Secretary-General, to take all necessary measures to protect civilians and civilian populated areas under threat of attack in the Libyan Arab Jamahiriya, including Benghazi."

Anders Rasmussen attempted to justify military intervention, stating that, "our goal is to protect civilians and civilian populated areas from attack by the Gaddafi regime. NATO will implement all aspects of the UN resolution, nothing more, nothing less."[331]

The international operation started from Benghazi and towns in the east, while Gaddafi had strong and tight control over the capital Tripoli and parts of the West. After almost nine months of a bloody struggle, Libyan revolutionaries killed Gaddafi on 20 October in 2011 in the city of Sirte, northwest of the country. However, the killing of Gaddafi did not end the violence in the country. In fact, the country has plunged into a prolonged regional and international fed conflict between the revolutionary forces in Tripoli and the counter-revolution forces in Tobruk, dividing the country into west and east.

Yemen

In Yemen, the situation was also complicated due to many factors such as military loyalty, tribal influence, and the split between north and south Yemen. The country is enjoying a great degree of political freedom compared to many countries in the region. Independent civil society organizations and authentic opposition parties were functioning actively in the country. Bonnefoy and Poirier pointed out:

> In the early 1990s, after unification of north and south, the Republic of Yemen embarked itself in an outstanding democratization process that no country in the region had yet experienced. The constitution, approved by referendum, appeared as particularly liberal, granting civil society and opposition parties a wide range of rights and a share of the exercise of power in the county for years.[332]

---

[331] Andre Rasmussen, "NATO Security General's Statement on Libya", 27 March 2011.

[332] Laurent Bonnefoy & Marine Poirier, "Civil Society and Democratization in Contemporary Yemen", Humanist Institute for Co-operation with Developing Countries, the Netherlands, 2009.

In 2006, the country underwent a presidential election described as an authentic and openly- contested process representing a milestone in the process of democracy in the country. All political parties participated, and the candidates were free to assemble and express their views.[333] However, Ali Abdullah Saleh won the election.

Consolidating his power was due to many factors: military loyalty, tribal support and corruption and patronage networking. He appointed members from his family to very high and important positions in the military, and security[334] in order to eliminate the inner threats, and to secure a power succession to his son Ahmad. However, he could not undermine the influence of his half brother and right-hand man General Mohsen al-Ahmar in the army, who opposed the power succession process. On the other hand, Ali Abdullah Saleh long enjoyed the support of his tribe, al-Ahmar tribe of Haashed, the most influential tribe in the country.

The revolution in 2011 was a broad based movement, as Sheila Carapico explained. It contained Al-Hirak Movement[335] of the separatist South Yemen, students and intelligentsia.[336] They occupied Al-Tagheer Square adjacent to the University of Sana'a, and main streets in other major cities such as Ta'izz, where the revolution started. Meanwhile, Saleh's supporters rallied in

---

[333] Yemen Final Report Presidential and Local Council Election, European Union Election Observation Mission 20 September 2006.

[334] Ahmed Ali Abdullah Saleh, the president's son, commander of the Republican Guard and Special Forces. Khalid Ali Abdullah Saleh, another of the president's son, commander of the Mountain Troops Armored Division. Yahya Mohammed Abdullah Saleh, the president's nephew, Central Security chief of staff. Tariq Mohammed Abdullah Saleh, another of the president's nephew, commander of the Special Guard. Ammar Mohammed Abdullah Saleh al-Ahmar, another of the president's nephew, national security chief. Mohamed Saleh Abdullah Al-Ahmar, the president's stepbrother, commander of the Air Force.

[335] Al-Hirak Movement: is a coalition of different fractions from South Yemen established in 2007, and calling for the separation of South Yemen and the return of People's Democratic Republic of Yemen.

[336] Interview with Sheila Carapico on the Uprising in Yemen (conducted by Sharam Aghamir), Jadaliyya. 16 April 2011.
http://www.jadaliyya.com/pages/index/1259/interview-with-sheila-carapico-on-the-uprising-in, viewed on 02 April 2014.

Al-Tahrir Square in central Sana'a.[337] Therefore, the lack of a spirit of solidarity was obvious among the Yemenis. However, the biggest blow for Ali Abdulla Saleh was the defection of General Ali Mohsen al-Ahamr, and to announce along with the leaders of al-Ahmar family their support and allegiance to the uprising. Such a situation divided the army, and erupted violent clashes between the two wings, hence transforming the peaceful youth uprising into an elite power struggle.[338]

Violence was used by the regime and the opposition alike, injuring and killing thousands of people including Saleh himself. He suffered extensive injuries including severe burns in an attack on his Sana'a palace in June 2011. Therefore, the country fell into crisis and political stalemate, urging the Gulf Cooperation Council and the United Nations to intervene through diplomatic and political means, and to secure a peaceful transition of power from President Saleh to his deputy, and granting him immunity from prosecution. Eventually, after months of escalating violence, Saleh signed the Gulf Initiative,[339] in November 2011. However, the departure of Saleh was not accompanied immediately with the departure of his sons from the key military and security posts. He then discarded the Gulf Initiative, forming an alliance with Houthi, his old enemy, against Al-Islah Party and other revolutionary forces in order to defeat the revolution. He supplied Houthi with heavy weapons and handed them some vital military bases used to belong to the state. But when he tried to turn against them, they killed him in December 2017, and Houthi has emerged as the strongest militia in the country, and was able to control Sana'a and North Yemen gradually through brutality and violence. Consequently, the country became divide between north and south, and has plunged into complicated long conflicts with the

[337] Al- Tagheer Square in Sana'a, Aljazera.net, 15 March 2011, Viewed on 1 June 2014. http://www.aljazeera.net/news/pages/a5d3d2c5–49de-4166-bddd-cd02884f9513.

[338] Tobias Thiel, "Yemen's Arab Spring: From Youth Revolution to Fragile Political Transition", LSE Publications, London, unknown date.

[339] Full details of the Gulf Initiative in Yemen can be found on this link: http://www.aawsat.com/details.asp?section=4&article=651308&issueno=12049#.U5A9w5RdUVg.

involvement of certain regional powers such as Saudi Arabia, Iran, Emirates, and Qatar.

Bahrain

The uprising in Bahrain was another piece of the Arab Spring puzzle. Peaceful protesters rallied in Lu'lu'a Square in the capital Al-Manama, demanding reform and change. However, Bahrain is a monarchy, unlike the rest of the Arab Spring countries (republics), so "the Arab monarchies have utilized to stay in power."[340] No doubt, the people of Bahrain, Sunnis and Shias, like the majority of Arab people were ambitious for freedom, reform and regime change. Moreover, there were great public grievances in the country among Shias and Sunnis alike. Both tried to promote democracy in the country,[341] so the uprising was understandable. However, social harmony was lacking in the country, making the uprising appear to be a sectarian struggle. The country is divided between Shia and Sunnis. "Some 60% of Bahraini national are Shia, the ruling Al Khalifa family, who are Sunni Muslims, control all key political government posts, security positions, and important economic institutions,"[342] as observed by Human Rights Watch. However, civil society organizations and opposition parties have great space for independence and freedom in comparison to other Gulf States.[343]

Civil society organizations contributed heavily to the uprising, including such organizations as the Bahrain Teachers Society, and

---

[340] F. Gregory Gause, "Kings for All Seasons: How the Middle East Monarchies Survived the Arab Spring?", Brookings Doha Center Analyses Paper, Number 8, September 2013, viewed on 12 August 2014. http://www.brookings.edu/~/media/research/files/papers/2013/09/24%20resilience%20arab%20monarchies%20gause/resilience%20arab%20monarchies_english.

[341] Frederic Wehrey, "Bahrain's Lost Uprising", Carnegie Endowment for international Peace, 12 July 2012, viewed 1 June 2014. http://carnegieendowment.org/2012/06/12/bahrain-s-lost-uprising/bkgu

[342] "Interfere, Restrict, Control: Restraints on Freedom of Association in Bahrain", Human Rights Watch, 2013.

[343] "Strong Civil society, but", Bahrain Monitor, unknown date, http://www.bahrainmonitor.org/monitor/m-018–01.html, viewed on 01 June 2014.

Bahrain Medical Society. Moreover, the General Federation of Bahrain Trade Unions (GFBTU) called for mass labor strikes during the uprising.[344] In addition, the main Shia opposition parties also participated in the uprising. Meanwhile, some Sunni opposition formed Al-Fatih Assembly to confront the protesters.[345] The country was deeply divided into two semi-balanced camps with an external political dimension as Iran supported the revolution, and Saudi Arabia supported the regime. Violence and dialogue were what the regime used with the protesters in order to stop the uprising.[346] However, the regime found itself faced with no alternative but to seek foreign military support from the Gulf Cooperation Council (GCC) in order to crush the uprising, and restore law and order.

> On March 14, the Gulf Cooperation Council (GCC) sent in its Peninsula Shield Force to help restore stability in Bahrain. In reality, this consisted of 1000 men of the Saudi Arabian National Guard and a contingent of military police from the United Arab Emirates. They provided the essential backbone while the Bahrain Defense Force pursued and arrested thousands of people across the country.[347]

The uprising in Bahrain risked mobilizing the Shias in the other Gulf States, and attracting great support from Iran. This would have placed the security of the entire Gulf region in jeopardy. The quick military intervention of Saudi Arabia sent an indication as to how important Gulf security was globally and regionally. The international system could not afford the destabilization of the Gulf region, as that would disrupt oil flows to the international

[344] "Interfere, Restrict, Control: Restraints on Freedom of Association in Bahrain", Human Rights Watch, 2013.

[345] Abdulnabi Alekri, Bahrain: the role of the Islamic movement in the uprising of February 14, Bahrain Center for Studies in London, 22 October 2012. http://www.bcsl.org.uk/en/studies/roleislamic-mov-feb14/1580-roleislamic-mov-feb14, viewed on 1 June 2014.

[346] Ibid.

[347] Kristian Coates Ulrichsen, "Bahrain's Aborted Revolution", LSE Publications, London, unknown date.

markets. In addition, Saudi Arabia would not allow the fall of a fellow ruling family in the Gulf, as such an event would shake the whole system in the region.[348]

The great noticeable absent from the Arab Spring was Algeria. A public revolution is always foreseeable as the county has been under a ruthless military elite rule for decades. However, its absence was understandable and was not a surprise as the country went into a bleak decade of unrest and bloodshed from 1992 to 2002 after the army coup on the Islamists after winning the elections in December 1991.

Most Arab regimes, including monarchies such as Saudi Arabia[349] and Morocco[350] have taken pre-emptive measures to stave off prospects of revolution. These include announcing reform policies, increasing state benefits to the people and raising salaries. However, in Syria, the regime did not offer any sort of concession, or show any sign of flexibility in order to deter the uprising, and immunize the country from the Arab Spring upheaval. Although the regime used authoritarian upgrading in the past for power succession and to deter the international threats, the regime at this crucial time failed to do so. Bashar Assad relied on his legitimate and overwhelming popular foreign policy as an automatic immunity against the revolutionary waves storming the region. However, the popular foreign policy could not help Bashar Assad against the uprising. Moreover, many people believe that Syria's stance toward Israel was not genuine, but for political regional gains. The borders between Israel and Syria were very safe since 1974, so instead of supporting Hamas in Palestine and Hizbollah in Lebanon, why did Bashar and his father before not plant a liberation movement on the occupied Golan Heights?

---

[348] Ibid.

[349] "King Abdullah issued a package of measures easing the citizens' lives", Al-wasat. 23 February 2011 http://www.alwasatnews.com/3092/news/read/528574/1.html, viewed on 13 March 2011.

[350] "The King of Morocco announces constitutional reforms", Aljazeera.net, 10 March 2011. http://www.aljazeera.net/news/pages/07d76ffc-34b9–411f-a0dd-0a26a4fd06ed, viewed on 13 March 2011.

The Arab Spring is Knocking on Syria's Door

In late January 2011, when the Tunisian and the Egyptian revolutionaries had won the battle over their leaders, President Bashar Assad expressed great confidence to foreign media outlets by assuring them that Syria was impervious to the Arab Spring and that he was always responding to his people's demands in relation to Israel. Syria's president stated that his nation was immune from the kind of unrest witnessed in Tunisia and Egypt. Syria was insulated from the upheaval because he understood his people's needs and had united them in a common cause against Israel.[351]

The Syrian people as well as the Syrian regime watched the events that took place in Tunisia and Egypt as political leaders were toppled by the power and will of the populace. While most of the Syrian people were eager to imitate and follow the Tunisian and Egyptian examples of peaceful revolt against their regimes, the Syrian regime was in shock and afraid to meet the fate of its counterparts in North African countries. Therefore, the Syrian regime and in particular Bashar Assad tried to invest at this critical time in his foreign policy toward Israel, implying that what happened in Egypt on 25 January 2011 was a normal public reaction to the close relationship between the Mubarak regime and Israel. In other words, it was the close relationship with Israel, rather than domestic concerns, that was the real motive for the revolution in Egypt; at least this is the myth that the Syrian regime tried to perpetuate in the aftermath of the Egyptian uprising in 2011. In a desperate move to protect itself from any public pressure, the regime in Syria manipulated the fall of Mubarak to portray it as a great victory for the Resistance Axis in the region (Syria, Iran, Hamas and Hezbollah) against the perceived moderate Arab countries, mainly Saudi Arabia and Egypt.[352] However, security

[351] Zeina Karam, "Assad says Syria is immune from unrest roiling Egypt", 31 January 2011, viewed on 31 January 2011. http://www.deseretnews.com/article/700105718/Assad-says-Syria-immune-from-unrest-roiling-Egypt.html

[352] "Has Syria benefited from the fall of Mubarak?", Aljazeera, 15 February 2011, http://aljazeera.net/news/pages/77dcdeb3-bdeb-41bd-8747-a83114a9a085, viewed on 15 March 2013.

forces in Syria were put on alert following minor incidents that happened in Damascus after the fall of Mubarak. Mr. Riyad Hijab, the defected prime minister, stated:

> Top leaders within the regime held many meetings after the events in Tunisia and Egypt to study the possibility of facing similar events in the country. After the events in Al-Hariqa Market in Damascus,[353] they formed a crisis cell headed by Said Bekhtian, the Assistant General Regional Secretary in the Baath Party, with the membership of all the managers of the security branches in the country.[354]

Many sincere friends of the Syrian regime and of Bashar Assad, such as the Turkish prime minister Recep Tayyip Erdoğan and the well-known Jordanian opposition figure Laith Shubailat, advised him to go ahead with some serious political and economic reforms in order to satisfy his people and eventually immunize his regime from the political tsunami that had affected the entire Middle East. Laith Shubailat visited Bashar Assad before the crisis and sent him a letter after the beginning of the uprising in Syria, urging him to make brave decisions before it was too late.[355] However, the events that followed showed that Bashar Assad never listened to such credible advice, which would have aborted the uprising. Bashar Assad did not resort to a pre-emptive strategy toward the Arab Spring through introducing some reform measures or adopting appeasement policies, as Morocco or Saudi Arabia did. Pettee stated, "A revolution represents at least the political failure of a government. In a great number of cases it represents the general failure of a social system. Every statesman would avoid them by

---

[353] On 17 February 2011, two policemen in Al-Hariqa Market in the center of Damascus beat the son of a shopkeeper after an argument. The police action caused a local public reaction that developed into a demonstration asking for accountability. However, the demonstration was dispersed after interference from the interio Minister.

[354] Interview with the author by Skype on 22 May 2013.

[355] Full of Mr. Shubailat's Letter can be found at: http://www.akherkhabar.net/content/view/16764/42/.

every means if he could."[356] For instance, on 10 March 2011, the king of Morocco agreed to a comprehensive constitutional reform ensuring more individual and collective freedom, more authority to the prime minister and more authority to the local councils.[357] Similarly, in Saudi Arabia, King Abdullah issued a number of royal decrees on 18 March 2011 to improve the living standards of Saudis.[358] Aristotle once stated, "Revolutions are effected in two ways, by force and by fraud. Force may be applied either at the time of the revolution or afterward. Fraud, [where] sometimes the citizens are deceived into accepting a change of government."[359] Bashar Assad could have contained the crisis in Daraa by interfering personally, and hence abort the uprising. Instead of involving himself with the subject of political reforms, he began preparing for a military confrontation with the revolutionaries. Two Iranian warships docked in the coastal Syrian city of Latakia on 17 February 2011, crossing the Sues Channel for the first time for almost 30 years carrying military equipment,[16] believed to be used against the demonstrators. Mr. Nassir al-Hariri, a resigned MP from Daraa, and the first defected politician from the regime, stated, "Bashar Assad promised me that he would visit Daraa and apologize to the people there, but that never happened."[360] In fact, Daraa received heavy fire from the regime, but not an apology.

After many failed attempts by young activists to create a major public rally and ignite public mobilization against the regime in Damascus and Aleppo, it was eventually the chaotic ordeal of Syrian children in the city of Daraa that ignited the

---

[356] George, Pettee, "The Process of Revolution" in Why *Revolutions*, Paynton, C & Balckey, R. Schenkman Publishing Co, Cambridge, 1971, pp.31–56.

[357] "The King of Morocco announces constitutional reforms", Aljazeera.net, 10 March 2011. http://www.aljazeera.net/news/pages/07d76ffc-34b9–411f-a0dd-0a26a4fd06ed viewed on 13 March 2011.

[358] "King Abdullah issued a package of measures easing the citizens' lives", Al-wasat. 23 February 2011. http://www.alwasatnews.com/3092/news/read/528574/1.html, viewed on 13 March 2011.

[359] Aristotle, "Man and Revilution", in *Why Revolutions*, Paynton, C & Balckey, R. Schenkman Publishing Co, Cambridge, 1971, pp.9–15.

[360] A Private Meeting, television program, Al-Aan, 25 May 2013.

revolution in Syria, and constituted the long missing spark for huge public mobilization in the city, and in the country soon after.

The Spark

By this stage in the conflict, tension was rising in the country. The story of Tal al-Mallohi, a young girl arrested in December 2009 by the security authorities, caused a huge public outrage in the country. Tal al-Mallohi became a symbol for the opposition and activists alike as a victim of the regime's repressive behavior. In this sense, she could be compared to Khalid Sa'id in Egypt. Scenes of Tunisians and Egyptians rallying in their capital cities revived the hopes of most Syrians that freedom and dignity could prevail in their own country, without resorting to an armed struggle with the regime. People could feel the winds of the Arab Spring blowing in Syria. Activists used Facebook to call for "Days of Rage" on 4 and 5 February 2011 in Damascus, but due to the low public response, the Days of Rage turned into a memorial event outside the Egyptian embassy in Damascus, where people lit candles in memory of the Tunisian and Egyptian martyrs. Many people were arrested by the regime.[361] On 17 February, policemen attacked the son of a shopkeeper in Al-Hariqa Market, one of the busiest areas in Damascus, after a dispute over a traffic matter. Spontaneously, more than 3000 people rallied against the policemen, calling them *Haramieh*, "thieves," and then chanted *Al-Sha'b al-Soory ma Beinzal*, "Syrian people will never be humiliated." It was the largest demonstration for decades. People stayed for a few hours until the arrival of the interior minister. He promised to punish the policemen who were responsible for the attack. People ended their rally, but the tension in Damascus and Syria as a whole never ended; in fact, it was escalating and spreading.[362]

---

361 "The Harbingers of Syrian Uprising", Alzaeera.net, 16 March 2011. http://www.aljazeera.net/news/pages/20f4114d-5f9e-43a7-abf1–8efe69b32a75, viewed on 18 March 2011.

362 "Al-Hariqa, the first protest against the regime for 40 years", ASharq Al-Awsat, 15 March 2012. http://www.aawsat.com/details.asp?section=4&article=668123&issueno=12161#.U5OPjZRdUVh, viewed 22 April 2013.

The complexity of the Syrian uprising was clear from the very beginning: It was activists, but not figures from the opposition or members from civil society organizations, who had the responsibility of attracting the public toward the uprising. The formal opposition in Syria was very weak and divided, and did not have the capability of mobilizing the masses. According to one group of activists, "The opposition is not strong enough to lead a street movement capable of changing the government,"[363] and this is where Syria was very different, and could explain the low public response toward the "Days of Rage" in February 2011. In Egypt, Tunisia, Yemen and even Bahrain, opposition and civil society in those countries was much stronger, and able to lead or have an influential role in the uprisings. In Egypt, for instance, activists and members of civil society were the catalysts of the uprising, but its strength stemmed from a strong informal coalition between activists, members of opposition parties and members of civil society organizations, all of which rallied in Al-Taharir Square in what was an unprecedented event. On the contrary, the Syrian revolt had to rely upon young activists only during its infancy, which led to a lack of momentum later on. Instead, it was the children's ordeal in the city of Daraa and the following consequences that ignited the revolution, a revolution that would prove to be the most costly and lengthy of all the Arab Spring revolutions.

In Daraa Province[364] the security services intercepted a phone call from a female doctor of the Aba Zeed family talking to a relative in Kherbet Ghazlah village about the downfall of Mubarak. According to records, this doctor reportedly said (*Ubal Aanna*) "the same to us hopefully." The doctor was arrested, detained for a few days, and had her hair shaved. The shaving of a woman's hair in such a tribal society caused an unprecedented outrage. A few days later, in the village of Adawan, to the west of

363 "Day of Rage for Syrians Fails to Draw Protesters", 4 February 2011, viewed 1 March 2011. http://www.nytimes.com/2011/02/05/world/middleeast/05syria.html?_r=0.

364 All the details of the early and the followed-up events in the Daraa have been gained through interviews with many local people in the city.

Daraa city, children wrote on the wall of their school *Al-Sha'b Youreed Isqat Al-Nizam,* "The people want to overthrow the regime." The same scenario was repeated in the city of Daraa itself, with children from Al-Arba'ain Elementary School writing on the walls of their school some anti-regime statements such as "your turn is due, doctor" (*ejack aldour ya dactor*), hinting at Bashar Assad's possible downfall, following Bin Ali and Mubarak. On the main gates of the school "go away" (*Irhal*) was written, as seen in photo below. The security services grew worried about the situation. On 27 February 2011, the security services launched a huge campaign, arresting eighteen children of the Al-Arba'ain School in the city of Daraa and detaining them. Responsible for this act was the political security division of the city, which was headed by Atef Najeeb, a cousin of Bashar Assad. He was appointed in Daraa in 2009, and was renowned for dealing with its people arrogantly, in that he took no consideration for the tribal structure of the society in that city. The parents were frightened to individually ask for the return of their children, so they formed a committee of prestigious tribal leaders and went to the mayor of Daraa, only for him to refer them to Atef Najeeb. The committee visited the director of the Military Security Division, Sohail Ramadan, many times without reaching a solution.

Upon the last visit to Sohail Ramadan, the parents were told: "If you are here about your children, I would advise you to forget about them; try to have children instead of them, and if you have no capacity to do so, bring your women to us, and we can do the job for you,"[365] a member of the committee claimed. A humiliating, provocative statement such as this cannot be accepted, especially in a tribal society, and would undoubtedly cause a backlash.

On 12 March 2011, the committee visited Atef Najeeb and warned him of unpleasant consequences if the children were not released by the weekend.

[365] Interview with the author by Skype on 24 September 2011.

Photo of Al-Arba'ain School in Daraa showing anti-regime writings on the main gate. (Irhal) "Go Away". A private photo was taken by one of the activists in February 2011.

Meanwhile, there was another call for a Day of Rage across the country on 15 March. Hundreds of activists in Damascus attended a demonstration outside the Umayyad Mosque. The security forces stormed the demonstration and arrested some activists, including Marwa al-Ghamian and Noura al-Refai.[366] On the following day, 16 March, a sit-in of academics, activists and families of political detainees took place in front of the Interior Ministry, demanding the release of the political prisoners. Many of these protesters were detained.[367] Although the antecedents that took place in Damascus were critically important, the spark of the revolution was in Daraa. Ironically, the revolution began in Daraa, a historic stronghold for the regime. Normally, in the event of a threat

366 The Campaign of Syrian Youth, the arrest of Marwa al-Ghamian and Noura al-Refai on 15 March 2011. Posted 21 March 2011, https://www.youtube.com/watch?v=xVMp5mADYp0.

367 "The Syrian Authorities suppresses a sit- in for the families of political detains in front of the interior minister", Levant News, 16 MRCH 2011. http://www.levantnews.com/archives/7575, viewed on 05 April 2013.

occurring from the outside or inside, regimes should reinforce their bases and increase their loyalists in order to be stronger and able to defeat the forthcoming internal or external threats. This is what the regime in Syria did in 2005, when the American threat was imminent. It strengthened its social base in order to respond more coherently to the American threats. However, the greatest mistake made by the regime in Syria in 2011 was impairing its social base. Daraa had been an essential social base for the regime since its establishment in 1963, so losing that social base forced the regime to rely mainly upon its own religious base (Alawis). Moreover, the regime and its allies conceived the uprising as a real threat to its very existence, a threat to the Alawi group and also a threat to the Shia community in the region as a whole, so he mobilized all of them and relied on the sectarian weapon from the beginning: a weapon that Syrian people have never been familiar with before and were not prepared for yet. Contrary to what his father Hafiz did in 1980s, Hafiz relied on the social base from the Baathist across all groups and communities in the country in his battle against the Islamists.

Muhammad Abu Rumyah, an MP from Daraa, made a huge effort to contain the crisis in Daraa. He declared in his statement in the People's Assembly on 27 March 2011 that his people remained loyal to the regime. He said:

> People of Horan are loyal, and they like Bashar Assad and the father of Bashar Assad for the great economic and social services they have offered to them. Horan was the only valuable area for Hafiz Assad and for Bashar Assad too, but what has happened in Daraa was because of the recklessness of Atef Najeeb.[368]

The regime, in such an anxious domestic and regional situation, should have resorted to a containment strategy rather than moving

---

368 FreeMediaSyria, MP Abu Rumyah demands the apology of Bashar Assad for the events in Daraa. Posted on 05 April 2011. https://www.youtube.com/watch?v=2dAUSuN32xg

toward a strategy of provocation or confrontation when dealing with domestic problems. In fact, early events demonstrate the absence of such a strategy in regime policies, a strategy that could have prevented subsequent events in the country. Although the grounds for revolution were mature and overripe in the country, revolution can always be avoided by a regime. Ironically, the events in Daraa instigated the revolution at a time when efforts must have been devoted to avoid it.

Overall, Bashar Assad's confidence in Syria's immunity against regional changes proved to be unfounded. In other words, "The Syrian regime in Damascus, which President Bashar Assad claimed was 'immune' from the political upheaval gripping the Arab world, [was] grappling with street protests on a scale not seen for a generation."[369] However, his misjudgment of the situation in the country was followed by his mishandling of the early events in Daraa. This forced the country to undergo the unnecessary phase of a very long internal war, costing lots of lives.

The Dramatic Developments of the Syrian Uprising[370]

What is clear from the Tunisian example is that revolutions need a spark, and it seems Assad had already ignited it in Daraa.[371] The Syrian uprising started in Daraa, but soon after it reached most of the Syrian provinces. Although they protested in solidarity with Daraa, every province had undergone different developments and witnessed different types of events that turned the the uprising into a revolution from below.

[369] "Arab Spring infects 'immune' Syria", UPI.com, 22 March, 2011, http://www.upi.com/Top_News/Special/2011/03/22/, viewed on 30 March 2011.

[370] I think it is very important to stand on the very early developments of the Syrian uprising in every relevant province in order to understand the expansion and increasing momentum of the uprising. Details in this section are derived from many interviews with the local people of the relevant cities or towns. YouTube was also a good resource.

[371] Maher Arar, "Deraa Protests are the Spark Syria Needed", The Guardian, 23 March 2011, viewed on 30 March 2011. http://www.guardian.co.uk/commentisfree/2011/mar/23/daraa-protests-syria.

Daraa. By Thursday, 17 March 2011 the detained children had not been released, and in fact, some leaks confirmed that they had been subjected to torture, and some of them had been moved to detention centers in Damascus. Such news increased the agitation of the people, so they agreed, in consultation with Sheikh Ahmad Sayasneh, a prominent figure in Daraa and the Imam of Al-Omari Mosque, to hold a demonstration at Al-Hamzah Wa al-Abbas Mosque in the city of Daraa.

On 18 March and immediately after the Friday prayers in Al-Hamzah Wa Al-Abbas Mosque, a young man called Ali al-Masalmeh chanted *Allah Akbar—Hurria*, "Allah is great—Freedom." People from many mosques congregated at al-Omari Mosque, their numbers reaching over 10000. The march was heading toward an area called Daraa Al-Mahatah, the market and the economic center of the city. People were only chanting against Atef Najeeb, the mayor and the corruption.[372] After reaching al-Seeba neighborhood, Atef Najeeb and Yasser al-Ali, the director of the military division in Daraa, and the mayor of Daraa met the protesters. While Mr. al-Ali and the mayor tried to calm the people down and listen to their demands, Atef Najeeb and his escort threatened and intimidated them. People could not allow this, and a clash between the protesters and the officials erupted, causing injury to the mayor, but Atef Najeeb successfully escaped. He requested reinforcement from Damascus, and helicopters carrying Special Task Force troops landed at the sports center (Panorama) in the city center. The troops were conveyed by buses to the location, where the march was still going on. Checkpoints were posted to prevent people from going further, but after a short while they started shooting at the protesters, killing two young men, Mahmoud al-Jawabra, and Hossam Ayyash, immediately, along with injuring three more who later died. Omar Allouh, an eyewitness, stated, "We were shocked; chaos prevailed, the shooting was by live bullets, and the instruction was shoot to kill, as most injuries were fatal injuries."[373] The protest was dispersed and

---

[372] Syrian Pulse, Demonstrations of Daraa, the Syrian Revolution, Posted on 21 March 2011, http://www.youtube.com/watch?v=SP4sdDucMZg.

[373] Interview with the author over Skype on 06 March 2013.

hundreds of people were arrested. On the next day, 19 March, thousands of people participated in the funeral services, demanding punishment for the killers. Sheikh Bassam al-Masry was the first to chant after burying the dead *al-qasas min man atlaqa al-rasas,* "punishment for those who fired the bullets." The revolution at this stage entered a new phase; demands developed from releasing the detained children, to requesting punishment for the killers. As a tribal and family-like society, punishment for the killers could not be compromised.

The regime wanted to use violence at this stage as an intimidation tactic to stop the protests and to abort the possibility of further public mobilization. The Chinese proverb "kill just one and frighten ten thousand others" clearly echoed the strategy adopted by the Syrian regime. The strategy was shoot to kill. However, the killing was a means and an end at the same time. It was a means of intimidation, and an end to kill the activities. The situation in Daraa became more complicated, so two top security officers, Rostom Ghazaleh from Daraa, and Hisham Bekhtiar, arrived in the city in order to meet with tribal leaders in the mayor's office.[374] They listened to the people's demands and promised to respond. They arranged for a delegation of tribal leaders and sheiks to meet with President Bashar Assad in Damascus. The convoy was successful in placing some demands at Bashar Assad. Mr. Motee al-Bateen, a member from the delegation, summarized their demands: 1) Release of the detained children; 2) Punishment for the killers; 3) Withdrawal of all kinds of military from the city; 4) The abolition of law 26; 5) The return of fully covered female teachers to teach in the schools.[375] Soon after the meeting, most of the children were released. However, the protests continued to exert pressure upon the regime to fulfill all the remaining demands. People took the backyard of Al-Omari Mosque as a center for their protests and sit-ins. They called it Dignity Square. Yet, responding negatively to most of these demands constituted a tipping point in

---

[374] almugtarep's channel, Rostom Ghazaleh admits the detention of children. http://www.youtube.com/watch?v=6Ziadi_M6dM.

[375] Interview with author over Skype on 25 March 2013.

the Syrian uprising as most people began to believe that Bashar Assad was fully aware of the critical situation in Daraa, and to blame for the deteriorating situation in the city. Prior to the meeting with President Bashar Assad, people were blaming the security offices in the city. On 23 March 2011, a mock raid was undertaken by the Special Task Force to storm the Al-Omari Mosque.[376] People responded by throwing stones on them, yet the operation escalated, and led to the killing of six more people and injuring dozens. Among the dead was Dr. Ghassab al-Mahameed and Ashraf al-Masri. Dr. al-Mahameed was the first doctor to be killed in the uprising. He was rescuing injured people. Mr. al-Masri was a famous contractor in Daraa. Syrian official TV claimed that armed militias were terrifying the people in Daraa, and their arms and money were found in Al-Omari Mosque.[377] The regime furthered its strategy of indiscriminate violence against the people of Daraa, so people were yelling and calling for solidarity and help (*Faz'a*). Snipers were deployed and positioned on the buildings and began to shoot at the people and at the ambulance crew. This was accompanied by a power cut throughout the city. The operation lasted for three hours until early morning. People were in a state of shock. Eleven people were killed in this campaign, including a couple of men who were found dead in the hospital after being taken there for treatment from minor wounds. Violence served as a means to suppress the protests, killing the activists and non-activists alike. This kind of indiscriminate killing was analyzed theoretically by Stathis Kalyvas:

> The logic of indiscriminate violence is: if the "guilty" cannot be identified and arrested, then violence ought to target innocent people that are somehow associated with them. The underlying assumption is that the innocent will either target the "guilty" to alter their behavior or the guilty will

[376] anahorani2011, The Night when Al-Omary Mosque was stormed, Posted on 22 April 2011, http://www.youtube.com/watch?v=8SSZLHu3rf0.

[377] oran show, weapons inside Al- Omary Mosque 23 March 2011. Posted on 23 March 2011, http://www.youtube.com/watch?v=ULzVj11XE7g.

> change their course of action when they realize its impact upon innocent people they care about—or both.[378]

On the next day and after the funeral, people started chanting different words *yali be'tol Shaboo Khaen*, "the killer of his people is a traitor", and *al-Sha'b yoreed isqat alnizam*, "people want to overthrow the regime." The people's demands went even further; calling for regime change. Again, this started another new and important phase in the uprising. Regime change was another new demand for the people. The forces responded by opening fire at people, and causing more fatalities.

Division 15 of the army was recalled from the neighboring city of As Suwayda and deployed in the city of Daraa. Many villages in the countryside responded to the appeal from the city, so many people walked more than 20 km from their villages such as El-Hrak, Izraa and others.[379] Indiscriminate shots were fired at them when entering the city at al-Kaziat neighborhood, killing 25 people and injuring dozens. People called this event the massacre of Al-Faz'a.[380] This event galvanized Daraa as a whole, as the people who were killed belonged to the city and its nearby villages. This was the point when the uprising started to extend beyond Daraa city. On the next day, 24 March, while people were returning from the funeral services in the village of Izraa, they were shot at by the security forces, and more than 20 people were killed in an event labeled the Massacre of Hajez Izraa.[381]

The quick spread of the uprising in Daraa can be attributed to the special social structure of that region. Although Daraa is classified as a tribal society, its social structure pivots rather upon

---

[378] Stathis Kalyvas, *The Logic of Violence in the Civil War*, Cambridge University Press, Cambridge, 2006, p.150.

[379] Khalid Al-horani, 23 03 2011, The Martyrs of Faz'a, Posted on 22 March 2013, http://www.youtube.com/watch?v=wuikdMcx1qw.

[380] Darra Coordination, some images from Al-Faz'a Massacre, Posted on 23 November 2011, https://www.youtube.com/watch?v=HhSB-geZDvI.

[381] Feras al-Hamed, The massacre of Hajez Izraa, posted on 30 June 2011, http://www.youtube.com/watch?v=Q6dD4O9K9b0.

extended families than tribes, making the relationship between the people more concrete. Leenders and Heydemann observed:

> Daraa's social networks certainly are not confined to ascriptive, kinship or communitarian ties, but the region's family clan structure and its significance in daily life is remarkable. Daraa's clan structure is essentially comprised of networks based on extended family ties.[382]

The violence strategy as a means only or a means and a goal failed in Daraa. The more violence that was used against the people of Daraa and the more massacres were committed against them, the more they mobilized the public. Their mobilization spread from the city of Daraa to the villages, and their demands changed from releasing the children to the punishment of the killers to a promise for regime change.

In the afternoon of 24 March 2011, Buthaina Sha'ban, a special adviser for Bashar Assad made a very important statement conveying the decisions that had been taken by the regional leadership of the Baath Party. It contained the following points:[383]

1) The formation of a supreme committee to investigate the crisis in Daraa and punish the people who were responsible, along with addressing the negative implications inflicted on the people.
2) Increase in the wages of all state employees.
3) Finance health insurance for the state employees.
4) Create more job opportunities for unemployed people and appoint temporary workers.
5) Embark upon an evaluation of government performance, local and administrative leaders.

[382] Reinoud Leenders & Steven Heydemann, "Popular Mobilization in Syria: Opportunity and Threat, and the Social Networks of the Early Risers", Mediterranean Politics, Volume 17, issue 2, 2012.

[383] Press conference to Buthaina Sha'aban, the private advisor to President Assad, 24 March 2011. https://www.youtube.com/watch?v=3rTl0JDKzTQ.

6) Set up new and effective measures for fighting corruption.
7) Carry out an urgent study regarding the termination of the state of emergency in the country, and issue legislation that is necessary to ensure the security of the nation and the people.
8) Prepare a new draft law for political parties in Syria.
9) Issue a new law for media responding to the citizens' aspirations for more transparency and more freedom.
10) Amend legislative decree 49 in order for it to respond to the people's complaints in the Kurdish area in the north.
11) Strengthen the authority of the judiciary and prevent indiscriminate arrests.

The regime through these concessions wanted to make a U-turn toward authoritarian upgrading to contain the uprising and limit its spreading across the country, but it failed to convince the people. However, taking such decisions was a great achievement, and could have ended the crisis if they had been accompanied by the withdrawal of the security forces and the military from the city of Daraa, and if there had been a restoration of the trust between the regime and the people. In addition, such decisions aimed to strengthen the credibility of the state and its institutions all over the country. The decisions responded to the most important demands to the people in the country, so it was not about Daraa only. On Friday, 25 March, the people in Daraa received the leadership decisions with doubt as the security forces were still stationed in the city, so they continued their protests and reached the center of Daraa city (Al-Mahata) chanting, "Oh Buthaina Sha'ban, Daraa's people are not hungry" (*Ya Buthaina ya Sha'ban, Sha'b Daraa mu joa'n*),[384] remarks that addressed the wages increase. They wanted to demonstrate to the authorities and to the whole world that their mobilization was about dignity and freedom, rather than bread or hunger. They were chanting "Death

[384] Fadi Al-Mahamed, Oh Buthaina Sha'ban, Daraa people are not hungry. Posted on 14 November 2011. https://www.youtube.com/watch?v=MfpLfsf OCG0.

rather than humility", imitating Fanon's axiom "Hunger with dignity is preferable to bread eaten in slavery."[385] Meanwhile, another massacre was committed in Assanamayn,[386] halfway between Damascus and Daraa, where security forces fired at crowds of people that gathered after the Friday prayer in solidarity with their fellow citizens in Daraa. Dozens of people were killed. Such news fueled the situation in Daraa city, so people stormed the mayor's office, tore up the largest picture of Bashar Assad, and attacked the statue of Hafiz Assad in the city center. Snipers opened fire, killing a few people and injuring dozens. At this important juncture, the people of Daraa reached the point of no return, and the uprising started to spread to most of the provinces in the country. The regime confirmed the operation of storming the city of Daraa, but claimed it was to suppress and destroy the terrorist groups.[387]

Indiscriminate violence proved to be a counter-productive strategy despite the high imbalance of power between the regime forces and the civilians in Daraa. Such fact and outcome was not unique to Daraa or to Syria. Henriksen claimed, "In revolutionary warfare reprisals serve the rebel cause,"[388] and Kalyvas again explains:

> The most infamous example of the futility of indiscriminate violence is possibly the Nazi reprisal policy in occupied Europe, aimed at deterring resistance against occupation. Reprisals appear to have been an utter and complete failure: they simply did not stifle resistance activity and, more importantly, they appear to have actually induced people to join the resistance.[389]

---

[385] Fanon Frantz, *The Wretched of the Earth*, Grove Press, New York 1961, p.147.

[386] Jassas Channel, The Syrian Revolution, The Massacre of Assanamayn Posted on 15 March 2011, http://www.youtube.com/watch?v=qeBmY7iirJE.

[387] 14march.org, The Authorities storm Daraa to Crush Terrorists Groups Posted on 26 April 2011, https://www.youtube.com/watch?v=spY2RF6iFfA.

[388] Thomas Henriksen, *Revolution and Counter-revolution: Mozambique's War of Independence, 1964–1974*, Greenwood Press, Westport, 1983, p.129.

[389] Kalyvas, op, cit, p.151.

Storming the city of Daraa potentially sent an indication to Syrians that the regime wanted to repeat the city of Hama's scenario from 1982, when security services and military divisions suppressed the uprising through violence and brutality. In fact, some sources close to Hezbollah leaked information about a meeting that took place in Damascus on 28 March 2011 between Qassem Sulimani, the leader of the Iranian Revolutionary Guard, representatives from Hezbollah and leaders of the regime, including Bashar Assad. In that meeting, a decision was taken to crush the uprising at whatever the cost. Bashar Assad was quoted as saying, "In Hama in 1982, we silenced them [the Syrian people] for thirty years, but now we will silence them for one hundred years." This quotation was leaked from some sources very close to Hezbollah. However, even the events on the ground and the heavy participation of Hezbollah and Iran within the battle against the revolutionaries can, to an extent, prove that such a meeting did take place, and that such a decision was taken. Such a meeting declared the decline of the state in Syria as it lost its monopoly on using violence within its border by inviting regional non-state actors to help the regime to suppress national protests. The involvement of Iran and Hezbollah, or any outside forces helping the regime, means the army was weak and unable to protect the regime, or full military loyalty (all soldiers and officers) was not guaranteed, so hiring foreign forces or mercenaries from outside the country was essential to the regime's survival. Gaddafi hired foreign mercenaries to protect his regime, and I think he could have stayed longer in power fighting his people if the West did not intervene militarily.

Resorting to excessive violence had implications beyond suppressing the early stages of the uprising in Daraa. It aimed to prevent the rest of the country from participation. Gagnon explains: "Images of threat and violence create silence and marginalize those who disagree with those in power; it demobilizes people who may in other circumstances have mobilized against the regime and effectively prevents their political participation."[390] The regime in Syria was

[390] V.P. Gagnon, *The Myth of Ethnic War*, Connell University press, London, 2004, p.28.

successful at silencing and demobilizing some areas in the country such as Aleppo for some time. However, Bashar Assad failed to suppress the peaceful uprising in Daraa. He was unlike King Louis XVI in 1789, who failed to use adequate force to suppress the revolution in France, nor like Napoleon, who succeeded in beating civilian resistance through the use of adequate force in 1848. The events in Daraa created huge levels of public solidarity in many places across Syria. It was different from what happened in Hama in 1982, when public solidarity was weak. The clashes in Daraa were not between the regime and a certain political movement. The cause was a public cause, and the regime's campaign was against the public in Daraa. On the other hand, the public consciousness in the aftermath of the Arab Spring revolutions in Tunisia and Egypt was more focused upon confrontation with the regimes. People had changed psychologically, and when they chanted "Death rather than humiliation," they meant it. The access of information also played a role in spreading the events in Daraa instantly, allowing the people to mobilize and demonstrate in solidarity with other fellow Syrians. However, public solidarity in Syria was nowhere near the public solidarity in Tunisia or Egypt during the uprisings of 2011 because of the fragmented society in the country, which constituted a very great obstacle in the face of revolution.

News sources close to the Syrian regime such as Zanobia and Aldunnia TV stated that the events in Daraa had been exaggerated and manipulated by misleading and prejudiced television channels in order to destabilize the country, serving Israeli and American interests in the region. They claimed that Bashar Assad had dealt with the events in Daraa very appropriately from the very beginning, so he sent his special convoy to express his own condolences to the families of the first young men who were killed in the events (Mahmoud Al-Jawabra, and Hossam Ayyash). The families accepted Bashar Assad's condolences, but regional and international powers manipulated these events to plot against Syria through different types of agents and terrorist militias.[391] Those

[391] Chaîne de jubaarin, The Fact about Darra's Events, Posted on 13 December 2012, http://www.youtube.com/watch?v=XX4lNHirM-0.

groups consist of 5000 people, and started moving from place to place in the country, from Daraa to its suburbs, to the suburbs of Damascus, to Homs, to Baniyas and then to Latakia,[392] as sources claimed. It was a state of denial.

Baniyas. This coastal town became very important to the Syrian conflict for many reasons, the first of which concerned Baniyas' complicated sectarian structure. Adnan al-Sheghri, the head of Baniyas Council at the time of the uprising, but who subsequently defected, claimed: "Baniyas contains a complicated religious structure. We have Alawis at 40 %, Sunnis, 56%, and Christians 4%. We used to live in peace, but real harmony and cohesion never existed, especially between Alawis and Sunni."[393] The second reason is the history of clashes between Alawis and Sunnis before Baath rule in the town. And third, Baniyas has a very important political position in terms of the past and the future; it is the home of many well-known politicians, such as Adnan Othman. Fourth, Baniyas was the most heavily impacted coastal settlement during the events of 1982, as it was a hotbed for the Muslim Brotherhood in the nearby area. Finally, it is the city where Abdull Halim Khaddam comes from, so he still has some influence among the people of his town.

As the uprising reached Baniyas, the crisis in Syria was reignited, in particular issues pertaining to sub-state identity. The situation in Baniyas was much more complicated than in Daraa, where the struggle was merely between the people and the regime. In Baniyas, identity, and sectarianism featured greatly in the struggle. The uprising in Baniyas led to a double crisis, as a prime moderate Sufi sheikh (Anas Ayrout) spearheaded the uprising in the town. This led to concerns from Alawis and Christians. The town accordingly divided into Sunnis supporting the uprising, Alawis supporting the regime, and very concerned Christians. It was the largest setback for the already fragile national unity.

[392] Addounia, Daraa, The Failure of Conspiracy, Posted on 04 May 2011.https://www.youtube.com/watch?v=CwXpKLLybcE.

[393] Interview with the author over the phone on 4 May 2013.

On 11 March 2011, Sheikh Ayrout made a sermon during Friday prayers entitled *Alsidq Maa Allah*, "Honesty with Allah." The sheikh called for reform in the country before it was too late. Most people reacted with vehement support. Sheikh Ayrout ig nored any pressure that was exerted on him from statesmen and from many personal delegates.[394] On Friday, 18 March, his sermon was about *Tsunami Alhukkam,* "tsunami of the rulers." People gathered almost from all over the town to this mosque, planning a large demonstration after Friday prayers. Once the prayers had finished, a young man called Anas al-Shegri led the demonstration, chanting: *Sunniyeh Alawiyeh nehna bedna al-Huryyia*, "Sunnis, Alawis, all of us need freedom."[395] The protesters were fully aware of the sectarian division and the difference in loyalties within the town, so they attempted to display unified slogans and to assure other sectarian communities that the issue was not about identity, but about freedom for all the people in the country. Clashes broke out between protesters and the security forces, along with regime loyalists, consisting mainly of Alawis. Sheikh Ayrout gave a speech wishing for a positive response from the

[394] Sheikh Ayrout ignored calls from Muhammad Ismael, mufti of the city of Tartus, and refused the warnings of Mudar al-Sayyed, (Mudeer Al-Awqaf) the manager of endowment directorate in the city of Tartus. He refused the invitation of the mayor to meet in Tartus. In fact he demanded the mayor to come over to Baniyas. The minister of endowments Muhammad al-Sayyed invited sheikh Ayrout to meet in Tartus, the sheikh refused initially, but he responded eventually under the condition that the mayor would not attend the meeting. The minister has told the sheikh about the impact of his activities upon the leadership in the country and asked him to put an end to the protests. The minister tried to appease him, but the sheikh showed no interest. A private envoy from Bashar Assad, Abdul Kader Sabra, an honorary consultant in Turkey, he tried to convince sheik Ayrout to give the regime another week and to refrain calling people for protest on the following Fridays. Another envoy from Maher Assad, Naeem Zuraiq, met with Sheikh Ayrout in order to convince the people of Baniyas to stop protesting. Another envoy from Damascus was Bassam al-Sabbagh, from Kufftaro institution; he tried to advice sheikh Ayrout and to warn him that Maher Assad's special snipers might attack him, but Sheikh Ayrout showed no great flexibility.

[395] ahlg, Demonstrations of Baniyas 18.03.2011 Posted on 19 March 2011, http://www.youtube.com/watch?v=qW7y1uSzxBE.

government toward the people's demands of reform. Abu al-Abbas, the head of state security in the town, contacted Sheikh Ayrout and invited him to visit their headquarters and to write down the demands of the people in Baniyas. Almost all of the people who were protesting followed the sheikh and waited for him outside. He later appeared from the balcony of the branch to read the people's demands:[396]

In the name of Baniyas or the Syrian people we demand the following:

> 1) No for all mixed-gender schools; 2) Monitor and decrease the electricity bills; 3) The return of (*Munaqabat*), fully covered female teachers to the education sector; 4) Refrain from arresting any protesters; 5) Release all political prisoners from Baniyas and all of Syria, especially Tal al-Mallohi; 6) Create more jobs and find proper solutions for unemployed young people; 7) Sack the seaport manager in the town [for adopting restrictions on the fishermen in the recent years]; 8) Remove the state imposed status of emergency in the country; 9) Allow all dissidents to return home; 10) Freedom of expression; 11) Open a religious school in the town.

He concluded that the regime had one week to respond to these demands, otherwise a much larger protest would take place within the town. The head of state security was not happy with such a conclusion, which included a blatant warning to the regime. However, none of these demands hinted at support for a regime change or the ousting of Bashar Assad, or indeed major political reforms. They instead focused upon political amnesty for the opposition, and socio-economic demands. However, some demands were inconsistent with the secularist orientation of the state, and this posed a great concern to the regime and other sectarian communities in the country.

[396] rojdar roj, The Demands of Baniyas People. Posted on 18 March 2011.http://www.youtube.com/watch?v=g6Avw2ama30.

The Grand Mufti Hassoun made an effort at this stage through one of his followers in the city to reconcile with Sheikh Ayrout, but he failed to persuade him. The grand mufti called Sheikh Ayrout and had a long phone conversation; Sheikh Ayrout eventually showed signs of slight flexibility. On Friday, 25 March, Sheikh Ayrout tried to calm the situation, but the people went to a demonstration at another mosque.

On Saturday, 26 March, a very big demonstration happened in the town followed by a sit-in in Al-Saraya Square. Sheikh Ayrout received lots of pleas from people affiliated with the regime to end the sit-in. Some security leaders warned that the sit-in could be stormed, but the young protesters were defiant. The sit-in eventually ended, but the sectarian tension remained in the town, and clear enmity between Alawis and Sunnis prevailed. The situation in Baniyas echoed the words of MacGinty, "Deeply divided societies are likely to have an enduring culture of violence."[397]

Overall, the uprising in Baniyas was the first real threat to state formation in Syria as a territorial state. National unity proved to be nothing more than rhetoric or empty words. Sub-state identities emerged, reflecting the internal social fragmentation and disintegration that threatened a looming vicious sectarian war in the country, and by default, in the region. Such an outcome would reshape the whole region demographically, socially and politically.

[397] Roger MacGinty, "Ethnonational Conflicts, Democratization, and Hate Crime", in *Violence and Politics*, Worcester, Bermanzohn, and Ungar (eds), Routledge, London, 2002, pp.165–183.

Picture from Baniyas on 6 May 2011.

Damascus and its Countryside. On 18 March 2011, people from Damascus and its suburbs gathered for Friday prayers in the Grand Omayyad Mosque. After the prayers, people started chanting for freedom.[398] The security forces entered the mosque and started beating the protesters. Dozens of people were arrested. On the following Friday, 25 March 2011, a large demonstration took place in the Grand Omayyad Mosque in Damascus in solidarity with Daraa and for freedom too,[399] and went through Al-Hamidiyah Market to some main streets in Damascus. The same was going on in the suburbs of Damascus, mainly in Duma,[400] so people from

398 SyrianFreePress, the Demonstration in Umayyad Mosque, Posted 18 March 2011, http://www.youtube.com/watch?v=hapQdvfvrTo.

399 The demonstration of Omayad Mosque 25 03 2011. Posted on 12 April 2011, http://www.youtube.com/watch?v=Dxlj_FJSxF0.

400 TalNews, the demonstration of Duma 25 03 2011. Posted on 27 March 2011, http://www.youtube.com/watch?v=1qZe5s8-qgk.

Duma itself and surrounding villages attended a large demonstration in the town center. The suburbs of Damascus and many parts of Damascus city center continued to protest persistently. The mosques of Al-Hasan in Al-Midan, and the mosque of Al-Rifai in Kafar Sousah witnessed continuous demonstrations. In spite of all the mobilization in the city of Damascus, the uprising remained very weak compared to other cities and provinces experiencing revolt, excluding Aleppo and Tartus. Thousands of people from the city of Damascus traveled to areas in the suburbs, such as Zamalka, Barzah, Darayya and Al-Qabon[401] in order to participate in the large demonstrations there. Many young protesters offered cold water and flowers to the security forces in an attempt to win over their hearts and minds. Those young protesters were influenced by the doctrine of Sheikh Jawdat Sa'id, who opposed using any aspect of violence in the political struggle. In fact, he emphasized peaceful means to achieve political change. Demonstrators in many parts of Damascus and its suburbs had been recorded holding roses as a sign of peaceful protests.

These attempts had no impact upon the regime forces in Syria, who responded to the protesters with bullets and fire. Such a scenario happened during the early days of the uprising in Darayya,[402] a western suburb of Damascus. There was a sincere intention by all protesters to keep and preserve a peaceful uprising. Violent reactionary behavior was perceived as being very dangerous and capable of creating more violence. The lesson of Hama in 1982 was always present in the minds of Syrians, so the protesters were aware of the regime trap that could push them toward violence.

The weakness of the uprising in the city of Damascus was mainly due to the military strategy of the regime. The regime had

[401] Interview with Mr. Jamal over Skype on 13 February 2013. Mr. Jamal said that he used to go from Baghdad Street in Damascus, where he lives to Zamalka, an eastern suburb of Damascus, in order to participate in the demonstration there. He added: many of his friends and neighbors do the same, and go to different areas in the suburbs of Damascus, where demonstrations are active.

[402] Razan Zaitouneh, "Darayya", The Damascus Bureau, 30 December 2012. http://damascusbureau.org/arabic/?p=2772, viewed on 01 June 2014.

learned the lessons of Egypt and Tunisia, where protesters occupied the main squares in both Cairo and Tunisia, so the regime in Syria devoted the majority of its security and military divisions to controlling the capital and its borders in order to prevent large demonstrations and sit-ins within it, or demonstrations coming from outside the city from the eastern or western suburbs. The merchant community in Damascus in general was also against the uprising. The business network that was established during Bashar Assad's era, where Alawis had great influence upon business as well as the military, had served the regime in its campaign against the uprising. However, history witnessed a similar stance before, when the merchant community of Damascus supported Hafiz Assad after the events in Hama in 1982.[403] Sunnis dominated the business sector at that time. The religious institution in Damascus was greatly divided. While Kufftaro Institute[404] and the administration of Al-Fatih Institute[405] were supportive of the reform process of Bashar Assad, Jama't Zayd[406] and some other sheiks were outspoken and very critical of the regime, but not as Thomas Pierret labels them as rebellious. Their mosques were magnets for demonstrations in the capital, and dozens of their students and disciples were killed in the demonstrations. In fact the rebellious

---

[403] Hafiz Assad hailed in a speech the merchant community of Damascus for their stance.

[404] Established in 1971by Sheikh Ahmad Kufftaro, the previous grand mufti of Syria, he was very close to both Hafiz and Bashar Assad. This institute was very strong and very loyal to the regime. However, after the death of Sheikh Ahmad, the institute became divided and weak.

[405] This institute was established by a *Hanafi* Sheikh; Saleh Farfur in 1956. His sons and prime students took control after his death, and became very popular in Damascus and its suburbs in early 1990s. After 2000, Al-Fatih became one of the most important religious institutes in Damascus, and its suburbs competing with Kufftaro institute. Its prime sheiks (Husam al-Farfur, and Abdull Fattah al-Bezem) are supporters of Bashar Assad, while most second row sheiks in the institute are among the opposition groups.

[406] It was established by Sheikh Abdul Karim al-Rifa'i in the 1940s, but revived in 1994 on the return of his sons (Osama and Saryah) from exile. Jama't Zayd has grown dramatically in the past few years, and gained good social base among the people and the merchant community in Damascus and its suburbs.

sheikhs in Damascus and its suburbs were from the second-row sheiks and many Salfai sheikhs. Many of them led the peaceful demonstrations, and became militants in the Free Syrian Army or judges govern the Sharia Courts in the areas under the Free Syrian Army control. The influential religious figures in Damascus were also deeply divided. Sheikh Kurayyem Rajeh[407] was supportive of the uprising, while Rateb al-Nabulsi[408] preferred silence. To the contrary, Sheikh al-Bouti was a flagrant supporter of the regime. He later issued a *fatwa* calling the public up to stand with the national army against the enemy.[409] As for Al-Qubaysiat, the regime had invested in their loyalty hugely. Basher Assad held many meetings with their seniors, but without their founder Mrs. Al-Qubaysi, as she chosen isolation. He allowed them to have their religious parties in the Grand Ommayad Moasque just few miles away from Ghouta, where people was suffering from Bashar Assad's war and starvation. However, many members declared their defection from this group in support for the revolution.

The old-new traditional alliance between the merchant community and sheikhs in Damascus played a negative role in the revolution. Moreover, the brutality of the regime in Daraa and in a suburb of Damascus also played a major role in demobilizing the people of Damascus, as Gagnon explained earlier. The images of violence and bloodshed that flooded out of Daraa and other places in the country silenced and marginalized the majority of people in the capital. The current demographic and social structure of Damascus also did not favor the revolution. The non-Sunni

---

[407] Krayyem Rajeh, he is a very respected and popular figure, known as sheikh of reciters of Al-Sham. He was the preacher of Al-Hasan Mosque in Al-Midan neighborhood in Damascus when the uprising began in March 2011.

[408] Rateb al-Nabulsi has a different religious discourse to most clerics, concentrating on treating the problems through better understanding of the Quran. He had the ability to attract lots of people in Syria and in the Arab world. Al-Nabulsi had a daily ten-minute religious program on the state radio for years before the uprising.

[409] Souria Ya Habibati, al-Bouti calls the public up to stand with Bashar's army. Posted 08 March 2013, https://www.youtube.com/watch?v=Hj_GJOVHJMQ.

population in Damascus cannot be underestimated, especially Alawis, who are surrounding the city from all directions.

Homs. The first demonstration calling for freedom took place in the city of Homs on 18 March 2011, located at the Khalid Bin al-Waleed Mosque. It lasted for an hour before dispersing. On 25 March 2011, two large demonstrations from Khalid Bin al-Waleed Mosque and Al-Kabeer Mosque took place; people were chanting against the mayor of the city *Al-Sha'b Yoreed Isqat al-Mohafez*,[410] "The people want the removal of the mayor." They wanted his removal due to a long-existing problem regarding the reconstruction of the old city of Homs. The two demonstrations met at Al-Sa'ah Al-Jadida "the New Clock Square." Some of the protesters[411] were overzealous and they entered the Officers Club, destroying a picture of Bashar Assad and kicking and destroying the picture of Hafiz Assad.[412] Some clashes took place between the people and the security forces, but no serious injuries were recorded. The sheikhs of Homs were on the frontline of the protests and the sits-in in the city.[413] Their position was different from the sheikhs of Damascus and the sheikhs of Aleppo. This probably was due to their weak relationship with the merchant community in the city, and their weak bonds with the security officials. Another explanation suggests that the sheikhs' positions were probably a reflection of a great relationship with the merchant community in the city, who had a problem with the mayor regarding the Dream of Homs Project in the old town, which would affect their businesses.

The footballer of Homs, Abdul Baset al-Sarout, has become the hero of all Syrians who stood against the regime, and a great icon for the revolution. He sang for Homs, for Syria and for the

[410] syrianstranger2000, The demonstrations of Homs 25.03.2011. Posted on 25 March 2011, http://www.youtube.com/watch?v=bsDBvPmptNQ

[411] His name was Kheder Al-Akidi Al-Hajji.

[412] thehoawkofSyria, This is how the revolutions started in Homs Posted on 25 March 2011, http://www.youtube.com/watch?v=dz56DBwjLdQ.

[413] Syria2011X, the Sheiks of Homs in the sit-in, Posted on 18 April 2011, http://www.youtube.com/watch?v=XCL-0jKWD9E.

revolution. His songs portrayed the suffering and the sacrifices of the people, their homesickness, their determination for victory over Assad, and the willing for martyrdom for that sake. He was later at the frontline against the regime military campaigns in Homs and across the country, but died fighting Assad's forces in June 2019.

Demonstrations were also remarkable in the towns and villages of Homs, especially Talbiseh and Ar Rastan, where the two towns were competing in the ability to arrange the biggest demonstration. The situation in the town of Talkalakh was dangerous as it is surrounded by Alawi villages. However, its people were brave enough to arrange many demonstrations against the regime despite the risk of their neighbors' attacks from the Alawi community.

Latakia. This is a mixed sectarian province to which the Assad family belongs. They descend from the village of Al-Qerdaha in the mountains of Al-Alaween in the countryside of Latakia. The province of Latakia is divided between 50% Sunnis, 4% Christians and 46% Alawi.[414] The Alawis are centered primarily in the countryside. However, after Hafiz Assad seized power in Syria in 1970, Alawis have enjoyed greater control within the entire province; in the city as well as in the countryside.

The events in Latakia started very early when, on 29 December 2010, a young man from the Borro family destroyed a small statue of Hafiz Assad in Sooq Al-Tujjar, "the Merchant Market," located in the center of Latakia. He headed later to destroy another statue of Hafiz Assad, a larger statue in al-Sheikh Daher neighborhood. The security forces arrested him, creating tension in the city, due to the belief that opponents of the regime were being unfairly discriminated against. On 25 March, thousands of people demonstrated in solidarity with Daraa. Many observers considered the demonstration in Latakia as a type of social suicide due to the big Alawi influence in the city.

---

[414] This statistic is an estimate as no reliable statistics are available, and have been provided by Mr. Adnan al-Sheghri, the head of Baniyas Council. There is a semi-balanced structure between Alawis and Sunnis in Latakia.

The situation in Latakia was very similar, but more dangerous than the equivalent in the town of Baniyas. Sub-state identities were evident since day one of the uprising, despite the great attempts from the protesters to portray their mobilization in the collective identity framework of being Syrians, rather than Sunnis.[415] Such attempts did not deny the fact that the protesters were overwhelmingly Sunni, while pro-regime supporters were not Sunni, but mainly Alawi.

Deir ez-Zur. This city responded promptly to Daraa. On 25 March 2011, people of Deir ez-Zur, went to the streets demonstrating in support of Daraa and denouncing the regime's cruelty against its people. Demonstrations became frequent daily rituals not just in the city of Deir ez-Zur, but extended rapidly to the towns and villages in the whole district such as Muhasan, Al Mayadin, Al Shheell and Al Quriyah. Deir ez-Zur occupies a large part of the eastern province which has a unique vital importance for the country in terms of food security and energy resources, particularly oil wealth, so high-ranking security officers such as Jameh Jameh were in charge of the city and showed zero tolerance toward the peaceful demonstrations.

Idlib. The villages and towns of Idlib preceded the city in the early demonstrations. Villages such as Binsh, Taftanaz, Kafar Nabl and not to forget the big towns of Ma`arat al-Nu`man, Saraqib, Khan Shaykhun, and their suburbs, have become strongholds for the uprising. The demonstration in Idilb were so distinctive in everything, from slogans to songs, and to cartoons. The village of Karfar Nabl was famous in its cartoons reflecting the Syrian suffering and the international position.

[415] Latakia Coordination, Latakia: the first demonstration, Posted 03 December 2011, http://www.youtube.com/watch?v=ukyFIhRtvjA.

Hama. People in Hama were a bit cautious at the beginning due to the past bloody experience of Hama massacre, where Hafiz Assad stormed the city, killing around 40000 people in February 1982. However, when the people decided to protest, their demonstrations were the biggest in the country. More than a million rallied in Assi Square in the city center calling for Bashar Assad to leave. Robert Ford, the American ambassador, visited the city and the demonstrators welcomed him and assured him that their protests were peaceful. I think welcoming Mr. Ford was a big blunder because it validated and supported the regime claims that the uprising was a US plot against the regime. The villages and towns of Hama such as Suran, Tayyibat al Imam and Halfaya were also brave in their demonstrations.

Ar Raqqah. It stayed a relatively calm city in the first few months of the uprising as a regime loyalist city, so Bashar Assad was comfortable to give the first Eid Al Adha prayer after the uprising in the city on 06 November 2011, challenging the uprising in the other parts of the country. However, the situation in the town of Al Tabqah was different. Demonstrations were accompanying its counterparts in the country. The main reason for Ar Raqqah calmness was the great alliance between the authorities and some major influential loyalist tribes in the city. However, in early 2012 huge protests burst in Ar Raqqah. In early 2013 state and security institutions fell into the hands of the armed group and the statue of Hafiz Assad was destroyed.

Al Hasakah and Qamishli. The protests in this area had a unique important nature as Arab, Kurds and Assyrians came together in protest against the regime. The spirt of unity among the people was high and recognizable. It was a true translation of the famous uprising slogan "The Syrian people are one." However, Kurds insisted to raise the Kurdish flag during the protests, which symbolized the Kurdish State, a state the vast majority of Kurds are dreaming of. This Kurdish enthusiasm supported the regime's narrative portraying the uprising as an international conspiracy aiming to divide Syria.

The Kurdish Flag.

Aleppo. The greatest shock for the revolutionaries was that Aleppo did not join other cities in the early stages of the uprising, as the roots of revolt in Aleppo were believed to be very strong. Aleppo was a great base for the Muslim Brotherhood in Syria and had witnessed bloody battles with the regime in the 1980s. In the early days of the uprising, hundreds of young people interconnected through Facebook and agreed to gather in Sa'ad Allah Al-Jabiri Square. The security services intercepted their communication and trapped most of them. They were arrested, beaten and then released after pledging not to protest again,[416] according to Abdull Karim, an activist from Aleppo. However, many students from the University of Aleppo protested for freedom and in solidarity with Daraa.[417]

The disengagement of Aleppo in the early months of the uprising can be attributed to many factors: Firstly, the security grip was firm, as the regime expected the uprising to take hold in either Hama or Aleppo, so it applied full control over the city. Secondly, the majority of the business community in Aleppo was against the revolution. Tycoons in Aleppo such as Shihabi (sons of

[416] Interview with the author over Skype on 22 March 2013.

[417] syrianagen2011, the demonstration of Aleppo University 13 April 2011, Posted on 13 April 2011, http://www.youtube.com/watch?v=d847hcLE1_Y.

Hikmat al-Shihabi, the former chief of staff), Krayyem and Nahhas were great allies of the regime. They pushed their employees to cooperate with the regime forces in suppressing the demonstrations in the suburbs of Aleppo. Others, such as Zedo, Mansour, Sekhneh and Barri recruited gangs to intimidate and threaten people who were attempting to march against the regime in the city.[418] Finally, the religious community was predominantly against the uprising. According to Pierrext, "When, in April 2011, Aleppian intellectuals published an open letter to the President calling for democratic reforms, the *Ulama* were absent,"[419] apart from two scholars. The formal religious institution in Aleppo was almost captured by two pro-regime sheikhs: Hassoun, the grand mufti, and Sohaib al-Shami. On the other hand, the overwhelming majority of sheikhs in Aleppo were traditional Sufis. They feared the threat of Salafism as a result of revolution. Sheikh al-Shihabi stated, "We prefer the hell of Bashar Assad to the paradise of Salafis,"[420] according to Issam Eido, a Syrian specialist in Islamic studies from Aleppo. The relationship between most sheikhs in Aleppo and some top security men in the city was significant. It was a relationship of mutual interests, which ultimately served the regime's interests.

Bashar Assad Begins to Talk

On 30 March 2011, after almost two weeks of clashes and bloodshed in Daraa and around the country. Bashar Assad gave his first speech before the People's Assembly.[421] Syrians were looking forward to his speech with hope that his wisdom would overcome the recklessness of the security leaders and thus put an end to the crisis. Unpredictably, the speech was shocking and

[418] God Lover, The most dangerous Businessmen supporting Bashar Assad Posted: https://www.youtube.com/watch?v=kRbxjOu3NR8.

[419] Thomas Pierret, *Religion and State in Syria*, Cambridge University Press, Cambridge, 2013, p.229.

[420] Interview with the author on 13 April 2013.

[421] Full speech can be found on the following link: http://www.voltairenet.org/article173297.html, viewed on 2 June 2014.

disappointing. During the speech, Bashar Assad was seen as making a mockery of the revolution, rather than acknowledging the enormity of the events. His appearance was lacking seriousness in many ways, but he admitted in his speech that the changes in the region were affecting Syria, contradicting his interview with the *Wall Street Journal* almost two months prior, about the immunity of Syria to the radical changes in some Arab countries. He also recognized the authenticity of the majority of protesters, although he believed in the existence of some infiltrators among them who had a foreign agenda. The foreign conspiracy as usual had great presence in his speech. Claiming that a conspiracy is not a theory, but a reality, Assad perceived Syria to be the victim of outside powers who had links within the country and aimed to destabilize it.

Reform and its necessity to fight and beat the *Fitnah* (internal strife) was one important part of the speech, admitting the delay of applying reform policies, which was mainly due to unfinished international and regional challenges. He also pointed out that the people surrounding him were not obstacles to the reform process, but rather the drivers of new progressive policies. Bashar Assad concluded this important speech by stressing the necessity of aborting the *Fitnah* as a national, religious and ethical duty, but he expressed his readiness for war if it was imposed on him, and accepted no place in the middle.

Comparisons between Buthaina Sha'ban's statement on 24 March 2011 and the president's speech on 30 March 2011 allow the observer to notice a sizable rift within the regime regarding how to deal with the crisis. Two opposite wings inside the regime can be seen as attempting to manage the crisis:

1. Containment wing, supporting a political solution to the crisis.
2. Confrontation wing, supporting a military solution to the crisis.

It appears that the speech of Bashar Assad declared the victory of the confrontation wing inside the regime, which supported a military solution to the crisis. The excessive violent and catastrophic events that happened in many cities and provinces across Syria shortly after his speech support this assumption. The regime had chosen a military solution for dealing with the uprising in Daraa, and with the increasing public revolt in the country.

Post-Speech Fueling of the Uprising

After the speech, the regime had shown more inclination toward violence, the use of state terror and indiscriminate attacks in order to suppress the uprising. The regime declared a war on what it called clients of the West and clients of Israel. Bashar Assad's speech was used to provide legality for the regime's behavior and its strategy rather than as a means of treating the problem and ending the crisis peacefully.

Major events took place allowing the crisis to plummet into more violence and more bloodshed, making the revolution more understandable and more popular. The violence had several forms:

1. Indiscriminate attacks on all demonstrations in Duma, Latakia, Daraa, Homs and other areas which took place on 01 April 2011, killing hundreds of people and injuring thousands.[422]
2. The battle of Al-Jiser, "the bridge" in Baniyas on 12 April 2011 after the murder of a security recruit, Nidal Jannud, a member of Alawi community. Clashes erupted between the security forces and young people, killing almost 26 people from the security forces and four people from the town.[423]
3. Storming the sit-in at the New Clock Square on 18 April in the city of Homs killing dozens of people.[424]

---

[422] Syrian Revolution, 01 April 2011, http://syrianrevolution.org/?page_id=1709, viewed on 13 April 2013.

[423] Interview with Sheikh Anas Ayrout over Skype.

[424] OsmanMash, Homs: the Massacre of Clock. The moment of shooting Posted 21 April 2011, https://www.youtube.com/watch?v=033dKTwqb1A

4. On 22 April 2001, Good Friday, tens of thousands of people decided to head on foot from the eastern suburbs of Damascus (Duma, Harsta, Erbeen, Saqba, Hamoriya, Kafarbatna, Hazza, Ein Tarma and Zamalka) toward the center of Damascus. Some of them crossed a distance of 15 km, but when they reached Jober and Zablatani, where the border of the city starts, snipers fired at them, killing dozens.[425]
5. The siege of the city of Daraa in late April 2011, forcing some public figures to announce the Declaration of Milk, in solidarity with the children of Daraa.[426]
6. Storming the village of Al-Bayda in Baniyas in early May 2011, the security forces embarked on humiliating the people. Some security forces were seen trampling over the young men in the village.[427] A few days later, the security forces shot some women in Baniyas who were calling for the release of their sons from the detention center.[428]
7. The Battle in Jisr Ash -Shughur in June 2011, which led to the killing of over 200 security men and the displacement of thousands of people from that area. In fear of retaliation from the regime, they entered Turkey and stayed in camps, creating a refugee crisis.[429]

[425] ABN-SYR, Good Friday demonstrations in in Easten Ghouta Posted 23 April 2011. https://www.youtube.com/watch?v=W1kUL5kMzOY.

[426] "Calls from Syrian actors and intellectuals to provide Daraa with food aid", Sryia-news.com, 3 May 2011.http://www.syria-news.com/readnews.php?sy_seq=132186, viewed on 13 April 2013.

[427] "The Syrian Army enters Baniyas", Aljazeera.net, 07 May 2011. http://www.aljazeera.net/news/pages/60209b0e-0993–4b73-b95d-8ad118dfc208 viewed on 1 June 2014.

[428] Freedamasyria, Killing the Women of Baniyas, Posted on 13 May 2011, https://www.youtube.com/watch?v=54phvBfTUlI.

[429] Syria: the killing of 120 from army and security forces in Jisr Al, BBC Arabic, 06 June 2011. http://www.bbc.co.uk/arabic/middleeast/2011/06/110606_syria_deaths.shtml, viewed on 1 June 2014.

8. Storming the city of Hama in July 2011, where almost half a million people congregated in Al-Asi Square.[430] The American and French ambassadors visited the scene as a sign of solidarity. However, the visit was manipulated by the regime to support its continuous claims that a Western agenda was behind the events and the uprising in Syria.[431]
9. The security forces committed a massacre in Deir-Zur city's Al-Hawaiqa neighborhood in late July 2011, shooting on a peaceful demonstration.[432]

Many promising presidential decisions and concessions accompanied these events, such as the abolition of the emergency law, the government reshuffle, granting citizenship for the Kurds, issuing new laws for free media, the withdrawal of the decision to ban fully covered female teachers from schools, allowing religious TV channels and many promises about new reform measures to be implemented in the near future. However, these goodwill policies and procedures were meaningless due to the non-stop violent crackdown on the peaceful demonstrations, rendering the trust in the regime very low. In other words, authoritarian upgrading may prevent revolutions from occurring, but it is unlikely to be able to stop an already started revolution, especially when bloodshed is still the overwhelming practice.

The military and security institutions were the only governmental and formal instruments to deal with the uprising. There was a noticeable absence of Baath Party involvement in any political solution. In fact, some top leaders of the Baath Party were among the supporters of the regime's military policy against the peaceful demonstrations. Bekhtian, the assistant general regional secretary

[430] ShaamNetwok S. N. N Hama: Storming Hama on Sundy's down 30 July Posted 30 July 2011. https://www.youtube.com/watch?v=7Mx-2I5rZt4.

[431] "Syria says US interfering as ambassador visits Hama", BBC, 08 July 2011. http://www.bbc.co.uk/news/world-middle-east-14074257, viewed on 01 June 2014.

[432] alfurat2freedom, The view of Al-Hawiqa after the Massacre, Posted on 01 August 2011, https://www.youtube.com/watch?v=25d8sr0LIHU.

in the Baath Party, told Nawaf al-Bashir, a prominent figure in the opposition: "We would kill a third of the Syrian people in order to suppress the uprising."[433]

Engines of the Revolution

Unlike the situation in Tunisia, Egypt, Yemen or Bahrain, the environment in Syria was dry in terms of independent and active opposition parties and civil society organizations. The opposition figures, and the grassroots of some opposition parties such as the Muslim Brotherhood, were limited in the country and weak, and unable to constitute a starting engine for the uprising. Similarly, civil society organizations, as mentioned in Chapter Two, are contained and lacking independence and public regard. Such a situation urged activists to establish forms of civil society organizations since the beginning of the uprising in Syria in order to mobilize the people and organize the uprising. This is what can be considered the mechanism of the uprising. Two pillars can be noticed at this stage of the uprising: 1) Activists inside Syria who plan and organize the demonstrations; 2) Activists outside Syria, mainly the children of Syrian dissidents, who provide different types of support such as media and information technology. For instance, the establishment of the formal Syrian Revolution page on Facebook; "*The Syrian Revolution against Bashar Assad 2011*," was created by Syrian activists outside the country. It turned out to be the most important media outlet about the revolution.[434] It also took the responsibility to choose a name for every week in the revolution trajectory in order to unite the people on certain issues believed to be very important, or to convey a

433 "The leader of Al-Baqqarah Tribe seeks refuge in Turkey after a journey of detention and persecution", 17 January 2012, viewed on 1 June 2014. http://www.aawsat.com/details.asp?section=4&issueno=12103&article=659302#.U5X7QZRdUVg.

434 "The Syrian Revolution page turned to the first news outlet about the revolution", Asharq Alawsat, 31 May 2011. http://www.aawsat.com/details.asp?section=4&issueno=11872&article=624347#.U5adY5RdUVg, viewed on 3 June 2014.

political message.[435] Civil society organizations from different orientations were established on the ground to manage the uprising affairs, where the opposition was relatively absent and divided. Antony Shadid observed this situation, so he stated:

> An opposition drawing its strength from Syria's restive streets has begun to emerge as a pivotal force in the country's once-dormant politics, organizing across disparate regions through the internet, reaching out to fearful religious minorities and earning the respect of more recognized, but long divided dissidents.[436]

Most of these organizations such as the Tsunami of Freedom movement, Pulse Gathering for Syrian Civil Youth (Nabed), Local Coordination Committees (LCC) and the Syrian Revolution General Commission are of secular orientation and work to build a civil and democratic Syria in the future. Their activities were important at this stage of the uprising. However, their discourse of secularism was met with dissatisfaction from the majority of people, and that contributed heavily to their weakness. On the other hand, the regime's brutality against the activists has undermined the influence of these organizations. Moreover, the radical proliferation of such organizations has divided the people and created an atmosphere of competition rather than cooperation. Hussam, an activist since the early days of the uprising, stated: "Every day, a handful of people from different groups used to come to our area, and invite us to join their group."[437] The overwhelming secularist trend of these organizations was confronted with an overriding religious discourse presented by a dissident Syrian Salafi Sheik

---

[435] List of weeks' names since the beginning of the revolution till 22 December 2011. http://the-syrian.com/archives/55433, viewed on 3 June 2014.

[436] Antony Shadid, Coalition of Factions From the Streets Fuels a New Opposition in Syria, The New York Times, 30 June 2011. http://www.nytimes.com/2011/07/01/world/middleeast/01syria.html?pagewanted=all&_r=0, viewed on 03 June 2014.

[437] Interview with the author over Skype on 01 June 2014.

resides in Saudi Arabia: Adan al-Arour. He was fairly unknown among Syrians, but he became popular. Despite being a Salafi, his discourse was comprehensive. He was able to polarize the majority of the demonstrators. They used to follow his TV program conveying advice to the people in Syria, and instructions to the activists and demonstrators.[438] However, some of this advice was catastrophic for the uprising and jeopardized many of demonstrators' safety, leading to their capture by the regime forces. Some people argued that his role at this stage was destructive rather than constructive, especially in the efforts to attract and assure the minorities.[439]

Manny observers labeled the uprising as an Islamic uprising. I think this is an unfair and unfounded claim. In fact, it was an uprising by Muslims, where people used to gather in mosques for Jumm'a (Friday) prayers[440] and then go for demonstration. Hadi, one of the demonstration's organizers from Zamalka stated, Razan Zaitoneh, one of the secularist activists, visited them and requested them to avoid chanting *Allah Akbar* (Allah is great), but to chant *Hurria* (freedom). They refused her request, saying that protesters were confronted with live bullets from the regime forces and facing death anytime, so they wanted to die chanting *Allah Akbar*, but not *Hurria*. They wanted to be *Shahieds* (martyrs), not a waste.[441]

The female participation in the peaceful demonstrations was noticeable, but restricted due to many reasons: First, the regime brutality; second, the culture restriction, where mixing is not permitted, so women used to join the end rows of demonstrations or sometimes had their own demonstrations.

---

[438] FreeMediaSyria, Sheikh Adnan al-Arour directs tips and important instructions for the revolutionaries, Posted 03 July 201, https://www.youtube.com/watch?v=Yqjgzmdr-_0

[439] Today Meeting, Television program, Aljazeera, 19 May 2012.

[440] Protestors used to go out from Jumm'a prayers for demonstrations. During Ramadan, protestors used to gather after the daily Taraweeh prayers. Few Christian young men used to wait outside mosques to join the demonstrations. This was seen noticeably in Homs

[441] Interview with Hadi on 13 May 2011 via Skype

The Obstacles of Revolution

The seeds of counterrevolution were planted deeply in the country even before the start of the revolution due to a fragmented society obstructing mass mobilization.[442] Indeed, Syria is a deeply divided country ethnically and religiously, and contains disciples of different types of ideologies. Martha Kessler also noted the existence of such a situation: "Contemporary Syria suffers in many respects from its legacies: It still lacks internal cohesion, its population remains diverse and factious; it is a defensive, suspicious country."[443] Therefore, the main obstacles before the uprising were indigenous actors making the success of the revolution highly unlikely. This is where Syria is also different from Tunisia and Egypt. The uprising brought about dangerous rifts in most social groups in Syrian society, so the country became divided as never before. Some people were in favor of the uprising, others of the regime. The Syrian Revolution caused vertical structural divisions within each of the different ethnic and religious groups that formed the Syrian society. Those divisions, in turn, caused a real and intense polarization state within each group. The intensity of this state varied between different groups depending on the religion, sect, ethnicity, or even on the regional and socio-economic circumstances.[444]

In fact, Syrian society has been divided horizontally and vertically. Interests, identities and fears of uncertainty and the regime's brutality are the main factors behind dividing the Syrian people. Nonetheless, the Syrian people were divided into three groups at this phase of the uprising. The first group was the pro-revolution group desiring a regime change and nothing less than that. Although great numbers of this group did not participate effectively in the demonstrations, fearing the wrath of the regime,

---

[442] Raymond Hinnebusch, "Authoritarian Upgrading and the Arab Uprising: Syria in Comparative Perspective", a paper was presented at BRISMES Conference, London, March 2012.

[443] Martha Kessler, *Syria: Fragile Mosaic of Power*, University Press of the Pacific, Hawaii, 2002, p.14.

[444] Wael Alheji, "The Social and Psychological Implications of the Syrian Revolution", All For Syria, 18 March 2013, viewed 20 March 2013.

they did and do support a regime change. The second group would be the pro-regime group, aiming to protect itself or protect its various interests. Under this category there is the Alawi sect, big parts of minorities, the majority of Sunni aristocrats in Aleppo and Damascus and some prominent religious figures from all religions and sects, in addition to some tribal leaders. The third group is characterized as ambivalent regarding who might be uncertain or perhaps more than neutral. Some elements of society showed neutrality in order to avoid the cost of possible miscalculations.

Tribal Society

The Syrian opposition and the Assad regime recognize the political importance of the tribal networks that cross Syria and extend into neighboring countries because millions of rural and urban Syrians express an active tribal identity and tribal affiliation.[445] Therefore, the weight of tribes in the balance of power between the regime and the revolution cannot be underestimated. Although many top tribal leaders have joined the revolution, others have chosen to support the regime.[446] The division among tribal societies regarding the revolution was evident and has caused considerable harm to the revolution's trajectory. The division was not only between the tribes, but also within them, so every tribe was divided into three parties: with the revolution, against the revolution and neutral.[447] These divisions can be attributed to many factors such as differing interests, differing loyalties and safety concerns.

Many members of the tribal society have benefited from the land reform policy, so they believe that any change in the system would lead to the loss of their acquired lands. Most tribal leaders allied to the regime are the beneficiaries of the land reform policy.

---

[445] Carole A. O'Leary and Nicholas A. Heras, "Syrian Tribal Networks and their Implications for the Syrian Uprising", Terrorism Monitor Volume: 10 Issue: 1, June 2012.

[446] Ibid.

[447] Sami Al-Sami, Sheikh Ahmad Fahed al-Karkh, al-Hadidi. Posted on 02 August 2012, https://www.youtube.com/watch?v=nAvECxOisKQ.

They would support the regime by any means necessary out of fear of losing the lands they have acquired and the prestigious position they have enjoyed for decades,[448] as Mr. Salem from Al-Naser, a branch of Al-Boshaban, a large tribe in al-Tabaqa town (Al-Thawra) in Ar Raqqa province, stated. Some tribes share mutual interests with the regime, so a regime change means a threat to their survival. Dr. Al-Nuaim, a member of Al-Nuaim Tribe, explained that some tribal leaders have deep overlapping interests with the regime. They run legal or illegal businesses in partnership with some key men in the military and in the security service.[449]

Some tribe's members in Aljazeera province have adopted Shiism with the support of Iran and Iraq; they have become very loyal to the regime.[450] Salem claims that some regional and national actors took advantage of the increased poverty in the region recently to promote Shiism among the tribal society in Aljazeera province.[451] Therefore, the uprising was a great opportunity for those tribes opposing the increasing Iranian influence among the tribal society. As said by Mr. Amir al-Dandal, from the al Eqidat Tribe, tribes in the past few years were targeted by the regime and Iran; there was an evident pro-Shiism campaign. Such activities created a great deal of anger and anti-regime sentiment among the tribal society in general.[452]

The neutral stance of some tribal men was due to a lack of confidence in the possibility of the revolution being victorious. In fact, some tribes believed the regime had the ability to crush the revolution as it did in Hama in the 1980s.

---

[448] Interview with the author over Skype on 6 May 2013.

[449] Interview with the author over Skype on 22 April 2013.

[450] Khaled Sindawi, "The Shiiat tune in Syria, Current Trends in Islamic Ideology", volume 8, Hudson Institute, Washington DC, 23 June 2009.

[451] Interview with the author over Skype on 06 May 2013.

[452] Interview with the author over Skype on 07 May 2013

The Kurdish Issue

This became one of the most critical issues in Syria after the uprising. It has to do with identity and irredentism. Kurdish people in the north have their independent identity and aspirations for local governance if not total independence. The Kurds have felt alienated in the region for decades. The notion of Arab nationalism, which was adopted by the regimes in Syria and Iraq, had tremendous social and demographic implications for them. Hundreds of thousands of Kurdish people were denied Syrian nationality, which added more problems to the already existing economic and social grievances. Moreover, Law 49 had enormous ruthless economic and social implications for the people in that region. They rebelled against the regime in 2004, but the regime's brutality and the regime–Arab tribes alliance aborted their rebellion. Mr. Sheikho, a Kurdish politician stated, "The notion of Arab nationalism left us alienated in our lands and in our country. Therefore, we support and will join any uprising against the Baath Party and the Baath ideology."[453]

The majority of Kurdish people joined the uprising at the beginning, and this was a great asset for the uprising. The town of Amuda, for instance, was a theater for large demonstrations in the Kurdish area.[454] However, the regime reaction toward them was remarkably different from the rest of the revolting areas in the country. The regime's brutality to suppress the uprising that was exerted in Darra, Homs and Baniyas was not applied against the Kurdish areas. The regime strategy was to contain and appease the Kurds in order to neutralize and utilize them. Many concessions were offered to them during Buthaina Sha'ban speech. Moreover, In July 2012, the regime withdrew most of its soldiers and local authorities from Afrin, Ayn al-Arab and parts of Aljazeera region, and handed them over to the Kurdish Worker Party's (PKK) affiliate, the Democratic Union of Kurdistan (PYD), to control

---

[453] Interview with the author over Skype on 18 May 2013.

[454] Mesa Amude, The demonstration of Amuda 01 April 2011. Posted 01 April 2011, https://www.youtube.com/watch?v=HGaNg6DV-nA

and administer these areas.[455] The regime in Syria appeased these two factions in order to exert pressure on Turkey, and to fight the Free Syrian Army and the Jihadist groups. Khaddou and Mazur argue:

> By using Kurdish identity to foment division in regions that it cannot control outright, the Syrian regime has taken lemons of its own cultivatio—Kurdish resentment and solidarity—and concocted a marginally less sour tonic: the perpetuation of its regional system.[456]

The irredentist trend among the Kurdish people was a burden on the revolution, and deepened the divisions among the opposition and the revolutionaries. The Kurdish opposition formed their own National Congress in order to unify their views on the Syrian opposition and on the future of Syria. This move encouraged other ethnicities such as Turkmen to form their own blocs in the opposition with considerable support from Turkey, creating even more fragmentation inside the revolution.[457]

The Christian Community

Christians had always been in the frontline of politics in the country prior to the Baath Party taking control. All Syrians can remember reputable names such as Fares al-Khoury from Damascus and Mikhail Lyan from Aleppo during the post-independence period. The harmony between Christians and Muslims in Syria has always been an ideal and unique one in the Arab world.

455 Shirawan Shaheen, "The Kurdish Issue in Syria", Azzaman.com, 16 September 2012. http://www.azzaman.com/?p=13779, viewed on 04 June 2014.

456 Kheder Khaddou and Kevin Mazur, "Struggle for Syria's Regions", Middle East Research and Information Project, volume 43 winter 2013.

457 Abd Al-Naser Sinky, "The announcement of the Syrian Turkmen Bloc in Istanbul", BBC, 16 February 2012, http://www.bbc.co.uk/arabic/middleeast/2012/02/120216_syria_turky_opposition_group.shtml, viewed on 15 August 2014.

In light of the uprising in March 2011, Christians, like most social groups in the country, were divided. Although hundreds of Christians participated in the demonstrations, the mainstream political line for them was neutrality. There are many Christians serving in the field hospitals as doctors and nurses, in the media (such as Basel Shehada), in the political opposition (such as Georg Sabra and Abdullah Turkmani), as members of the Syrian National Congress and as fighters, though in very limited numbers, in the Free Syrian Army in Hama, Idlib and Daraa for example.[458] Some Christians have issued a clear statement in support, declaring that they were joining the uprising.[459] Meanwhile, there are other Christians who decided to fight with the regime until the conclusion of the conflict, for example the former minister of defense Dawoud Rajeha, who was killed along with some security leaders in an attack targeted at the National Security Building on 18 July 2012. The limited involvement of the Syrian Christians in the uprising is attributed to the failure of the Church and its leaders to convey the right message about the situation to the Christians[460] as Georg Sabra, a Christian opposition figure, argued. The Church, he said, is a respectable religious institution; most Christians abide by its rules and instructions. Josef Olmert has a different explanation:

> The Ba'th regime, itself based on an alliance of minorities, mostly Alawites, but also Druze and Ismailli Shi'ites, has diligently tried to foster good relations with the Christians, particularly the Orthodox communities of Aleppo and Damascus. It pays off these days, when the vast majority of

[458] Sunnarevolution1, Christians in FSA Posted on 18 September 2012. http://www.youtube.com/watch?v=QY6Q6gQgBdM Objection, television Program, Al-Arabiya, 03 February 2012.

[459] "Statement of Syrian Christian in Support of the Revolution", Jadalliyya, 19 July 2011. http://www.jadaliyya.com/pages/index/2181/statement-of-syrian-christians-in-support-of-the-r, viewed on 3 June 2014.

[460] Objection, television program, Al-Arabia, 03 January 2012.

> Syrian Christians are taking a passive, onlooker view of the uprising and stay outside of it.[461]

In general, the Christian community in Syria had and still has a great fear of the unknown future, bearing in mind the situation in Iraq and the fate of Christians in that country, where most of them were forced to leave their homes and their country. Mr. Aleji, a Christian psychologist from Syria, explains the fears of Christians more closely:

> Christians in the country were under the influence of a mental filter, which filtered out all good things about an event, so they thought about the dark aspects and the bad outcomes of the revolution, leading to a bleak view on it. Their views or stances were based on concerns and fears and not on events going on the ground.[462]

Christians are a minority in Syria, and divided into many different churches, so they cannot afford to enter a battle and lose it. They decided to bond their future with that of the country, but with neither one of the conflicting parties, contrary to the Alawi decision. However, their mainstream demobilization was another obstacle for the uprising and contributed to the regime propaganda of facing an Islamic revolution.

The Druze Community

On the 28 March 2011, a sit-in was organized by the solicitors of the city of As-Swayda, the main region of Druze, in solidarity with the revolution. A demonstration of almost 160 people went out onto the streets of As-Swayda in August 2011, but the security

[461] Josef Olmert, "Syria's Christians and the Uprising", Your Middle East, 29 April 2013. http://www.yourmiddleeast.com/features/syrias-christians-and-the-uprising_6516, viewed on 03 June 2014.

[462] Interview with author over Skype on 08 May 2013.

forces intervened and dispersed the protest.[463] Moreover, Muntaha al-Atrash, the granddaughter of the Druze leader Sultan Pasha al-Atrash who led the 1925 revolution against French colonization, was on the side of the revolution from the first day. She criticized the regime and visited the grieving families of men killed by the regime forces.[464] Nevertheless, some observers consider that neutrality is the mainstream Druze stance. "Claims that the Syrian Druze community is shifting its support to the opposition are off the mark. No more than a trickle are joining the rebellion,"[465] as Gambill has stated. Mr. Mallak, a pro-revolution politician from the Druze community, attributes the general neutral position of the Druze to "the fear of unknown future and to the sect's sheikhs who are utterly loyal to the regime, and enjoy a great influence over the people in the community."[466]

Still, the Druze community had great grounds to join the uprising and be an important part of it. Its historical role in revolutions and politics in the country and in the region is momentous. Considerable numbers of effective leaders in the Baath Party and in the army were from the Druze community such as Salim Hatoum, Fahed al-Shaer, Abed Kareem Zaher al-Aldeen, and Hamad Obied. However, the Druze role in military and politics was significantly undermined after the coup of 1966, where Alawis have won the struggle for power in the country. Therefore, the uprising in Syria in 2011 was an opportunity for them to restore their historical political role in the country, but they missed it.

Ismaili Community

"Salamiya [the center of Israelis in Syria], in eastern Hama province, was one of the first cities to stage anti-government

[463] "The Role of Druze in the Syrian Revolution", Masar Press Agency, 31 October 2013. https://www.masarpress.net.

[464] Ibid.

[465] Gary C. Gambill, "Druze: Toward Defiant Neutrality", Middle East Forum, March 2013.

[466] Interview with the author over Skype on 29 April 2013.

protests, but has steadfastly refused to take up arms in demanding the toppling of the regime"[467] claims Williams. Thousands of people in the city of Salamiyah and some villages of Masyaf participated in the demonstrations from the very early days of the uprising, challenging the dangerous sectarian structure of their region, as Masyaf and Salamiyah are religiously diverse provinces. Great numbers of intellectuals from the Ismaili community have been engaged in politics and in the opposition for decades. The community was a great base for communism and socialism, and harbors many pro-democracy activities. Moreover, great numbers of Ismaili intellectuals and intelligentsia suffered persecution and intimidation during Hafiz Assad's era. Mr. Yahia, a politician from Salamiyah, attributed the participation of the Ismailis in the peaceful uprising against the regime to:

> Their ever heavy involvement in politics and opposition, in addition to the miserable situation of the town of Salamiyah as no governmental development plan was implemented there for decades. Moreover, the historic tension between Alawis and Ismailis cannot be dismissed here, however, it was not overwhelming factor.[468]

Therefore, it was not unusual for the Ismaili community to engage in the peaceful uprising against the regime. However, the Ismaili community in Syria does follow the Ismailis' world spiritual leader, Imam Agha Khan, who rarely spoke about the situation in Syria, but issued a statement prior to the Geneva Conference[469] in January 2014, promoting a peaceful solution in Syria.[470]

---

[467] Lauren Williams, "Agha Khan Urge Syrians to seek peace through dialogue", the Daily Star, 18 November 2013. http://www.dailystar.com.lb/News/Middle-East/2013/Nov-18/238135-aga-khan-urges-syrians-to-seek-peace-through-dialogue.ashx#axzz34b0sIKO7, viewed on 04 June 2014.

[468] Interview with the author over Skype on 22 May 2013.

[469] The Geneva Conference was held in Geneva in late January 2014 between the Syrian regime and the opposition, and sponsored by the United Nations, in order to reach a political solution to the Syrian conflict.

[470] Williams, opt, cit.

The Alawi community

While the revolutionaries were chanting in their demonstrations at the beginning of the revolution "One, one, one, the Syrian people are one" (*wahhed wahed wahed alshab asory wahed)* in an attempt to remove any sectarian dimension from the uprising, the regime adopted rhetoric suggesting that the uprising was a sectarian conflict from the outset. Buthaina Sha'ban declared clearly that some people were planning to ignite a sectarian *Fitnah* in Syria.[471] Moreover, the revolutionaries had chosen the name of Saleh al-Ali, an Alawi leader during the French Mandate, as a name for one of their weeks[472] in order to reassure the Alawis, distance their fears and attract them, but the revolutionaries failed. Some members of the Alawi community, most of them communists, such as Habib Saleh, who suffered for a long time in prison during Hafiz Assad's era, continued to express support for the revolution. However, the vast majority of the Alawi sect showed unlimited loyalty to the regime in the conflict against the uprising. Furthermore, they pushed their sons to fight for the regime's cause. The situation of the Alawi community was very complicated and their support to the regime can be attributed to three main factors. The first factor is that they conceived of the uprising as a movement against the Alawis, but not against the regime. It was solely in the interests of the regime to portray the uprising as a movement against the community, but not against the regime. This portrayal pushed them to arm themselves with the help of the regime, and to develop radical anti-Sunni sentiments. The regime provided the Alawi neighborhoods in Damascus and Homs with military protection, so they became segregated areas, causing the sectarian tension in the country to escalate further.[473] Second, the majority of Alawis have enjoyed unique advantages during the reign of the Assad family in the

[471] Jassas Channel, The decisions of the Baath Party after the events in Darra, Posted on 24 March 2011, https://www.youtube.com/watch?v=3rTl0JDKzTQ.

[472] List of weeks' names since the beginning of the revolution till 22 December 2011. http://the-syrian.com/archives/55433, viewed on 3 June 2014.

[473] AlAan TV, Alawis and the Syrian uprising, Posted on 07 April 2013, https://www.youtube.com/watch?v=H4Cp0vBP3JE#t=1799.

military, in education and in terms of job opportunities and promotions. Therefore, the collapse of the Assad regime means losing all these advantages. This made them adamant in defending their long-enjoyed gains and interests. Third, the Alawi's beliefs contains huge hatred toward Muslims. Such hatred can explain the brutality, the torture sessions in prisons and the massacres that have been committed by them across the country. However, Dr. Suqrat Ba'aj, a mixed Alawi-Sunni pro-revolution politician, did everything in his power to convince the Alawis to join the revolution, and to bring about the criminalization of sectarianism. He argues, "the failure of the opposition to offer a national mature initiative that can dissipate their fears and eliminate their concerns has also played a great role in their demobilization."[474] However, such claims can be refuted when observing the formal national broad discourse of the opposition.[475]

The loyalty of the Alawi community to the regime in Syria can probably be considered the largest burden on the Syrian uprising. Their opposition of the uprising was a huge obstacle to the uprising itself. The regime in Syria employed instrumentalism, where ethnic or religious tensions or conflicts are driven by the manipulation of ethnic or religious identities by political leaders for their political or economic gains. This strategy sustained Alawi loyalty and made the trajectory of the uprising very complicated.

Two other main actors influenced the role of minorities in Syria:

1. Cross borders loyalties: All the minorities in Syria have great regional or international connections, and such connections do influence their behaviors and stances within the country.

[474] Interview with the author over Skype on 7 May 2013

[475] The opposition since its very early conferences never ignored to stress heavily on the national unity of Syria and the rights of all minorities, and Alawis in particular.

2. The geographical presence of the minorities in Syria is unbalanced. The Kurdish presence in the north is very dense, and Alawis constitute almost 40% in the coast and drop to 0% in many areas. And while the Druze are centralized in As-Swayda in the south, the Ismailis are in Salamiyah in the Suburb of Hama in the mid-country. Such situation would endanger the unity of Syria heavily.

THE SYRIAN OPPOSITION

The Syrian opposition joined the uprising in the same feeble and divided state mentioned in Chapter 2: deeply fragmented, with no vision, no public support and most importantly no harmony between them. The Damascus Declaration and the Muslim Brotherhood were the main elements of the opposition despite the fact that the Muslim Brotherhood is part of the Damascus Declaration.

The Damascus Declaration detected the waves of change within the country as an extension of the Arab Spring, so its members issued a statement on 25 January 2011 to all Syrians and especially the youth, calling on them to stick to peaceful mobilization and for the common purpose that preserves national unanimity, which is building a civil democratic state, and not to be dragged into any kind of violence or retaliation.[476] The Muslim Brotherhood was in a difficult position as they were still constrained by their pledge to stop their opposition activities against the regime following the Israeli war on Gaza in 2009. Moreover, on 15 December 2010, almost three months prior to the uprising, Mr. Reyad al-Shaqfa, the general guide of the Muslim Brotherhood in Syria, announced their acceptance of giving up their political activities and returning to Syria as imams or ordinary people as a form of appeasement to the regime.[477] On 1 May 2011, more than two months since the uprising started, the Muslim Brotherhood decided to disregard all of its commitments to the regime and formally join the uprising.

[476] George Sabra, "The Syrian Revolution and the Political Parties", A paper was presented at The International-Arab Relations Formula Conference, Doha 2012.

[477] The Guest of the Program, television program, Aljazeera, 15 January 2011.

Nevertheless, its grassroots members were involved in the uprising from the early days.[478]

The opposition managed to hold several conferences in Turkey during this phase of the revolution, but it failed to form a strong cohesive opposition body able to represent the revolution.

The Opposition Conference in Antalya, 1 June 2011

The opposition conference was a very important stage where all different backgrounds of Syrian opposition met publicly for the first time in decades: Islamists, leftists, Kurds, tribal leaders and independents. On the other hand, the Antalya Conference enjoyed a public support from the revolutionaries, but far less support from the Inside Opposition.

The Syrian regime considered the conference as a political danger, so he tried to appease the opposition. Bashar Assad issued a presidential decree in the eve of this conference diminishing Law 49 of 1980, which stated that members of the Muslim Brotherhood must be executed.

The final statement of the conference included the following points:

1. The conferees are committed to the demands of the Syrian people in ousting President Bashar Assad, overthrow the regime and support the peaceful revolution of the Syrian people.
2. The conferees called on Bashar Assad to resign and to hand over the power to his deputy, Farouk al-Sharaa.
3. Refuse foreign military intervention and emphasize on the peaceful and nationalizing nature of the revolution, and on the unity of Syria. It was the people's demand not to accept any kind of foreign military intervention in Syria in the early months of the revolution. Syrians in the beginning always criticized the Libyan scenario of having foreign military intervention to remove Gadhafi.

[478] Ibid.

4. Guarantee the equality between all Syrians in the country.
5. Build a civil democratic state in the future.
6. Work for economic prosperity and scientific advancement in an environment of justice, safety and peace.
7. Call on the Arab people, the Arab League, the Islamic Conference Organization and the international community to stand beside the Syrian people against the brutality of the regime.

Despite the great efforts that were exerted to reach a successful conference and to respond to the hopes and the demands of the revolutionaries in Syria, the conference was not fruitful and productive. Dr. Abdul Razzaq Eid, a main figure in the conference, attributes the failure of the conference to some reasons:[35]

1. The absence of a clear common vision among the main participants on the best way to help the revolutionaries in Syria. Some of them wanted to form a representative body for the revolution, while others wanted to have the conference as a meeting in solidarity with the revolutionaries.
2. The plan of the Muslim Brotherhood (Aleppo Branch) to hold a follow-up conference in Brussels dispelled the efforts between the two conferences and weakened Antalya Conference.
3. The opposition inside Syria, mainly the Damascus Declaration, did not offer a great support to the conference.

The Brussels Conference, 4 June 2011

Immediately after the Antalya Conference, another conference was sponsored by the Muslim Brotherhood (Aleppo Branch) in Brussels. No major outcomes were reached in Brussels. In fact, the Brussels Conference increased the division among the already divided opposition. It was the first major sign of a divided opposition since the beginning of the revolution. The division among the opposition was great and quite evident when they called for the Brussels Conference just days after the Antalya Conference in

June 2011.[479] It was a major setback for the opposition and the revolution alike. Their unity now was a necessity more than at any other time in the past.

The National Coordination Body for Democratic Change in Syria (NCB), 25 June 2011

This body was established by some political powers belonging to Arab nationalists, leftists, Marxists, some Kurdish parties and national symbolic figures in Damascus. It is chaired by Hasan Abdul Azeem, an Arab nationalist and Nasserist who defected from the Damascus Declaration in 2009. NCB aimed to end authoritarian rule in Syria, but did not adopt violence as a mean for change. Its members promoted civil resistance, so they denounced the formation of the Free Syrian Army, and refused suggestions of any kind of foreign military intervention. They also opposed any Islamic trends within the revolution. However, their political discourse was vague and the radical demands that they made of revolutionaries rendered them unreliable opposition. The NCB refused to reconcile with or join the SNC, and its vague discourse regarding the fate of President Bashar Assad made it very unpopular among the revolutionaries. Major controversies have affected the two bodies, leading the international community and the Arab League to complain about the deep divisions among the Syrian opposition. Such division was also used as a pretext to justify the low international involvement in the Syrian Crisis.[480]

The National Salvation Conference in Istanbul, 16 July 2011

The idea behind this meeting was to have a Skype conference between the Outside Opposition and some Inside Opposition

---

[479] "A Conference for the Syrian Opposition in Brussels", Aljazzera.net, 04 June 2011. http://www.aljazeera.net/news/pages/0907b859–0dbf-4895–8251–0f7f815e51f0, viewed on 03 June 2011.

[480] Inside Syria, television Program, Aljazeera English, 20 May 2012.

figures (traditional opposition not revolutionaries). Yet, the regime attacked the place where the Inside Opposition was due to meet, killing 19 revolutionaries mainly from Damascus and its suburbs that had come to protect the place for the opposition. The Skype conference failed, but some figures from the Inside Opposition gave a supportive speech, such as the Kurdish leader Mish'al Temmo, who was killed months later at his home in Al Qamishli.

Haitham al-Maleh was proposing to form a government in exile from the opposition. Yet this proposition did not enjoy great support among the conferees. The conference in its final statement called on Syrian people and their national bodies to achieve the following goals:

1. Escalate the democratic peaceful struggle, which is a combined effort of the traditional opposition who has been struggling for decades and the revolutionaries who are struggling now.
2. Calling on the regime in Syria to transfer power peacefully to a national temporary government able of dismantling the security state and establishing a constitutional life, and calling for parliamentary and presidential elections.
3. Form a civil democratic state based on citizenship and on a contemporary constitution that can respond to the aspiration of Syrian people.
4. Emphasize the equality between all Syrians and respect their ethnic and religious backgrounds, and the peaceful harmony among the Syrian people.

The most important point in the final statement was drawing the rug from under the revolutionaries by considering their uprising as a continuation of the long struggle of the opposition. The revolution belongs to all, revolutionaries and opposition, Outside Opposition and Inside Opposition. However, the opposition overriding and hijacking the revolution was the greatest problem for the revolution, which made it longer and more complicated, hence the cost was higher.

THE ROLE OF INFORMATION TECHNOLOGY

Just days before the uprising, the authority in Syria lifted the block on some internet sites such as Facebook, tempting the people to use it for their communications, so the authority could intercept and monitor them easily. In the beginning of the revolution, the prevailing perception among the people was that Bashar Assad would not follow his father's footsteps and repeat the Hama scenario from 1982. Telecommunications, media and information access were different from earlier times, so photos or videos showing the regime's brutality would spread globally in seconds, making the regime crack down mostly on media activists. Mr. Feras stated, "All my fellow inmates in the jail were freed apart from a few young men accused of communicating with TV channels such as Aljazeera and Alarabiya."[481]

Facebook was the online arena for the revolution, so every village or neighborhood in Syria participating in the uprising against the regime had a page on Facebook under name of Coordinate delivering its local revolutionary news and other news, which were important for them. On the other hand, the regime loyalists used Facebook for their campaign supporting the regime. Moreover, Facebook became an online battlefield between pro-regime and anti-regime activists. Mutual cyberattacks have caused the disappearance of many Facebook pages belonging to both parties.

Internet communication among the revolutionaries, or between them and their supporters, were running through a satellite system, as no national government or non-government supplying service was available in their areas. Activists and fighters in the Free Syrian Army and the various Jihadist groups were also using Thuraya phones and talkies as an essential means of internal communication for all purposes. They relied predominantly on Skype as the safest and most secure way to communicate despite warnings from some experts that Skype was not secure against the

[481] Interview with the author over Skype on 25 May 2013.

regime's interception due to the war on terrorism's globally adopted measures. According to the adopted privacy policy:

> Skype will not sell, rent, trade or otherwise transfer any personal and/or traffic data or communications content outside of Microsoft and its controlled subsidiaries and affiliates without your explicit permission, unless it is obliged to do so under applicable laws or by order of the competent authorities.[482]

This means that Skype could potentially help the regime by revealing information on its users if this were to be portrayed as part of the war on terror. The US listed some fighting groups and people in Syria such as Jabhat Al-Nusra and the Islamic State in Iraq and Asham as terrorist groups.[483]

Hussein Jabry, an internet activist, used to make internet calls to high-ranking officers in the government and the security services such as the Republican Guards office intimidating them and providing them with false information about the uprising and provoking them through using humiliating language against Bashar Assad and his father, Hafiz. His tactic was so smart they never been able to intercept or locate him. It was a simple mean of expression, but was so brave at the time and very influential, targeting the regime symbols, which was a taboo for more than forty years.

Overall, information technology, media and telecommunications had both positive and negative roles in the Syrian uprising. On the one hand, they helped the Syrian activists and revolutionaries spread their message globally, and provided them with alternative forms of communication and information access after such services were suspended formally in their areas. On the other hand, thousands of activists and revolutionaries fell victim to the regime's advanced monitoring and tracking systems.

---

[482] Skype privacy Policy, "What Information Does Skype Collect and Use" http://www.skype.com/en/legal/privacy/#collectedInformation

[483] Foreign Terrorist organizations, US Department of State. The report can be found on: http://www.state.gov/j/ct/rls/other/des/123085.html.

ASSAD'S BRUTALITY

From day one the regime has resorted to all methods of brutality in order to intimidate people and kill them. Orders were clear: shoot to kill, bomb to kill, torture to cause suffering and kill and rape to humiliate. The main aim at the beginning was to suppress the people, forcing them to end the uprising, but later the aim changed to force people out of their homes and their lands in order to bring about a social demographic change in the country. Millions of Sunni Muslims left their homes and their areas as a result.

The brutality was systemic and indiscriminate, but had never been individual acts. Images of children, women, elders and men have been leaked by Caesar,[484] a defected Syrian officer, showing thousands of tortured bodies in different prisons and detention centers. Also, the Gravedigger has spoken in his testimony before Congress and at German Court Rivals Horrors of Nazi Crimes about the mass graves he witnessed and about the sadistic methods of torture inside Assad's jails. The methods of torture were brutal and inhumane, from lashing to beating to burning to nail removal to electric chairs to burying alive. For instance, my cousin Rouhi Naddaf was killed by electric chair in two hours while he was fasting during the month of Ramadan in 2011, and my own brother Mouaz was killed from lashing, torture and negligence in Sednayah Prison 2011–2014. Horrific and heartbreaking stories were told by Hasna al-Hariri,[485] a previous detainee in some of Assad's prisons, about the cruel and despicable treatment of women by the regime offices inside Assad's prisons.

[484] All leaked images can be found on https://leaks.zamanalwsl.net/tortures.php

[485] Alhurra, الحكي سوري - خنساء حوران تحكي قصة تعذيبها في سجون الأسد, Posted on 3 April 2011, https://www.youtube.com/watch?v=EF15FyUhq-k.

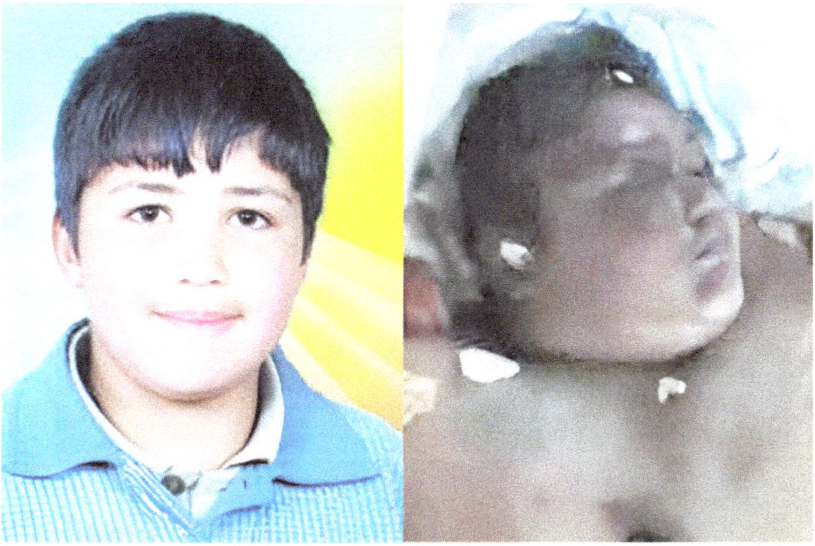

Images of child Hamza Ali Al-Khateeb, 13 years old from Daraa tortured to death in Assad's prisons in May 2011.

Torture, humiliation and rape took place. Children were born in prison as a result of rape. Dr. Rania al-Abbsi, a Syrian chess champion, is still detained, along with her husband and six children. The eldest was 13 years old and the youngest was only 20 months old in March 2013. Children in Syria have paid the ultimate price for Assad's brutality, leading to people in the Arab world calling him a child killer.

Moreover, barrels of bombs and missiles were the main weapons used to target schools, hospital, markets and congested streets in order to cause great causalities and death, and force people out of their lands. The use of banned cluster bombs, and white phosphoric attacks have been witnessed frequently in Hama, Idlib, Daraa, and Deir ez-Zur provinces. As a result, great number of Syrians suffer now from permanent physical and psychological problems and disabilities. Such massacres have been committed by the regime forces, the Iranian militias and the Russian airstrikes in the villages, towns and cities that revolted against Assad's regime.

The Beautiful Syria has been destroyed. Neighborhoods in the rebellious regions have turned into rubbles, and became unrecognizable especially in Jobar, Zamalka, Ein Tarma, Al Mleha, and Harasta in east Damascus. Also, in Darayya in west Damascus, and Al Yarmouk Camp area in south Damascus. The situation was the same in Idlib, Deir ez-Zur, Hama, Homs, and Daraa. The destruction was always associated with burning the land registry office in many places in order to destroy the title deeds. It is all about a demographic change in Syria and changing Syria's identity.

Aleppo (the oldest city in the world) has suffered so severely from the barrel of bombs, missiles, and airstrikes. The Umayyad Mosque and the old market in the city have been destroyed considerably. The amazing ancient citadel of Aleppo was also damaged. Similarly, the great mosque of Khalid Bin Al-Walid in Homs was destroyed significantly, and the tomb was vandalized. Graves and shrines which belong to Umayyad age in Damascus and Idlib were exhumed and desecrated. The grave of Imam Ibn Taymiyyah in Damascus has been entirely demolished. It is a blind malice and an inherent hatred.

Bashar Assad's image has become an icon for the destruction of Syria.

MASSACRES AND GENOCIDES

A large number of massacres have been committed against the Syrian people by Assad and his allies, but here are some of the massacres that Syrians people will never forget ever:[486]

- The Massacre of Houla in Homs, 25 May 2012, where some Alawi militias (Shabbiha) have slaughtered 109 people, including 49 children.
- The Funeral Massacre of Zamalka, 30 June 2012, where Assad regime has targeted a funeral by a car bomb. More than 105 people have died as a result and hundreds were injured. Ironically, this massacre happened on the same day as the Geneva Meeting was taking place to discuss an end to the war in Syrian.
- The Massacre of Daraya, 25 August 2012, where some Assad's militia stormed the town of Daraya and killed more than 220 people mainly women and children.
- The Massacres of Queiq River in Aleppo, January 2013, where some regime forces killed more than 200 people including children and women and threw them in the river.
- The Tadamon Massacre in Damascus, 16 April 2013, where regime forces have captured random people from the street in Tadamon neighborhood in Damascus, blindfolded them, then asked them to walk toward a giant hole filled with a pile of bodies before shooting them. The victims were mainly Palestinians, and I think it was meant to be. Palestinians constitute a semi-majority in this neighborhood.
- The Massacre of Al Bayda in Baniyas, 2–3 May 2013, where Assad's forces and some supporting militias have killed more than 248 people, including 210 children.

Another method of brutality was besieging some towns and cities for many months, imposing total isolation on them. Food and raw materials were completely unavailable. In some closed areas such Homs, Zabadani and Madaya growing and farming independently

[486] All of the massacres and violations that have been committed by the regime against the Syrian people have been monitored and authenticated by the Syrian Network for Human Rights.

was so difficult due to the limited size of land in control, so starvation has spread among the people, pushing them to eat grass and cats in order to survive. Many children and elderly people passed away as a result. Meanwhile, in Ghouta, the situation was much better. The land in control was relatively much bigger, so people resorted to growing their food and raising some small animals such as rabbits and chicken to rely on in order to survive.

The besiege of Al Yarmouk Camp neighborhood in south Damascus was notorious for its ruthlessness and its severity.

A Palestinian man from Al Yarmouk showing his refugee card requesting to go to Israel.

Besieged Palestinian people of Al Yarmouk are waiting for aids, February 2014.

An image of a child dead from starvation in Madaya, January 2016.

Some images from the Massacre of Houla, 25 May 2012.

Some images from the Massacre of Al Bayda in Baniyas, 2–3 May 2013.

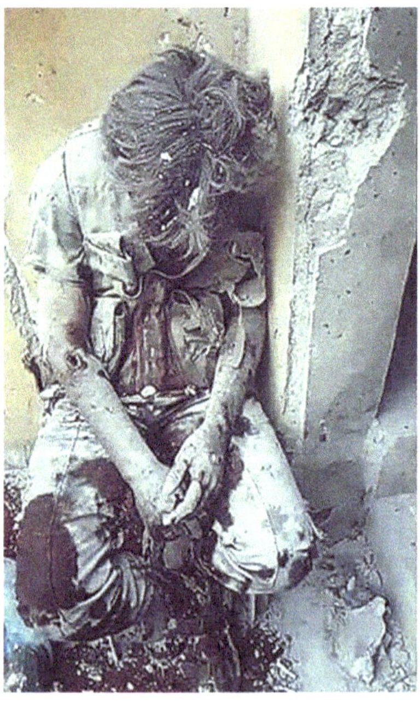

A child has been killed by an Assad's barrel of bombs thrown on a family shelter in Ghouta, east Damascus.

A pro-Assad Alawi officer torturing some civilians then burning their bodies with pride!

Issam Zaher al-Deen, a prominent leader in the Syrian republican army and belongs to the Druze community is butchering some Muslim detainees.

Hundreds of thousands of people were on the edge of real death as starvation and diseases have spread among them. Ironically, the vast majority of this neighborhood are Palestinians, where Assad always claims protecting them and defending their rights against Israel.

CONCLUSION

After the beginning of the uprising, where Bashar Assad was proved wrong in his prediction about the immunity of Syria against the Arab Spring, the regime resorted to authoritarian upgrading through offering concessions in order to discontinue the uprising. However, it has been shown that authoritarian upgrading may have been able to avoid uprising, but in no way is able to stop it once it has started, especially where bloodshed is ongoing. Similarly, violence is not the best means of facing a public uprising, particularly when the people are chanting "Death rather than humiliation."

By the beginning of September 2011, the uprising was already spreading to almost all parts of the country. However, Syrian society was divided horizontally and vertically, making the uprising endure formidable obstacles. The spirit of solidarity that was seen among the Tunisians and Egyptians was not great among the Syrian people. Interests, identities and ideologies among Syrians undermined the uprising. Moreover, the weakness of civil society in the country in comparison with Tunisia, Egypt, Yemen and Bahrain, and the weak divided opposition, added even larger burdens to the Syrian uprising.

The demobilization of the city of Aleppo and to some extent the city of Damascus was a major setback for the uprising, but it harmed the regime's legitimacy too. In other words, the mobilization of most rural areas while Aleppo and Damascus stayed calm made it very difficult for the regime to maintain any semblance of legitimacy, because it had always relied on the rural areas to be presented as a populist regime. Theoretically, it was problematic for both the Baath Party and the regime for aristocrats to be seen supporting the regime while members of the working class, and grassroots activists, were seen to be supporting, or, in fact, creating the uprising. But, in practice, the regime needs business support to survive such a great challenge. The rural areas formed the core and the main prevailing element in the uprising across the country apart from the coast, where Alawis are dominant. Mubarak and Bin Ali surrendered power when the uprisings occupied the capital city centers. Even Gaddafi was captured when Tripoli was liberated from his control. On the contrary, the demonstrators in Syria failed to make such an achievement and occupy the center of Damascus due to the military tactics from the regime, surrounding the city center with military checkpoints and snipers.

People used mosques as meeting points in order to organize large-scale demonstrations. At this stage, it was in no way evident that any particular ideology might be driving the revolution. The revolutionaries were descended from different affiliations, but the mainstream was made up of non-ideological revolutionaries. Having mosques as centers for rallying and mobilization did not imply the presence of any particular ideology, but rather that of courage and enthusiasm. In other words, the mainstream revolutionaries at this stage were Muslim, but not Islamist. The uprising at this stage was overwhelmingly public and peaceful despite some sporadic violence in many parts of the country. There was a prevailing determination among the revolutionaries to keep the uprising peaceful despite the brutality of the regime forces. The revolutionaries tried not to repeat the experience of Hama 1982, which cost tens of thousands of victims. President Bashar Assad admitted that the revolution started peacefully, "The uprising was public and peaceful, and when it failed to change the regime, they [the revolutionaries] turned to an armed struggle after Ramadan [August 2011]."[487] However, the peaceful revolution failed against the regime's force and brutality. Most of the first revolutionary generation was detained or killed, putting the revolution at risk. The death toll among the revolutionaries reached almost 5000 by the end of August 2011, and the number of detainees reached over 100,000, most of them doctors, media experts and peaceful protesters,[488] so resorting to violence against the regime was an inevitable reaction.

---

[487] RT Arabic, Assad: The blood of Martyrs will not go in vain, Posted: 3 June 2012. http://www.youtube.com/watch?v=I_neAoOOpc4.

[488] The Martyrs of Syrian Revolution, 31 August 2011. http://ahrar-syria.com/archives/1503, viewed on 4 June 2014.

Chapter Four

FROM REVOLUTION TO INTERNAL WAR

INTRODUCTION

The peaceful uprising could not achieve regime change in Syria. Likewise, the regime could not suppress the peaceful uprising, so repeating the Hamas scenario failed. By August 2011 the revolution in Syria had entered a new dramatic phase, a phase of formal internal violence starting an internal war within the country. Revolutionaries, both civilian and military, had adopted violence. Although peaceful demonstrations continued in almost every revolutionary city or village, Syria had now entered a stage where arms did the talking, not peaceful demonstrations. This chapter begins to explore the reasons behind the failing of peaceful protests to change the regime, making resort to violence inevitable. Also, I will discuss defections from the army, and the establishment of the Free Syrian Army. The political opposition and its divisions are also deeply focused on.

THE MOVE TOWARD VIOLENCE

As President Bashar Assad admitted, the revolutionaries turned to violence after Ramadan in August 2011. People adopted violence openly after approximately six months of public and peaceful demonstrations, during which the revolutionaries had been the recipients, and not the perpetrators, of violence. They resorted to violence as a reaction response and a method of last resort. The regime in Syria had pushed the revolutionaries to use violence. Assad pushed them to a place where he was much stronger and could beat them,[489] as Mr. Subhi al-Toufaiyli, the former Hezbollah leader, has stated. Scholar Gene Sharp observed this situation years ago from a theoretical perspective. He explained: "Military resistance against dictatorships does not strike them where they are weakest, but rather where they are strongest."[490] Evaluation and hindsight both suggest that the regime forced the revolutionaries to enter and accept a realm in which it could attract international legitimacy with regard to its violent campaign against them, portraying the revolution as a violent struggle between the government and some Islamist rebels. The regime succeeded in its tactics, and the prevailing picture of the Syrian Revolution in the world's media was, and still is, one of a regime fighting Islamist rebels.

By adopting violence, the revolution in Syria validated the views of many scholars who conceive of violence as a means for change, such as Huntington, Johnson, Sorel and others. Huntington defined revolution as "a rapid, fundamental, and violent domestic change," while Johnson conceived it as "a change, effected by the use of violence in the government, regime, and society." For Sorel, he endorsed violence as a means for mass social movements to bring about the downfall of the state.

WHY DID NON-VIOLENCE FAIL IN SYRIA

Although the non-violent approach failed to persist in Syria, it did not fail in achieving some of its political aims, such as refuting Bashar Assad's allegation about the immunity of Syria to public uprising. Moreover, the peaceful demonstrations undermined the regime's legitimacy nationally and internationally. Still, the most important achievement of the peaceful and popular uprising was that the regime became uncertain of the loyalties of its supporters,[491]

---

[489] Objectively, television program, MTV Channel, 25 February 2013.

[490] Gene Sharp, *From Dictatorship to Democracy*, Albert Einstein Institution, USA, 2010, p.29.

[491] Maciej Bartkowski and Mohja Kahf, "The Syrian Resistance: a Tale of two Struggles, Part 2", Open Democracy, 24 September 2013. http://www.opendemocracy.

especially among the Baathists. However, such achievements and gains could not equate to victory in the long run, ensuring that violence was inevitable in order to achieve the opposition's concept of total victory. This notion of an inevitable descent into violence was hypothesized by David Schwartz when he wrote: "It does seem both clear and important that the failure of non-violent politics causes the transition to internal war."[492]

There are many factors that contributed to the transition from non-violent struggle to a violent campaign waged against the regime:

1. Although the mainstream revolutionary discourse and behavior did not pertain or resort to violence in the first phase of the revolution and rejected any kind of foreign military intervention (the Libyan scenario), their demands started to change gradually after August 2011. In the second phase, there were blatant calls for foreign military intervention and the use of any kind of violence against the regime.[493] The excessive use of violence by the regime ensured that the revolutionaries possessed only one option, which was to defend themselves and appeal for help from any external sources. In a sense, it was a natural reaction in order to protect themselves, their families and their properties. It is as Robert Gurr once explained, an innate response activated by frustration. According to John Keane, "Individual victims of violence find in effect that they are treated, as Aristotle put it, 'like a wild animal meant to be hunted'."[494] Al-Kawakibi also points out that people will

net/civilresistance/maciej-bartkowski-mohja-kahf/syrian-resistance-tale-of-two-struggles-part-2, viewed on 01 October 2013.

[492] David Schwartz, a "Theory of Revolutionary Behavior", in *When Men Revolt and Why*. James Davis(ed), The Free Press, New York, 1971, pp.109–132.

[493] The revolutionaries called for international protection on Friday, 9 September 2011, and for a no-fly zone on Friday, 28 October 2011.

[494] John Keane, *Violence and Democracy*, Cambridge University Press, Cambridge, 2004, p.38.

resort to violence as a reaction after an outrageous bloody scene committed by the authoritarian ruler against them.[495]

2. Gandhi's and Jawdat Said's[496] way of change betrayed the civilian and peaceful protesters in Syria as the regime forces showed no respect for lives and the regime showed no regard for human values. For example, the children of Daraa were on the verge of death after milk was not allowed by the regime to reach the city in the early months of the uprising. Activists in many parts of Syria such as Al-Qabun and Darayya used to offer the regime forces cold water and food, but they got bullets in return immediately.
3. The absence of a strong civil society and strong opposition in Syria made non-violent means of struggle at worst impossible and at best rare and ineffective. Moreover, all the social, educational and economic institutions are fully monitored, controlled and infiltrated by the security services, rendering civil resistance futile. Erica Chenoweth and Maria Stephan suggested that "non-violent campaigns achieve success through sustained pressures derived from mass mobilization that withdraws the regimes' economic, politics, social, and even military support from domestic populations and third parties."[497] Such a scenario is inapplicable in Syria due to the regime's security, military and business networks. In this context, Syria is very different from the other Arab Spring countries, where civil society organizations and political

---

[495] Abd –al-Rhaman al-Kawakibi, "*The Natures of Despotism*", Dar al-Nafa's, Beirut, 2006, p.183.

[496] In his controversial book, *The Doctrine of the First Son of Adam*, Jawdat Sa'id argues that Muslims should follow the examples of the first killed man on earth (Able), so not to react violently against oppression and suppression, not to treat violence with counter violence, and not to use violence when tackling the regimes. He stated, "Muslims should not involve in the guilt of committing killing or assassination, or calling people for such acts or behaviors." Jawdat Sa'id tried in his book to distance Muslims who work for Islamic society from resorting to any sort of violence when trying to change the current society.

[497] Erica Chenoweth and Maria Stephan, *Why Civil Resistance Works*, Columbia University Press, New York, 2011, p.44.

opposition enjoy some freedom and independency, which enabled them to play an effective role in the uprising, and have the awareness of the danger of descending to violence against the regimes.

4. The resilience of the regime has created an impression among the revolutionaries that Bashar Assad would not be defeated via non-violent means, but through forceful confrontation. The testimony of Mr. Karim, an activist from a suburb of Damascus, emphasizes this point: "The more peacefully we protest, the more brutality we receive from the regime; so we had to deter them and protect ourselves. The regime forces are defeating us so easily."[498] Bartkowski and Kahf believed that Mr. Karim's view was one of fatal beliefs during an armed response debate. They write that "armed protection came at a collective price exacted by the regime, resulting in more civilian losses in the long run as whole neighborhoods were demolished in pitched battles between armed combatants."[499] Sharp shares Bartkowski's and Kahf's view, believing that violent rebellions can trigger brutal repression that frequently leaves the populous more helpless than before.[500]
5. The inactive stance of the international community. The support of the international community and Western powers is so essential for the success of revolution in the age of globalization. The majority of Syrians were unsurprised by the regime's cruelty against the peaceful demonstrators, yet they were staggered by the stance of the international community toward the regime's obvious crimes. Therefore, a common conception became ingrained among the revolutionaries, namely that help was not forthcoming and nobody was going to prevent the regime from attacking them. Taking this into account, they decided

[498] Interview with the author over Skype on 15 July 2012.

[499] Bartkowski and Kahf, op, cit.

[500] Sharp, op, cit, p.12.

to resort to violence and deal with the regime using their own resources.

6. Violence was not adopted as a primary tactic, but as a reactive strategy. The revolutionaries had no knowledge of Karl Marx and his view that "violence is the midwife of every old society, pregnant with a new one." They had no knowledge of Lenin's maxim that declared "you cannot make an omelet without breaking eggs." They had no knowledge of Mao Tse-Tung's adage "political power grows out of a barrel of gun." Furthermore, the people of Syria, in general, were ill informed about the concept and the duty of Jihad against oppressive rulers. The Jihadists ideology against the rules has been absent from the Syrian public and religious society for decades The idea of Jihad against the regime was not organized by religious leaders, but it was an individual initiative announced by the people to defend themselves and their families. None of the formal *Ulama* declared Jihad against the regime until 13 June 2013, at the Cairo Conference.[501]
7. The concept of Jihad was heavily associated with using violence against the regime. Yet, resorting to Jihad was not necessarily connected to any affiliation with Jihadist groups, but rather, it can be viewed as an individual religious reaction. In other words, the concept of Jihad was not institutionalized at the beginning of the uprising. Syrian people wanted to defend themselves in the name of Jihad; they wanted to die as martyrs. Mr. Hadi, when he was asked why he was holding an Islamic banner expressing anti-regime sentiments, responded with the words, "I may protest and struggle for freedom and dignity, but I do not want to die for their sake. I want to die as a martyr for the sake of Allah."[502]

[501] AljazeeraMubashar, The Muslim Scholars declare Jihad against the Syrian Regime. Posted on 14 June 2013. https://www.youtube.com/watch?v=ZtYdAP6gae4.

[502] Interview with the author over Skype on 15 September 2011.

8. The revolutionaries' mistrust in the regime made them unable to believe any further promises, discourses or even decisions the regime that has taken implying reform. This mistrust played an important role in the revolutionaries' trend toward violence as no hope from the regime was expected. The regime's brutality against peaceful protest was increasing, and associated with no real trend toward genuine reform. Such hopelessness created hopes in violence as the only means to deal with the regime.
9. The revolution in Syria was propounded from below, rather than from above. In other words, the revolution was of a bottom-up typology, rather than being top-down in nature. The failure of the revolution in Syria to ignite a revolution from above such as coups due to the strength and robustness and above all the loyalty of the inner core in the military to Bashar Assad was crucial to turning the revolution into violent struggle. Mass protests would play a great role in preparing for revolutions from above,[503] but the Syrian uprising could not play such a role. This failure was one of the most calamitous elements of the Syrian Revolution, and has contributed heavily to its long trajectory. The inner concrete core of the regime in Syria has proven to be unbreakable,[504] so a possibility of military coup or a revolution from above would have been very unlikely at this stage, and proved to be concrete. The regime was a sectarian and family regime concentrated within the Alawi sect, and in the Assad–Makhlouf families. The inner concrete core of the regime relied on *assabya*, and the military is controlled by the Alawis as explained in Chapter Two. The loyalty inside the military that guaranteed the success of Bashar Assad's inheritance of power in 2000 was protecting his regime during the uprising of March 2011. Consequently, the revolution from below in

---

[503] Fred Halliday, and Mazine Molyneux, M. *The Ethiopian Revolution*, Verso, London, 1983, p 30–31.

[504] The Syrian Revolution, television program, Aljazeera.net, 12 November 2012.

Syria could not create a revolution from above. In fact, the regime was able to overcome the fragmented sociality and opposition by creating its opposite—a cohesive unitary regime—making it very difficult for anyone to attempt a coup without risking their own survival.[505] However, the revolution from below was able to provoke military defections, transforming the revolution into a formal "armed uprising,"[506] and an internal war between the revolutionaries and the regime. Military defections are problematic and damaging for any regime to cope with, but not enough to overthrow it if did not reach the top offices or the inner military core. Such a scenario has happened in Yemen, and constituted the main reason for Ali Abdullah Saleh to step down.

THE DEFECTION FROM THE MILITARY

Regimes depend upon military loyalty when attempting to crush or suppress a public uprising. It is the loyalty toward the regimes and the leaders, and not toward the state or the country, that is depended on. It is where the leaders can enjoy full obedience when giving orders. Gurr argues, "Maximum coercive control is likely to require maximum loyalty in both scope and degree."[507] The military's loyalty for the regime in Syria was shaken once the regime resorted to violence and showed no qualms about using violence against the protesters. Military loyalty is potentially more of an imperative for a regime when confronting an internal threat rather than an external enemy. Gurr builds on his coercive control argument, stating that, "The capacity of a regime to exercise any kind of persistent coercive control over its citizen, at any level of threat or severity of sanctions, depends on the loyalty of its

[505] Darwisheh, op, cit.

[506] A phrase of Hannah Arendt.

[507] Ted Gurr, *Why Men Rebel,* Princeton University Press, New Jersey, 1971, p.201.

military and internal security services."[508] The defection from the military in Syria started as early as April 2011, when a recruited soldier Walid al-Qasha'mi (from Daraa) and officer Ahmad al-Khalaf (from al-Rastan in Homs) individually declared their defection from the army.[509] The number of military defectors including soldiers, sub-officers and officers had reached almost 100,000 by July 2012, according to some sources.[510] A later report by the Syrian Network for Human Rights stated the number of recruits in the official army to be around 70,000 in August 2014, compared to 320,000 before the beginning of the revolution in March 2011.[511] The defections began in remote military divisions and on the battlefields, where higher-ranking officers were less able to exercise their power. Many officers and soldiers had reportedly been shot dead when attempting defection. On 23 June 2012, 48 people were killed in Syria, among them 10 soldiers were attempting to defect in the suburb of Damascus.[512] The defection of politicians and diplomats can embarrass the regime politically. Many top politicians have defected from Bashar Assad's regime, such as Prime Minister Riyad Hijab. However, to date, such developments have not served as anything other than an embarrassment to the regime, from which it quickly recovered.

---

[508] Ibid, p.251.

[509] "The Free Syrian Army and the Tipping point in the Syrian Revolution", Al-Midan, 10 October 2012. http://www.midannews.net/home/articleview/tabid/89/ArticleId/23/.aspx#.U_q2jLywKJs, viewed on 20 August 2014.

[510] Rawshan Qasem, "The Beginning of the End", Al-Majalah, 6 July 2012, viewed on 5 October 2012. http://www.majalla.com/arb/2012/07/article 55236807.

[511] "The regime arresting policy in 2014", The Syrian Network for Human Rights,17August2014.http://sn4hr.org/blog/2014/08/17/the-syrian-regimes-arresting-policy-in-2014/ viewed on 28 August 2014.

[512] "48 People were Killed in Syria among them 10 Soldiers were Attempting to Defect in the Suburb of Damascus", 24, June 2012, viewed on 3 October 2012. http://www.alrai.com/article/522468.html.

Why Defections?

Military defection is the worst nightmare for any regime at a time of war, and the regime situation is more critical when facing internal enemies than external enemies, but facing civilians is the most dangerous decision a leader can take. When the regime is facing an external enemy, loyalty is almost guaranteed, but when facing the public loyalty is on the line, and the risk of defection is very likely. In general, there are many reasons why military personnel made a decision to defect from the army:

1. Military personnel began to question the regime's discourse and its allegations regarding the existence of Islamic fundamental groups, determined to destroy the country and establish an Islamic regime. Colonel Riyad al-Ass'ad, the founder of the Free Syrian Army, stated, "We know this regime very well and we are used to such allegations and fabrications."[513]
2. Officers refused the regime policies and the orders to shoot protesters, opting instead to make their own decisions. They did this knowing that disobeying orders would lead to their death as punishment for treason. Defector Lieutenant Ahmad al-Khalaf, who died fighting for the revolutionaries in the battle of al-Rastan in Homs, stated, "I never conveyed the leadership orders to my soldiers to kill the people of Daraa, but when the leadership found out on 7 June 2011, they put me under arrest and planned to kill me."[514]
3. Military personnel opted to join the revolution after having suffered the same social and economic grievances as the protesters, and probably more. Captain M. al-Qadi, an engineer officer in the Military Academy in Aleppo, defected in February 2012, explaining the hardships experienced in

[513] Interview with the author over the telephone on 20 May 2013.

[514] Lieutenant Ahmad al-Khalaf, "The Security Controls the Army", Asharq Al-Awsat, 06 August 2011, viewed on 10 August 2011 http://www.aawsat.com/details.asp?section=4&article=634532&issueno=11939#.UmiFx5R4aDQ

the military sector: "We are suffering from religious, promotional, and scholarship-related discrimination. There is an inherent lack of trust between us as Sunnis and them as Alawis, and this makes us feel alienated."[515] Sunni officers have long been suffering from neglect and marginalization in the Syrian army.

4. There was a distinct lack of self-confidence and morale among the majority of soldiers serving in the regime army. The regime displayed a shocking neglect for their lives and interests. For instance, it refused many ransom deals that would have saved some of its soldiers, who were held as captives by the Free Syrian Army, returned or set free. Salem, a defecting officer, stated: "The regime has no value for our lives, he has agreed to exchange the Iranian captives, but not my colleagues who are still in the hands of the Free Syrian Army. The Iranian captives are worth more for our regime."[516] It is very important to emphasize in this context that defection from the army was not based on identity or on ideology. Although the overwhelming and prevailing defectors from the army have been Sunnis, the defecting officers and soldiers stated very clearly that their move came on principle due to the regime's brutality against the civilians and peaceful protesters, so it was not a move against the regime for being an Alawi regime.[517] And even though the defecting officers and recruits were overwhelmingly Sunnis, some Druze have also defected from the military,[518] in

[515] Interview with the author over Skype 5 June 2013.

[516] Interview with the author over Skype on 11 June 2012.

[517] The statements of the early defected officers such as Tlas and al-Qasha'mi confirms that the regime's brutality against peaceful protesters was behind their defection. Their statements can be found on these videos: https://www.youtube.com/watch?v=yxHKKW2lhHw https://www.youtube.com/watch?v=6U1o7a2Y5-Q.

[518] Orient news, Asswaydaa: The formation of the first FSA battalion. Posted 02 October 2012, https://www.youtube.com/watch?v=lvSXq7OHlfw.

addition to a handful of people from the Alawi community.[519] I note here that the social public base among the Sunni community have helped their sons or relatives to defect from the army, and were treated like heroes. However, other social communities did not welcome such action from its sons or considered it as treason to the regime or the national army.

Phases of Defection

The defection from the national army went through three phases:

1. The defectors left the army and hid in some place away from the regime, calling for their colleagues to defect from the national army. Most defectors stated that their defection was the only choice in front of them to avoid killing people and to avoid getting killed for refusing the orders of the leadership to fire at the demonstrators.
2. The defectors then started to protect the demonstrations, so there were two groups of people witnessed in the demonstrations at in this phase:
   - Peaceful demonstrators consisting of unarmed peaceful and civil protesters chanting for freedom and the regime fall.
   - Defectors from the army, and their duty was to protect the demonstrations against the regime forces, especially snipers. Their job was to defend only, not to launch attacks against the regime forces. They started to purge the revolutionary areas from the regime forces, so they established their own checkpoints to secure these areas. This is a remarkable phase, where control over the regime forces started to shrink, and thus, the sovereignty of the state started to diminish. Most state infrastructures and possessions had been captured and seized from cars to buildings including schools, hospitals, councils and police stations.

[519] The free Alawis, the Free Alawis front. Posted on 21 March 2012, https://www.youtube.com/watch?v=yGYkeofXPUw.

The defensive tactic that was adopted by the defecting officers and soldiers was attributed to many reasons: 1) No decision was yet taken by the revolutionaries or by the military defectors to start launching attacks against the regime forces. The aim was to protect the demonstrators and the civilians; 2) Many of the regime recruits were from the people, and many were serving the compulsory military service, so it was a big dilemma for the revolutionaries; 3) Many soldiers, sub-officers and officers had to overcome extreme danger and difficulties to defect from the army. The regime had a zero tolerance policy toward such behavior, so the revolutionaries appreciated the difficult circumstances surrounding the military personnel in the army. In fact, the military defectors had to secure his family and relatives before taking his decision because the regime might retaliate against the families of the defectors; 4) There were no proper military machines available in their hands enabling them to shift their plan from a defensive strategy to an offensive one. Most defecting military personnel defected with their rifles only.

3. The defectors started to form battalions and brigades with the revolutionaries as a framework in order get organized and prepare to fight the regime. In this crucial phase in late August 2011, some defecting officers and soldiers gathered in Turkey and agreed to form formal military bodies in order to support more defections, polarize new defectors from the army and train them for a long battle with the regime.

The Free Officers Movement

Defected Lieutenant Colonel Hussein Harmoush, along with 26 defecting officers, announced the formation of the Free Officers Movement on 28 June 2011. It was to serve as a shadow organization for all military defectors. Hussein Harmoush stated, "We are not aiming to fight the regime forces, they are our brothers and our sons. Our job is to protect the demonstrators and the civilians from the regime forces."[520] Harmoush's strategy was not well received among other officers, leading to disputes spreading and the decision taken by Colonel Riyad al-Asa'd to establish the Free Syrian Army (FSA) on 29 July 2011. According to Mr. Hemidan, a close officer to Harmoush, "Lieutenant Colonel Harmoush was planning to support military disobedience among the officers inside the army, but not to form an army against the regime."[521]

The Free Syrian Army (FSA)

Colonel Riyad al-Assa'd attributed the formation of the Free Syrian Army to many reasons, declaring: "From day one I was not convinced with the political solution in Syria, so I was planning to defect and to establish an army of defectors to fight the regime forces; an army to be the core of the future national army in Syria."[522] However, Riyad al-Assa'd wanted to form a national, non-ideological and non-partisan army. It was to be neither an ethno-national army similar to the Kosovo Liberation Army, nor an army that adopted a certain ideology as the IRA in Northern Ireland. On 29 August 2011, Lieutenant Colonel Harmoush was kidnapped in Turkey by some agents belonging to the Syrian regime, with the cooperation of Turkey, as many observers stated.[523] He later appeared on Syrian state TV giving a statement of confession. At the time of this writing, his fate is still unknown. After the kidnapping of Lieutenant Colonel Harmoush, the Free Officers Movement and the Free Syrian Army were united under the name of the Free Syrian Army and under the leadership of Colonel Riyad al-Assa'd.

The formation of the Free Syrian Army was the most harmful blow to the regime; it was a large-scale, unpredicted move. Tens of

[520] The News Hour, television program, Al-Arabiya Channel, 9 August 2011.

[521] Interview with the author over Skype on 9 June 2013.

[522] Interview with the author over the telephone on 20 May 2013.

[523] Many people think it was a coopeertvse operation between the Syrian and Turkish security services.

thousands of soldiers and officers had the courage to defect and the Free Syrian Army arguably shifted the balance of power in favor of the revolution. The regime lost the confidence in the Sunni officers; many of them were detained owing to the fear of defection. Some soldiers had started to leave the battlefield and join the Free Syrian Army, creating a major crisis for the regime. "Indeed, most defections were not from the top-ranking officers, but rather, stemmed from a vast quantity of low-ranking soldiers."[524]

The Free Syrian Army became the umbrella for every armed group and individual fighting the regime, whether it was of a military or civilian, secularist or Islamist nature. This situation can prove the fact that the Free Syrian Army is an idea, but not an army or organized and united guerrilla.[525] It was an idea that symbolized the violent struggle against the Syrian regime. Hassan Aboud, the former leader of the Ahrar Asham Brigade, one of the most powerful brigades fighting the regime in Syria, backs this view on the Free Syrian Army. He stated, "The FSA is more of a concept than a functioning body, it is not effective. It is more a general term."[526] There was no sort of coordination or connections between the thousands of battalions or brigades, and the leadership of the Free Syrian Army. For this reason, it was difficult for the leadership to implement a strategy or command certain tactics. Fragmentation and disorganization plagued the Free Syrian Army and made cooperation and coordination difficult on the battlefield, so its operational effectiveness was limited.[527]

Many battalions and brigades even adopted the name of the Free Syrian Army out of respect to its founder Colonel Riyad

---

[524] Munzer Eid Al-Zamalkani, "The National Free Syrian Army" Asharq Alawsat, 21 July 2012, viewed on 21 July 2012 http://www.aawsat.com/leader.asp?section=3&issueno=12289&article=687406

[525] Usahma Darrah, "Counterinsurgency Strategy of the Syrian Regime", a paper was presented at the Center of Syrian Studies in St. Andrews, Scotland 17–19 June 2013.

[526] Talk to Aljazeera, TV Program, Aljazeera English, 21 December 2013.

[527] O'Bagy, E. "The Free Syrian Army", Middle East Security Report 9, Institute for the Study of War, March 2013, viewed on 15 August 2014, http://www.understandingwar.org/sites/default/files/The-Free-Syrian-Army-24MAR.pdf.

al-Ass'ad and as a cover for their military activities against the regime. However, the defected Lieutenant Colonel Yaser Al Aboud in Daraa stated that the Free Syrian Army had a revolutionary nature and must be militarily organized. In the words of Wasel Chamali, an independent Syrian opposition member, the Free Syrian Army consisted of, "independent civilian armed groups and defected officers. They lack organization and cooperation."[528] The most important point worth noting here is that the violent struggle in Syria was formally portrayed as a conflict between two parties: the regime itself pitted against the Free Syrian Army as a united body. This is not an accurate depiction. The struggle was between the Syrian regime on one side, and hundreds of different independent and fragmented militias on the other. Every town or village had its own militias. All these militias operated under the Free Syrian Army's name. Nevertheless, they were not united or harmoniously organized. Such a situation made the internal war in Syria descend into uncontrolled violence, and encouraged some national, regional and international elements to penetrate some battalions and brigades on the ground. The fragmentation of the Free Syrian Army ensured that it lacked cohesive control and blunted the efficacy of its attacks against the regime.

The most popular and strongest battalions of the Free Syrian Army in this phase were the Battalions of Al-Farouq in Homs, renowned for fighting against the regime in the famous battle of Baba Amer in Homs during February 2012. It was a battle presenting the first big challenge to the regime in terms of military capability. The primary regime strategy against the Free Syrian Army was to strike their controlled areas and cause severe civilian casualties. This would have the effect of undermining public support for the Free Syrian Army. However, the regime's strategy later developed into attacking the civilians simply as a punishment for harboring the Free Syrian Army.

Syria, at this stage, plunged into uncontrolled violence between the regime and its supporters on one hand, and the revolutionaries

[528] Alzamalkani, op, cit.

and their supporters on the other hand. Every party sought the extermination of the other. "There was no alternative to victory" for either of them. It was a war between the anti-regime elements of society and the pro-regime elements within the society, so the struggle was based on loyalty, but not on identity. Identity was one element of the struggle, so the struggle as a whole was much broader. The revolutionaries started targeting every person that was loyal to the regime regardless of any other factor such as identity or class. Despite the heavy involvement of civilians in the war, and the deeply divided nature of societal groups, it is important to acknowledge that these societal groups were not at war. There was no declared war between Muslims and Alawis, Muslims and Druze, or Muslims and Christians.

Moreover, although Gurr and Sharp have placed emphasis upon external support for the revolutionaries, it is clear that the Syrian Internal War started with a very localized and privatized national support-base. Infiltrations and alleged support from regional countries occurred in later stages. During this phase of the revolution, the Free Syrian Army and the regime had the same adopted flag, which is the national Syrian flag. The revolutionaries and regime loyalists were still at this stage sharing the same slogans, the same ideas and the same war stories, but they were competing on legitimacy. The rift between the two factions had not yet grown, and ethno-symbolism, where every party has its own slogans, ideology and myths, had not yet ripened.

It is very important to mention here that the Free Syrian Army at this stage had gained great support and admiration among the public in the Muslim community, and where the uprising was active. Demonstrators used to greet them and hail their behaviors. They were successful in winning the public's minds and hearts. Some famous slogans in the demonstrations were: *Allha Mhayy Al-Jaish Alhur*, "Allah may greet the Free Army,"[529] and *Al-Jaish*

[529] Al-Qusaye Coordination, Allah may greet the Free Army. Posted on 26 November 2011, https://www.youtube.com/watch?v=puVrw5eOxEM

Alhur: Allah Yehmeh, "The Free Army: may Allah protect it."[530] Such a situation encouraged more military men to defect from the national army and to join the Free Syrian Army.

Both the Free Syrian Army and the regime used the Syrian National Flag in the beginning of the revolution.

THE POLITICAL OPPOSITION

Descending to violence made the need very serious for a formal political body to represent the revolution. On the other hand, the establishment of the Free Syrian Army posed a great challenge to the political opposition and its influence over the revolution.

The Syrian National Council (SNC)

After many failed attempts from the revolutionaries and the opposition to form a political representative body for the uprising

[530] ShaamNetwork SNN, Homs Bab Al-Sebaa, Posted on 30 January 2012, https://www.youtube.com/watch?v=k9HlqL-Q0j8.

abroad, on 2 October 2011, the establishment of the Syrian National Council (SNC) was announced. The revolutionaries inside the country welcomed the step very warmly. It was the most important achievement for the political opposition since the start of the uprising. The revolutionaries supported the formation of the SNC as a political body representing the revolution formally, regionally and internationally. Three revolutionary blocs were inside the SNC representing the revolution and the revolutionaries. It was a crucial achievement that can be viewed as a response to the exacerbated humanitarian and refugee crises in the country. Moreover, the establishment of the SNC was perceived by the revolutionaries as a signal that the differences and divisions among the opposition had been repaired. The SNC achieved a great deal in the first two months, especially in terms of meetings, designed to lobby support for the Syrian Revolution, being organized at the international level. However, the SNC was plagued by a plethora of problems which prevented it from reaching its sustained goals and targets. Some of these problems were structural while others were rooted in external factors:

1. The involvement of ideology in shaping the SNC was contrary to the nature of the revolution, which was intended to be non-ideological. The SNC polarized most ideologies and most opposition parties. Such a situation created unnecessary tensions among the core SNC factions,[531] often regarding power balancing within the organization. The Damascus Declaration and Muslim Brotherhood[532] dominated the SNC and influenced its decisions. The SNC

[531] The main component blocks were: 1) The 74 Block, the core of the SNC; mainly under the influence of Muslim Brotherhood. 2) The National Symbolic Figures Block. 3) Muslim Brotherhood. 4) Damascus Declaration. 5) The grassroots, which consist of separate bodies, and were representing the revolutionaries such as the Local Coordination Committees of Syria, the Syrian Revolution General Commission, and the High Council for the Revolution Leadership.

[532] The Muslim Brotherhood joined the SNC in three different separate blocs trying to be smart, so they could have a bigger representation in this body.

was a dishonest deal between the Damascus Declaration and Muslim Brotherhood in Syria.[533] On the contrary, the revolutionaries were non-partisan people, and revolted against the regime for freedom and dignity. The usage of mosques was not an expression of a certain ideology, but was in fact as an expression of strong unity and widespread protest.

2. By neglecting and alienating the political defectors from the regime, such as the defected Prime Minister Riyadh Hijab, and the defected councillor of Baniyas, Adnan al-Sheghri, and many defected diplomats and principals, the SNC failed to find a containment policy for the new defectors, hence failed to encourage further defection from the regime. Isolating the defectors created problems of efficiency within the SNC. It proved insufficient as an organization when dealing with humanitarian issues such as the refugee crisis, and the methods of governing the liberated areas. Mr. Hijab is on record as affirming, "I have no political ambition, but I am ready to offer my services and expertise to build a new Syria."[534] Such expertise was often wasted by the SNC.
3. The SNC was uncertain as to whether the Free Syrian Army should be supported, as, in contrast to the latter, it wanted the revolution to be a peaceful revolution. Colonel Riyadh al-Ass'ad complained many times regarding the lack of assistance from the SNC. He stated, "They never provided us with any support. Some of them even ignited disputes between officers in the Free Syrian Army for their own interests."[535]

The SNC may have conceived the leaders in the Free Syrian Army as a threat that wanted to dominate the revolution and undermine the political opposition's influence.

[533] Interview with the author over Skype on 22 February 2013.

[534] Interview with the author over Skype on 22 May 2013.

[535] Interview with the author over the telephone on 20 May 2013

However, the SNC responded to the revolutionaries' demands and formed a military bureau in March 2012,[536] designed specifically to liaise with the Free Syrian Army. The organization decided to support the Free Syrian Army after immense pressure from the revolutionaries, but I think it was not a strategy that they adopted independently or willingly.

4. No clear strategy or policy was implemented to deal with the emerging crises, including the refugee crisis, the treatment of injured people, support for the martyrs' families, the arrangement of medical aid or emergency food distribution. Instead of leading the revolution, the SNC was little more than a mouthpiece of the revolutionaries.
5. The SNC failed to be a proper hierarchical and democratic institution. The decision-making process was vague and lacked transparency. Burhan Ghalioun, the first SNC chairman, was not elected, but rather appointed after an agreement between the component blocs. He stated, "Internal disputes over the leadership were awful. The Damascus Declaration refused my appointment in the second term. Every leader of the component blocs wanted his turn to be the chairman of the SNC."[537]
6. The SNC adopted political stances not familiar to the public in Syria, evidenced by its decision to meet publicly with some figures known widely as supporters of Israel, such as Bernard Levy, John McCain and Josef Lieberman. Such actions were manipulated successfully by the regime and by Hezbollah alike, both of whom made allegations about an existing link between Israel and the opposition. In addition, such public meetings have damaged the image of the SNC as well as the revolution among the wider Arab audience, in particular the Palestinians. In fact, such policies

[536] "The National Council and the Free Army agreed on activate their cooperation", Dpress, 13 January 2012, viewed on 17 April 2014. http://www.dp-news.com/pages/detail.aspx?articleid=108423.

[537] Interview with the author over Skype on 11 June 2013.

have boosted Bashar Assad's legitimacy nationally and across the Arab world as an anti-Israel leader.

7. The SNC suffered from a lack of political support from the international community. Although many states welcomed the formation of SNC and hailed its very existence as an achievement, they did not back it with strong political and financial support. In fact, some political and diplomatic figures such as Robert Ford, the American ambassador to Syria, led a campaign against it, leading to the establishment of the National Coalition of Syrian Revolution and Opposition Forces in November 2012, according to Mr. Saher, a member at the SNC.[538]
8. Adopting the "Independence Flag"[539] as the national and revolutionary flag was a controversial move to copy Libyan revolutionaries. Such a move deepened divisions among the Syrian people, but made the struggle easier to define in terms of a conflict between two parties in the country: pro-regime loyalists versus anti-regime loyalties. Although the anti-regime forces possess the majority, the pro-regime forces have higher power capacities. Gene Sharp has observed such an imbalance carefully. He stated: "By placing confidence in violent means, one has chosen the very type of struggle with which the oppressors nearly always have superiority. The dictators are equipped to apply violence overwhelmingly."[540] Ethno-symbolism started now from this phase of the conflict. Both parties in the struggle were associated with different ideas, myths and symbols. The revolutionaries were aiming to return to the post-independence era, where freedom and democracy were the

[538] Interview with the author over Skype on 11 December 2012.

[539] The Independence Flag was first adopted in 1936 symbolizing the Syrian struggle against the French Mandate in Syrian. The flag was adopted then by the constitution and ratified by the parliament after independence and stayed the national flag until 1958 when the unity with Egypt took place, but adopted again after the collapse of the unity with Egypt until 1963 when Baath Party took over.

[540] Sharp, op, cit, p.4.

prevailing principles upon which society was built. On the other hand, the regime's loyalists showed more adherence to the formal national flag as a symbol of dignity, as it represented all the victories that the country had won in the past. Moreover, the adoption of the independence flag helped the regime to launch a propaganda campaign against the revolutionaries, describing them as a pro-French Mandate group claiming that the flag symbolized the mandate era. The independence flag was designed and adopted first during the French Mandate after signing the Independence Agreement in Paris in 1936, and Syria was then called the Syrian Republic, but not the Syrian Arab Republic. Ironically, the opposition wanted to have the independence flag, but to keep Syria as the Syrian Arab Republic. it was a big dilemma.

The Independence Flag that was adopted by the SNC as the Revolution Flag in December 2011.

9. After the beginning of the revolution, the opposition in general faced great problems relating to identity, ideology and irredentism. People in the opposition ceased to represent the revolution, but rather the ethnic and religious communities. Another group, the Kurds, announced their interest in Federal Syria; they wanted to see Syria without

an Arab identity. They established their National Council, and Burhan Ghaluion stated:

> Finding a conciliation with the Kurdish political parties took great time without reaching good outcomes. On the other hand, some Kurdish political parties have launched a big campaign against the SNC for refusing to accept their demand of self-determination.[541]

The SNC failed to be a non-ideologically based body like the revolution. The ideological struggle between the opposition inside and outside the SNC had a great impact on opposition's efficiency. In Ghaluion's opinion, "The SNC and the opposition in general was a victim of prolonged enmity between Hasan Abdul Azeem (NCB) and Riyadh al-Turk (Damascus Declaration)."[542]

The National Coalition of Syrian Revolutionary and Opposition Forces

It was established in November 2012 in Doha, with the presence of the prime minister of Qatar, Hamed bin Jasem, the main reason behind establishing this body was to enable more Syrian figures and more Syrian groups with different orientations to join the opposition in order to make it more inclusive, and more importantly to dilute the heavy influence of the revolutionary solid blocs in the SNC in order to make taking the decisions more flexible and more in line with the friends of Syria's interests. However, such a move made more divisions among the opposition. Therefore, the gap has widened between the opposition itself and between the opposition and the revolutionaries or the fighters on the ground. Moreover, the National Coalition is more problematic in terms of leadership, and suffers more foreign influence. Qatar,

[541] Interview with the author over Skype on 11 June 2013.

[542] Interview with the author over Skype on 11 June 2013.

for instance, imposed Sheikh Mouaz al-Khatib to be the president of this body, declining any other candidate, including Burhan Ghaliuon. Many opposition figures and blocs have left the National Coalition gradually in opposition to its policy, but some others joined the body to get their voice heard in this platform. On the ground, the coalition formed an interim government in order to ensure the continuation of public services, legal duties and basic services in liberated territories and to serve as temporary executive branch, as they stated.

Overall, it was clear that the US and its allies, and Russia, indeed do not want a strong opposition to Bashar Assad in order to boost his legitimacy by portraying the opposition as divided and unqualified, and hence unable to replace Bashar Assad. However, when the United States had the plan to invade Iraq in 2003, it worked so hard to bring together the fragmented Iraqi opposition in one strong united body. Similarly, when NATO had the plan to intervene in Libya to remove Gaddafi, a strong opposition body was built from some figures of Libyan oppositions and former state officials, and had international support.

The revolution in Syria did not want an opposition body, but a revolutionary political body to represent the revolution on the international stage and to convey its demands, but not be a theater for the old opposition disputes and clashes. This revolutionary body has the duty to appoint some technocrats in order to prepare the situation for the fall of Assad and start governing the country until proper elections could take place. But such an ideal scenario did not happen; because the opposition hijacked the revolution and the international community has aborted it.

CONCLUSION

Overall, for the revolutionaries resorting to violence was not a preferred option, but it was the only reactionary choice in the face of the regime's increasing brutality. The revolutionaries became more adamant, and came to realize that the struggle in Syria was about their existence as humans with dignity. Hussam, a former member of the Al-Farouq Brigade, stated, "If the revolution was defeated by the regime, we will be treated in humiliation as never before and forever."[543] The defection from the army was a great advantage for the revolutionaries, and a setback for the regime, but not to the extent of threatening its collapse as the inner core in the regime stayed very loyal. Nevertheless, the problems of political opposition reflected badly on the revolution.

The phase of internal war was, in fact, a transitional phase. During this phase, there were prevailing Islamic values among the revolutionaries and the officers, but these were waiting to be necessarily institutionalized or framed. The brutality of the regime made people seek refuge in religion and become more pious than ever. In the words of Sheikh Anas Ayrout, "If anybody at a moment of near death was not too close to his God and practicing his religion, so when will he be? The people in Syria lived under the imminent danger of random attacks from the regime forces."[544] Therefore, the revolutionaries in this phase became more attached to their religion, and they adopted more religious discourse, and became more ready to transform into real Islamist fighters and Jihadists, which occurred significantly in the next phase.

[543] Interview with the author over Skype on 23 June 2012.

[544] Interview with the author over Skype on 6 May 2013.

Chapter Five

FROM INTERNAL WAR TO HOLY WAR (JIHAD)

INTRODUCTION

Osama Bin Laden hailed the Arab Spring revolutions, even though the public uprisings' success in toppling long-standing dictators such as Bin Ali in Tunisia and Mubarak in Egypt undermined the concept of Jihad as the only means to depose regimes in the Arab world. In other words, the Arab Spring revolutions presented an ideological challenge to the Jihadist discourse. However, such a challenge was short-lived after the world has failed to stop Bashar Assad's brutality against the Syrian people and declined to support the Free Syrian Army, putting many people in a big dilemma and having no other alternative but to resort to Jihad in order to defend themselves and their families. "The West did not like our revolution flag, let them deal with the Jihad flag then,"[545] as a Free Syrian Army member has stated. On the other hand, Western support to the counter revolution in Egypt in July 2013, when the military deposed the elected president Muhammad Morsi, bringing back the country to its status before the 2011 revolution, and also the Western support for old regime restoration in Tunisia, have all revived the Jihadist ideology in the region as the only means for a real change. A change can put down the whole establishment and uproot the deep state, but not just the change of a president. Overall, resorting to Jihad after the Arab Spring was the result of another Western political failure in the region.

---

[545] Interview with the author in on Skype, 12 February 2013.

A Jihadist movement calling itself Jabaht Al-Nusra claimed responsibility for the huge deadly explosion that hit Midan neighborhood in Damascus on 6 January 2012 in which tens of *Shabbiba* were killed.[546] Meanwhile, in early 2012, dozens of videos of deadly attacks carried out against the regime forces by a movement calling itself Ahrar Asham Al-Islamiah were posted on the internet. It was an unannounced declaration of a new phase in the Syrian Revolution; a phase in which newborn Islamic movements, adopting the banner or the flag of the Islamic Army (*Al-Okab*), were taking the lead in the armed violent struggle against the Syrian regime. They belonged to all Islamic trends (Salafis, Sufis and Jihadists).

The black and white Islamic Army's flag or banner (Al-Okab), written on it in Arabic: No God but Allah; Muhammad is his messenger.

This chapter discusses how Jihad emerged after March 2011, and the origins of Jihadists in Syria, with concentration on some important Jihadist groups operating in the country, and also the backlash against adopting Jihad as a way of struggle against the regime. Moreover, it includes the fighting between some Jihadist groups which made the revolution trajectory more complicated,

[546] Al-Manara Albaida, The revenge for the Al-Asham's Women Posted 22 February 2012, https://www.youtube.com/watch?v=4dPbJkomu34.

and hence extended the regime's control as a result, and also prolonged the regime's days in power.

BACK TO IDEOLOGY

Whatever trends that groups belong to, using Islamic banners and slogans is somehow the most effective means of mobilizing the religious and non-religious people in Middle Eastern society. This is especially so in a society that is overwhelmingly flooded with ideology, faith and identity. In 2003, when the late Grand Mufti Ahmad Kufftaro declared Jihad against the American invasion of Iraq,[547] religious and non-religious people came forward zealously. Full buses of young Syrian people traveled to Iraq aiming to fight against the invasion, and a young Syrian who was in another bus claimed an American missile targeted one of those buses before reached the Iraqi border.[548]

Bernard Lewis once argued, "Islam could provide the most effective symbols and slogans for mobilization, whether for or against a cause or a regime."[549] The revolution at this stage started adopting ideology. It was transformed from being a non-partisan and non-ideological revolution into an ideological revolution, inspired by Jihad's doctrines and symbols. Jihad became a formal inspiration for political violence in Syria for the revolutionary side.

Resorting to violence was a natural response to the regime's cruelty as people had to defend themselves and their families, but resorting to ideology and beliefs was very important for mobilization and recruitment, and offers a great motive and concrete platform for more sacrifices. "People do not fight; do not risk their lives and those of their families for dry, distant, theoretical conception. We must search for something, perhaps a metaphoric element, which

---

547 Mufti Syria Calls for Martyrdom operations against the Invaders, Aljazeera, net, 27 March 2003. http://aljazeera.net/home/print/f6451603–4dff-4ca1–9c10–122741d17432/8cabc45f-ecce-4e64-b2fd-649c1b05cf1e, viewed on 11June 2014.

548 Interview with the author over Skype on 27 October 2011.

549 Bernard Lewis, *The Crisis of Islam,* Phoenix, London, 2004, p.19.

moves people's hearts as much as their hands,"[550] as Selbin explains. Islam does offer this platform and pushes people to sacrifice themselves for great rewards in the hereafter. Declaring Jihad was an indication that people had reached a point where they had nothing to lose. Their disappointment at international society's lack of support was unrecoverable. In fact, the claim of a global conspiracy against Muslims was an attractive claim among the Syrian revolutionaries, so they resorted to Allah's support only,[551] and adopted the ideology that Allah is pleased with most,[552] as Nidal, a member of a Jihadist group in Syria, has claimed. Gilles Kepel may have a better and more precise explanation for the Syrian revolutionaries becoming Islamists; he argued, "The Islamist way was attractive because God and the Holy Koran guaranteed its proper implementation on earth, unsullied by the provisions and manipulations of despotic generals, Kings, or Sultans."[553]

Ethno-symbolism at this stage divided the revolution, making its trajectory more complicated and more problematic. The Islamist way was the mainstream trend at this stage, where the Islamic ideas, symbols and aims constituted the prime inspiration for the revolutionaries. Meanwhile, the formal opposition along with the Muslim Brotherhood and the secularist revolutionaries kept the independence flag as their symbol. The ideas about freedom and democracy remained their ultimate aspirations and their ultimate aims.

The Concept of Jihad (Holy War)

The concept of Jihad is not restricted to any trend in any of the contemporary Islamic schools. All Sufis, Salafis and Jihadists

---

[550] Selbin, Eric. Theses on the Future of Revolution in the Future of Revolution, John Foran(ed), Zed Books, London, 2003, p.83.

[551] One of the most famous slogans in the revolution was "O Allah, we do not have someone else, O Allah."

[552] Interview with the author over Skype on 23 April 2014.

[553] Gilles Kepel, *Jihad: The Trial Political Islam*, IB Tauris & co Ltd, 2002, p.374.

believe in Jihad as a divine rule, but they differ on the causes of Jihad and on the applied circumstances. Traditional Salafis and traditional Sufis support Jihad only when it is launched against an outside enemy of the nation or aggressor, but they do not agree on waging Jihad against a ruler who did not declare an obvious *Kufur* (infidelity), making him a non-Muslim. On the contrary, Jihadists (Salafis or Suffis) believe in launching Jihad against a ruler if his policies, actions or behaviors—such as adopting principles contrary to Islamic law, or allying with an enemy of the nation (the Muslim nation)—demonstrate *Kufur*. Omar Abu Omar (Abu Qatada), a Jihadist theorist and a preacher, argued "The reasons for the existence of the Jihadist groups in our time in the world are: 1) Work to release the Muslim prisoners, 2) Support the oppressed Muslims, 3) Deter the oppressor."[554] Moreover, "to reform the inclusive contract for all Muslims in the world, which is Al-Khilafa,"[555] or we can call it the Islamic State. Sayyid Outb conceived Jihad as world revolution against the sovereignty of man:

> This religion is really a universal declaration of the freedom of man from servitude to other men and from servitude to his own desires, which is also a form of human servitude; it is declaration that sovereignty belong to God alone and that he is the lord of all worlds. It means revolution against all kinds and forms of systems which are based on the concept of the sovereignty of man.[556]

The concept of Jihad is twinned with the concept of Khilafa among the revolutionaries in Syria. It was not a sole effort of the Jihadist groups. In fact, Hizb Al-Tahrir (the Islamic Liberation Party) played a significant role in selling the concept of Khilafa

---

[554] Omar Abu Omar (Abu Qatada), *Jihad and Interpretation,* Dar al-Bayarek, Beirut, 1999, p. 113.

[555] Ibid, p.93.

[556] Sayyid Qutb, *Milestones*, Maktabah Booksellers and Publishers, Birmingham, 2006, p.67.

among the people in Syria. Although Hizb Al-Tahrir is not a Jihadist movement, its principles and concepts of establishing Al-Khilafa played a remarkable role in attracting the public to the Islamist way. Mixing with the public in an appropriate environment, away from regime surveillance, has contributed heavily to enable Hizb Al-Tahrir turning thousands of people away from the national framework of the revolution and the restricted national and public goal of changing the regime. It instead turned their consciousness to the broad and ultimate aim of establishing Al-Khilafa, as stated by Hazem,[557] a member of Hizb Al-Tahrir in Syria.

The Roots of Jihadists in Syria after the Uprising

There are two roots for the Jihadists in Syria after the uprising, the first being national roots, consisting of former Syrian Jihadists prisoners who were convicted of terrorism, but who were released from prisons in May and August 2011 after receiving presidential amnesty.[558] Many of them were previous fighters in Iraq or used to belong to some Jihadist groups. Their release served the regimes in two ways, first, as those individuals regrouped again to fight the regime, validating discourse about the existence of Jihadist groups in Syria threatening the country and the region as a whole. Second, those individuals belonged to different ideologies (traditional Salafis versus Jihadist Salafis), and had different views causing them to be divided in the conflict against Bashar Assad. However, the great achievements of the Jihadist groups such as Jabhat al-Nusra in attacking important sites for the regime led many people to admire their sacrifices and many youths to join this group. In a few months of its formation, the majority of its members were Syrian recruits.[559]

---

[557] Interview with the author over Skype on 15 June 2012.

[558] Assad issued a general amnesty includes political prisoners and the Muslim Brotherhood, BBC, 31 May 2011, viewed on 10 June 2014. http://www.bbc.co.uk/arabic/worldnews/2011/05/110531_syria_act49.shtml.

[559] Today's Meeting, television Program, Aljazeera, 19 December 2013.

The second root of the Jihadists in Syria was foreign roots, consisting of global Jihadists who arrived in the country for the long-awaited holy war in the Land of *Bilad Asham*. "Being a Jihadists on the Land of *Bilad Asham* was and still is the dream for the noble and most honorable people since the prophet's time,"[560] as announced by Abu Muhammad al-Jawlani, the head of Jabhat Al-Nusra, which was a branch of ISIS at this stage. The global Jihadists doctrine derived from the early days of Islam, where Muslims returned to Mecca from Medina "to spread the word of God through the blades of their swords, and to [spread] their system of governance [that established in Medina] in accordance with the teaching of Allah as revealed to Muhammad in the Quran."[561]

During this phase, the struggle had evidently gone beyond its national framework. Allies and supporters from outside the country have been heavily involved in the struggle in Syria on both sides: that of the regime and that of the revolutionaries. Regional states such as Saudi Arabia and Qatar started supporting some Islamic brigades and some battalions of the Free Syrian Army. Meanwhile, thousands of Sunni Muslims flooded many parts of Syria, particularly the north and west of the country in response to the call for Jihad and to help the Syrian people. Turkey turned a blind eye on the people coming for all over the world through its airspace and its land to join the Jihad in Syria. In contrast, Iran mobilized the Shias in the region (Iraq, Iran, Lebanon, Yemen, Bahrain and Afghanistan). In the name of protecting the Shia shrines in Syria, thousands of Shia traveled to Syria and fought beside the regime forces.[562] Therefore, Syria has become the theater for double Jihad from opposite parties; Muslim (Sunnis) versus Shias. Ironically, the West stood beside the Shia Jihad against the Sunnis.

---

560 JihadTV22, "We sacrifice ourselves for you O people of Asham", Posted on 27 December 2012. http://www.youtube.com/watch?v=LmBRUakQJRA.

561 Jarret Brachman, *Global Jihadism*, Routledge, London, 2009, p.41.

562 "The foreign fighters siding the regime, who are they'?, Asharq Al-Awsat, 19 February,2014, http://classic.aawsat.com/details.asp?section=45&article=761991&issueno=12867#.U7LlUo1dUVg, Viewed on 13 June 2014.

A battle in May in 2013, in the town of Al-Qusayer,[563] outside Homs, revealed Hezbollah's flagrant involvement in the Syrian conflict. Its leader Hasan Nasrallah admitted his party's involvement in the Syrian struggle on the side of the regime. He justified such behavior as an effort to support the Syrian regime against the Western–Jihadists conspiracy in Syria, and to protect the Shia shrines there.[564]

Although there are concrete reasons behind the struggle in Syria becoming a holy war, five important factors caused the internal conflict to spill out of the country and cross national borders:

1. Identity polarization and mobilization in the region, especially between Syria, Lebanon, Iraq and Turkey: For instance, clashes erupted between Alawis and Sunnis in the city of Tripoli in Lebanon after the uprising in Syria, and escalated to levels not seen in years.[565] Hezbollah allied with the regime, while some Lebanese Salafis such as Sheikh Ahmad al-Aseer allied with the Syrian Revolution.[566] These clashes put the country and the region on the verge of a sectarian war. It was another aspect of the weakness of the nation-state system in the region and a blow to state formation in the Middle East. The real boundaries in the region proved to be not the political boundaries between the different countries, but the social boundaries between the ethnic and religious groups in the region.

[563] Al-Qusayr: is a town located in Homs province; it is situated on the borders with Lebanon, and does contain Sunnis and Shias villages, but Sunnis are the majority.

[564] Shadi Zeid, Nassrullah admits for the first time his involvement in Syria. Posted on 26 May 2013, https://www.youtube.com/watch?v=ZF3KgWoZG2E.

[565] "The death toll rises in the Tripoli fighting in North Lebanon, Aljazeera.net, 15 March 2014", http://www.aljazeera.net/news/arabic/2014/3/15, viewed 15 June 2014.

[566] The Lion of Lebanon, Sheikh al-Aseer speaks to a sit-in supporting the Syrian Revolution in Lebanon 15 April 2012. Posted 13 June 2014, https://www.youtube.com/watch?v=twh8Z_AbHpg.

2. The interests of some groups and political parties in the region. The regime in Syria has political opponents outside Syria, such as the Coalition of 14 March in Lebanon.[567] They automatically support the idea of revolution against the regime. Meanwhile, the regime has powerful non-Syrian allies both within and outside the country, such as the coalition of 4 March in Lebanon including Hezbollah, the Republican Revolutionary Guard in Iran, the Shia militias in Iraq, and the Palestinian Public Front, the General Leadership of which, headed by Ahmad Jibreel, is based in Syria. Jibreel's militias fought alongside the regime's forces against the protesters.[568]
3. The lack of participation of non-Sunnis in the revolution and in the Free Syrian Army has led to the conflict being portrayed as a war against Sunnis only. The images and video footage of the regime's brutality and of the regime forces humiliating the religion's values, attacking mosques and minarets, have supported this depiction. This portrayal has provoked many Muslims worldwide to support and participate in the Jihad in Syria, to fight the regime and to defend their brothers and sisters in Islam, they claim. When the uprising escalated into an armed struggle, the level of participation by members of minorities was even lower, and when it turned into a holy war, the minorities turned against it. Many activists belonging to the minorities did not hide their concerns and opposition over the revolution turning to a purely Islamic struggle.
4. The ineffectiveness of international institutions and the "Great Powers" in putting an end to the bloodshed in Syria

[567] The main politics in Lebanon after the assassination of Rafiq al-Hariri in 2005 is divided mainly into two coalitions: 1- Group of 14th of March coalition, which includes opponents to Syria such as the Sunni leader Sa'd al-Hariri, and some Maronite leaders such as Samir Gaga. 2- Group of 4th of March, which includes mainly Hezbollah and its allies such as Michel Aoun.

[568] "The Militias of Ahmad Jibril fights Israel in Al-Yarmouk Camp in Damascus!!!" Orient, 13 November 2102. http://www.orient-news.net/?page=news_show&id=508, viewed on 13 June 2014.

and preventing the regime from attacking its people: In fact, people mistrusted the international community's efforts concerning the crisis in Syria. The theory that none of the world's states want to help the victims in Syria has occupied the minds of many Muslims since the conflict began.

5- The struggle in this phase is ideologically driven, so it is not just about changing the regime, but in fact about faith and ideology: immigration, Jihad and establishing Al-Khilafa or the Islamic State. Such developments have made Syria the main polarizing center for Jihadists across the world and a preferred destination for their families.

Syria is the center of *Bilad Asham* Land, the Levant or Greater Syria, which in the Islamic religion is the greatest land for Jihad. Many Jihadists have left their bases in other parts of the world such as Iraq, Chechnya and Pakistan to move to Syria. There are many sayings in the Hadith from the Prophet Muhammad (Peace Be Upon Him) about the holiness of *Bilad Asham*. Some sayings include recommendations and orders to immigrate to *Bilad Asham*. "From Abdulla Ibn Hawala, the Messenger said: 'You will be split up into groups of armies. An army will be in Asham, an army in Iraq, and an army in Yemen. Abdullah said: I stood up and said: choose for me oh Messenger of Allah. The Prophet (PBUH) said: 'Upon you is Asham, and whoever cannot, let him go to Yemen, and let him drink from its water, for Allah has assured (secured) for me Asham and its people.'"[569]

The concept of the Hijra (immigration) prior to Jihad is derived from Quranic text. "Indeed, those who have believed and those who have immigrated and fought in the cause of Allah—those expect the mercy of Allah. And Allah is Forgiving and Merciful."[570] The way to Jihad is Hijra (immigration). Therefore, Jihadists started to immigrate to Syria firstly in support of the

[569] Immam al-Albani (english) http://immamalbani.blogspot.co.uk/2011/05/virtues-of-al-sham.html.

[570] Quran, Surat Al-Baqara, verse 218.http://quran.com/2 verse 218/.

Jihad to help their brothers in Syria defending themselves against the Assad regime, and secondly to implement Sharia law both during and after the conflict. They brought their families with them, planning to reside in Syria (*Bilad Asham*) forever.

Such factors pose an important question about Islamic identity. Global Jihadists belong to dozens of different national identities. However, the Islamic identity has overridden other identities and imposed on them certain commitments that conflict with commitments toward their societies or their own states. Moreover, the *Al-Walaa-Wa-Al-Braa* (loyalty and disavowal) doctrine restricts Muslim identity to that dictated by religion, so adopting this concept renders Islam the defining force behind the identity of a Muslim. Many Jihadists have destroyed their national passports[571] and declare loyalty to the Islamic State in Iraq and Syria (ISIS).[572] Sayyed Qutb outlined the Muslim identity as he sees it:

> The homeland for the Muslim, in which he lives and he defends, is not a piece of land; the nationality of the Muslim, by which he identified, is not the nationality determined by the government; the family of the Muslim, in which he finds solace and which he defends, is not blood relationships; the flag of the Muslim; which he honors and under which is martyred, is not a flag of a country. Nationality means belief and a way of life.[573]

Jihadist Groups in Syria

There are many different Islamic groups fighting in Syria. They are different in their ideologies or schools of thoughts and orientations, different in origins, different in their aims and goals, different in

---

[571] The Future Syria, Egyptian Jordanian, Saudis, Canadian, and Tunisian destroy their passports in Syria. Posted 22 April 2014, https://www.youtube.com/watch?v=mqY9La5a-kE.

[572] The Islamic State in Iraq and Syria (ISIS) is the most powerful Jihadist group operating in Syria and Iraq. (See Jihadist groups in Syria).

[573] Qutb, op, cit, p.102.

resources of support and different in the field of activities and operations. Moderate Sufis, traditional Salafis and Jihadists, along with groups affiliated to the Muslim Brotherhood[574] in Syria, have gained ground and followers in the country. The adopted ideology can determine some other elements such as support and aid. Mainly, while moderate Sufis and traditional Salafis do enjoy private and governmental support from some countries in the region, Jihadists are self-funded, and relying on private and secret resources.

Ahrar Asham (Freemen of Syria)

This may be the third strongest group in Syria in relation to its operational activities. "Its operational and civil activities take place all over the country apart from in Tartus due to the regime's tight control in that city,"[575] as its former leader Hassan Abboud claimed. It belongs to the Salafi Jihadist trend. However, it can be considered as a national Jihadist group. In other words, its aim was initially to establish an Islamic State in Syria after the collapse of the regime; there is no global or regional agenda. The Revolutionary Pact, which was declared and signed by Ahrar Asham's leader, Hassan Abboud, and some other groups within and outside of the Islamic Front[576] in May 2014, emphasized its national and Syrian framework in terms of aims, operations and recruitments.[577] Its discourse in the pact seemed less-Jihadist than it used to be in the past. There was no hint of establishing an Islamic state in Syria in the pact. Instead, their aim was to establish the state of law and state of justice in Syria.[578] The changing

[574] Most groups affiliated with Muslim Brotherhood do no adopt the black and white flag. They still adopt the independence flag of the opposition.

[575] Today's Meeting, television Program, Aljazeera, 8 June 2013.

[576] The Islamic Front is a coalition of the main Islamic formations in Syria such as Ahrar Asham, Jaish Al-Islam, and others. It was established in November 2013.

[577] The Islamic Front, signing the revolutionary pact. Posted on 17 May 2014, https://www.youtube.com/watch?v=Mu4EaJkXh9U.

[578] Ibid.

discourse can be attributed to their foreign sponsors' demands.[579] This group has relied frequently on foreign aid from Saudi Arabia and Qatar. Diab, a member of a Jihadist group claimed: "Ahrar Asham and Jaish Al-Islam received missiles from Saudi Arabia, but not enough to liberate one neighborhood in Aleppo or a small area in Idlib."[580] In September 2014, more than 20 leaders of Ahrar Asham, including its main leader Hassan Abboud, were killed in a big and mysterious explosion in Idlib. However, Ahrar Asham's strategy kept its pragmatic transition from being a Jihadist movement to an Islamic movement. This transition was due to the mounting influence of the Muslim Brotherhood on its leadership. Their pragmatism reached a very strange point, so they offered full cooperation with the Americans to fight ISIS. I think such changing discourse was to assure the Americans about their identity and about their mission, which is a national mission inside Syria, and is only aiming to topple Bashar Assad and his regime.

Jaish Al-Islam (The Army of Islam)

It is a traditional Salafi group, operating mainly in the Ghouta, the eastern suburb of Damascus, and has had activities in many areas around Syria including the coast,[581] as Ahmad, one of its leaders, has claimed. In fact, its headquarter is in Duma, an eastern suburb of Damascus, long known as a strong Salafi base in Syria. Jaish Al-Islam is a solely Syrian group, and although its leader Zahran Alloush denies any foreign governmental support, and admitting receiving private support from outside and inside Syria,[582] many

---

[579] Hassan Hassan, "Islamic Front's new covenant is a step in the right direction", The National, 20 May 2014. http://www.thenational.ae/thenationalconversation/comment/islamic-fronts-new-covenant-is-a-step-in-the-right-direction, viewed on 16 June 2014.

[580] Interview with the author over Skype on 1 October 2013.

[581] Interview with the author over Skype on 15 February 2014.

[582] Aksalser.com, Zaharan Alloush in a long interview, Posted on 21 November 2013, https://www.youtube.com/watch?v=uiGWqzdh9mE.

observers and reports speak about Turkish, Qatari and Saudi support to this group.[583] In fact, many observers see that Jaish Al-Islam was a Saudi proxy.[584] The leadership structure inside Jaish Al-Islam is very strong, relying on three angles; Asabiya, regionalism, and Salafism. Its core consists of Salafi cousins from the town of Duma, making it very strong in the face of any kind of penetration or internal struggle.

Jaish Al-Islam has become a very strong army in Ghouta, east Damascus, and was able to acquire heavy weapons including tanks and some missiles, which were displayed in a military many times. All of these weapons were seized from the regime barracks directly or from other groups who acquired them from the regime. Jaish Al-Islam has fought many battles against the regime such as Alkimia and Allah Ghaleb, where few thousands of his fighters got killed. Most of them were young men, 18–20 years old. He targeted the regime's important sites in Damascus causing shock and awe, and imposing a curfew in the city. Zahrah has always pledged to liberate Damascus from Assad, and he was able to do so at some point, but apparently his Saudi sponsor did not allow such a move as the Saudis never intended to remove Assad. Their goals from creating and sponsoring Jaish Al-Islam were completely different and we will talk about it in the next chapter.

Jaish Al-Islam had another battle to fight with ISIS, who were successful in approaching east Damascus from the west and establishing a big base in the village of Mesraba. Alloush had pledged many times to crush the Islamic State, and to prevent them reaching Damascus. Furthermore, he prioritized fighting ISIS to fighting the Assad regime and he recruited young people in this campaign using a *fatwa* relying on some interpretations of

---

583 Lisa Lundquist, "Analysis: Formation of Islamic Front in Syria benefits Jihadist groups", The Long War Journal, 23 November 2013, viewed on 15 May 2014. http://www.longwarjournal.org/archives/2013/11/yesterday_a_new_isla.php#

584 "Saudi Arabia Funds Jaish Al-Islam Syria", Money Jihad, 20 November 2013. http://moneyJihad.wordpress.com/2013/11/20/saudi-arabia-funds-army-of-islam-in-syria, viewed on 15 June 2014.

Islamic texts.[585] In summer 2014, he launched a vicious campaign against the Islamic State in many areas in east Damascus. Eventually, he successfully defeated ISIS in Ghouta. On 25 December 2015, Zahran Alloush was killed by a Russian air strike, and his deputy Albouydani took over. The killing of Zahran came just after the Riyadh Conference in December 2015 to pave the way for political talks with the Syrian regime. His assassination was an indication of a new phase where arms must be put down and talks with Assad must start in order reach a political conciliation between the Assad regime and the opposition. Zahran was one of the most prominent heads in the armed opposition, so I think killing him was an important step in order to move toward negotiations with the regime, and it was an important intimidating message for other leaders in the armed opposition.

Needless to say, Jaish Al-Islam did not treat people under his control well and in dignity. In fact, it was a regime copy in the revolution area. People lost the freedom they enjoyed during the peaceful demonstration. Impressment was the fate to whomever criticized them and their policies. Al Toubeh prison was the most notorious place where people were tortured and killed.[586] Another kind of punishment for the prisoners was digging trenches in Ghouta.

In April 2018, Bashar Assad recaptured Ghouta after the Russians led negotiations with Jaish Al-Islam agreeing that they relocate to North Syria.

[585] He manipulated some Islamic texts that fighting Khawarej is more important than fighting the infidels, and the martyr has double reward when fighting Khawarej.

[586] Many people hold Jaish Al-Islam the responsibility for the disappearance of Razan Zaitouneh and her colleagues in Duma. They were recruited by some international bodies to recorded human rights breaches by Assad regime of by the opposition.

Ajnad Asham (The Soldiers of Syria)

This coalition consists of some groups adopting moderate Islam, and representing the prevailing Islamic orientation in Syria before the revolution, including the Muslim Brotherhood. In fact, the prevailing orientation for this group is the Muslim Brotherhood[587] as claimed by Khalid, one of its members. Ajnad Asham can be considered as the main rival for Jaish Al-Islam as they mainly centralized in the same area, eastern Damascus, but is supported by Damascus Sufi scholars. Moreover, Ajnad Asham's brand of Islamism appears to be more influenced by local Damascene Sufi scholars than by the Gulf-based hardliners favored by many commanders in the Islamic Front.[588] However, the main external supporter for this coalition is understood to be Qatar, as Khalid has claimed. However, Ajnad Asham became weaker due to the lack of support and consequently merged with Al-Rahman Legion under the leadership of Abd al-Nasser Shmer. Consequently, the Eastern Ghouta in East Damascus became under the control of Jaish Al-Islam and Al-Rahman Legion. They are two inharmonious and at odds groups, so their differences have developed into bloody clashes after the death of Zaharn, where hundreds of people were killed.

Lywaa Al-Tawhid (The Al-Tawhid Brigade)

After liberating many villages and towns in north Aleppo, local armed groups met and decided to form a united big group in order to enter and liberate the great city of Aleppo. It was headed by Abdul Qader al-Saleh, and militarily by Abdul Aziz Salameh. Al-Saleh was a small businessman from the town of Mare, and he belongs to the Suffi Islamic school. This group has become the strongest group in the north, and was able to fight and win many

---

[587] Interview with the author over Skype on 8 June 2014.

[588] Aron Lund, "Ajnad al-sham Islamic Union", Carnegie Endowment for International Peace, 04 March 2014, http://carnegieendowment.org/syriaincrisis/?fa=54750, viewed on 15 June 2014.

battles against the regime, liberating a great part of west Aleppo. Defected Colonel Youssef al-Jader (Abu Forat)[589] has joined this group and led the liberation of the Infantry School in Aleppo. The well-known leader Abu al-Tayyeb one of the most popular figures in the revolution. He was over 80 years old when he established the Grandsons of the Prophet Battalion from his sons, grandsons and nephews in order to fight the regime forces, and then joined this brigade until his death in the battlefield in Aleppo on 25 March 2013.

Leader Al-Saleh has always claimed that the regime has fallen already and the war is actually with Hezbollah and Iran. He stressed that Lywaa Al-Tawhid had never received any kind of military support from outside, and all the arms they possessed were acquired from battles with the regime.[590] Al-Saleh was assassinated in November 2013. He was buried in a grave that he built for himself in advance.

Faylaq Asham (The Legion of Syria)

It constitutes the armed wing for the Muslim Brotherhood on the ground. It was the first time that a bloc in the political opposition had a military wing on ground that followed its orders. It was established on 10 March 2014 from the Muslim Brotherhood affiliate groups mainly in Homs, Hama and Idlib. The Muslim Brotherhood since the transition to armed struggle against Assad's regime had an influence in many armed groups on the ground, so all these elements in those groups have been united in one sole Muslim Brotherhood armed group called Faylaq Asham.

[589] Colonel Youssef Al-Jader (Abu Forat) is one of most remarkable figures in the Syrian revolution. He defected from Assad's army in July 2012 after refusing orders to bomb some areas in Latakia where he was serving. He joined Liwaa Al-Tawhid group and participated in many battles to liberate Aleppo. He called upon the Alawis to not follow Bashar Assad, calling for the unity of all Syrian people. He was killed by a landmine immediately after leading the liberation of infantry school in Aleppo in December 2012.

[590] Today's Meeting, television program, Aljazeera, 14 August 2012.

Faylaq Asham is enjoying great support from Qatar and Turkey, and fought many battles against Assad's regime and ISIS in many areas. It also participated in some Turkish operations in North Syria, and used to accompany the Turkish convoys and patrols in Idlib, and the Russian–Turkish joint patrols on the Aleppo–Latakia international road (M4). On the other hand, Faylaq Asham has participated heavily in Astana meetings and constitutes the head of the opposition delegate team.

Lywaa Tahrir Al-Sham (The Liberation of Syria Brigade)

This group was established by the defected Captain Firas Bitar in Zamalka in Ghouta, East Damascus. He tried to establish a strong military base in order to push toward the center of Damascus, but was restricted by the overwhelming presence and power of Jaish Al-Islam and Faylaq Al-Rhamn, and the by the different agenda with them. So he had to move out toward Al-Qalamoun, where heavy fighting against the Assad regime was taking place in Yabrud and Rankos, and the surrounding areas. He once targeted Bashar Assad's entourage on the way to Eid Prayer with mortars from Zamalka in August 2013. Captain Firas never accepted any kind of foreign support, but relied on his gains from battles against the Assad regime. He refused to fight ISIS as he always believed that the battle was against the Assad regime only. Such stance made Turkey and Qatar ignore him and distance him from any military, political or social leadership. He ended up as a fuel vendor on the roads in Idlib.

Jabhat Al-Nusra (The Support Front)

This group was established in late 2011 by some Syrians and foreign (Arab) fighters serving in Iraq under the Islamic State of Iraq.[591] Its leader is Abu Muhammad al-Jawlani; he was a frontrunner in the Islamic State in Iraq. In fact, Al-Nusra was

[591] Today's Meeting, television program, Aljazeera, 19 December 2013.

initially a branch of the Islamic State in Iraq in Syria, but a secret branch, and enjoyed its financial support, but after the announcement of Abu Baker al-Baghdadi in April 2013, and the rebellion of al-Jawlani, Jabhat Al-Nusra relied heavily on private resources, mainly individuals in the Gulf countries. Moreover, Jabhat Al-Nusra has seized important oilfield sites in northeast Syria. In November 2013, it seized Al-Omar oilfield, one of the biggest oilfields in Syria.[592] Some of their recourses come from hard- fought efforts on the battlefields.

Jabhat Al-Nusra operated heavily in most parts of Syria, and has carried out many deadly attacks against the regime, and gained public support from the people. Moreover, Jabhat Al-Nusra has claimed responsibility for many attacks in Lebanon, including the suicide attack against some Hezbollah bases in Hermel in northwest Lebanon as revenge to its involvement against the Syrian people.[593]

The Islamic State (ISIS)

This was the strongest armed group on the ground, so it has extended on the ground fast and gained huge land in between Syria and Iraq reaching a size three times bigger than the size of England with two main centers: Ar Raqqah in Syria and Mosul in Iraq. It was headed by Abu Baker al-Baghdadi, and was initially originated in Iraq under the name of the Islamic Sate in Iraq in 2007, but after extending its operations to Syria, its name was changed in April 2013 to the Islamic State in Iraq and Syria (ISIS). Also, many Islamic armed groups in Africa, Afghanistan, Yemen, and Egypt declared their allegiance (*Bai'a*) to al-Baghdadi and to the Islamic State. It was the only group to pose a real threat to the regime by attacking its social base in the Alawi villages in 2014. Ironically, some Free Syrian Army groups that are supported by Turkey, Saudi Arabia and Qatar surrounded them from behind, forcing them to retreat from that area.

---

[592] SAQR Halab Al-Shahba, Jabhat Al-Nusra seized the biggest oilfield Posted on 23 November 2013, https://www.youtube.com/watch?v=ZrukwyFrhSM.

[593] Jabhat Al-Nusra claims responsibility for the Hermel bombing, Al-Sharq Potal, 16 January 2014. http://www.al-sharq.com/news/details/199253#.U6P77Y1dUVh, viewed on 19 June 2014.

ISIS went through many phases to reach its current form. It started on 15 December 2005, when six Islamic factions established the Council of Shura Al-Mujahedeen[594] in order to coordinate their efforts fighting the foreign troops in Iraq after the invasion in 2003. The council was chaired by Abdullah Bin Rasheed al-Baghdadi, then by Al Zarqawi, who gave Bai'a to Osama bin Laden. However, shortly after the death of Al Zarqawi, the council decided to disband itself and establish the Islamic State in Iraq as an independent entity free from Al-Qaeda in early 2007. They did not give Bai'a to Osam Bin Laden, so they elected Abu Omar al-Baghdadi as its leader. Therefore, the Islamic State in Iraq and Al-Qaeda were two different organizations at this stage. But what was the notion behind establishing the Islamic State in Iraq? Anwar al-Awlaki answers by saying:

> Whether the state survives and expands to the next Muslim Khilafa or it is destroyed by the immense conspiracy against the rise of any Islamic state. I believe this to be a monumental event. It represents a move of the idea from the theoretical realm to the real world. The idea of establishing Islamic rule and the establishment Khilafa on earth now. It is not any more talk, it is action, and it the reflection of the fact that this time the Mujahideen are not going to do the work and fight the fight only to let someone else bear the fruit of their efforts, but their intention is not just to drive the invaders out of their land just to have a *Monafic* (hypocrite) filling his place, but the process is a project of an Islamic state followed by the return to the system of Khilafa.[595]

After the death of Abu Omar by the Iraqi government in 2010, the members in the Islamic State elected Abu Baker al-Baghdadi, so shortly after the Syrian uprising he dispatched one of his recruits

---

594 The Islamic fractions are: Al-Qaeda in Iraq, Jaish *Al-Ta'ifa Al-Mansurah*, Katbiyan Ansar al-Tawhid wal Sunnah, Saray al-Jihad Group, Al-Ghuraba Brigades and Al-Ahwal Brigades.

595 A video clip was watched on twitter on 30 March 2023. Unknown link.

(al-Jawlani) to Syria in August 2011 in order to form Jabhat Al-Nusrah[596] and fight the Syrian regime. In April 2013, al-Baghdadi announced disbanding Jabhat Al-Nusra, and the formation of the Islamic State in Iraq and Syria.[597] However, his decision was rejected by al-Jawlani. He instead gave Bai'a to Sheikh Ayman al-Zawahiri,[598] the Al-Qaeda leader. al-Zawahiri has interceded to solve the problem, ordering that the situation return to what it was before both declarations,[599] but al-Baghdadi rejected the orders of al-Zawahiri in a challenging statement in which he insisted on pursuing his plan of establishing the Islamic State of Iraq and Asham and claiming that Alzawhiri's decision was somehow limited by the Sykes–Picot borders between Syria and Iraq. Such borders do not exist in the mind and realm of a global Jihadist.

In June 2014 Abu Baker al-Baghdadi declared Al-Khilafa in Mosul in Iraq, a declaration that polarized more Jihadists and some Muslims across the world to travel to Syria and Iraq and to be part of the new emerging state. The immigrants were people from different backgrounds: doctors, engineers, students, businessmen, professionals, and non-professionals.

Overall, ISIS is an independent group having no affiliation with Al-Qaeda, but shares the same ideology of Salafi Jihadism. Its members are of various nationalities from around the world, and its goal is to establish an Islamic State in the region. It has applied Sharia law in the areas that it controlled in Syria and Iraq.[600]

---

[596] Today's Meeting, television program, Aljazeera, 19 December 2013.

[597] Avicenna TV, Al-Qaeda announce the Islamic State in Iraq and Syria, Posted on 9 April 2013, https://www.youtube.com/watch?v=NvMp0rJDngs.

[598] Aleppo and Idlib, Al-Jawlani's Statement denying his knowledge about the state of Iraq and Syria decision. Posted on 10 April 2013, https://www.youtube.com/watch?v=pPFZ1_1AK7E

[599] The correction of Islamic State's trajectory, Al-Zawahiri cancels the Islamic State in Iraq and Syria. Posted on 27 December 2013, https://www.youtube.com/watch?v=Cax1C6ETCp0.

[600] Abu Alhasan Mohamed Bashan, the Islamic State in Iraq and Syria: Applying the Sharia Law Posted on 07 April 2014, https://www.youtube.com/watch?v=4KZEde-eDzQ.

It dominated and governed northeast Syria and northwest Iraq with a vast size of land rich in resources. Hence, I disagree with Gunter Meyer's claim that the Gulf States were funding or supporting ISIS to fight against the regime of Bashar Assad in Syria.[601] Although ISIS may have been secretly funded by a few wealthy individuals in the Gulf States who believe in its message and support its goals, the Gulf States have no interests to fund or support a group adopting Salafi Jihadism, and hold a flagrant enmity toward the regimes in the region and are working for their collapse. Moreover, ISIS has the ability to fund itself. It has made an effort to establish networks in society that generate a continuing flow of money.[602] In addition, ISIS secured massive cashflows from the oilfields of eastern Syria, which it had commandeered in late 2012.[603] When ISIS took over some parts of Iraq in June 2014, and seized Mosul Bank, many reported ISIS becoming the richest terrorist group in the world.[604]

The State Versus Al-Nusra. Al-Jawlani's rejection of al-Baghdadi's decision maybe was for a fresh new start in the Jihad trajectory. He maybe did not want the considerable mistakes of the Islamic State of Iraq to be a burden on Jabhat Al-Nusra, and on the Jihad in Syria in general. It is important to bear in mind that the Islamic State of Iraq had very low public support in Syria, and that many people regarded it with distrust. Moreover, al-Jawlani's strategy shows that he understands and appreciates the special way of life of the Syrian people, their entrenched moderate Islam and their unfamiliarity with radical Islam. He understood that the Jihad strategy adopted in Iraq cannot be implemented and will not be successful in Syria. However, all these assumptions faded away

---

601 Andrea Bicker, "Who Finance ISIS?", DW, 19 June 2014, http://www.dw.de/who-finances-isis/a-17720149, viewed on 19 June 2014.

602 Ibid.

603 How an arrest in Iraq revealed Isis's $2bn Jihadists network, The Guardian, 15 June 2014. http://www.theguardian.com/world/2014/jun/15/iraq-isis-arrest-Jihadists-wealth-power, viewed on 19 June 2014.

604 CIBOZ, ISIS Becomes the Richest Terror Group in the World Posted on 14 June 2014, https://www.youtube.com/watch?v=M2MSeiuW8no.

and proved to be wrong with the later consequent major changes of al-Jawlani's alliances and strategies

On the ground, both declarations have had many implications. The public support for Jabhat Al-Nusra has fallen considerably after the revelation of its affiliation to Al-Qaeda. People did not want to have, on the one hand, more international challenges and extra unbearable burdens on the Syrian Revolution to be added to those already existing. On other hand, the public support of Al-Qaeda in Syria was very low, and many people were skeptical about Al-Qaeda's agenda and strategy. In addition, the declarations caused a great rift among the grassroots elements of Jabhat Al-Nusra. Some of them were loyal to al-Baghdadi, but others stayed loyal to al-Jawlani. Such division has caused instability in the structure of Jabhat al-Nusra, and weakened it considerably, and needed some time to recover. However, such defection did not go peacefully, but developed into a severe armed fighting between the state and Al-Nusra.

There is also the fact that the relationship between Jabhat Al-Nusra and other Jihadist groups in Syria such as Ahrar Asham became weaker. Giving Bai'a to Al-Zawahiri meant that Jabhat Al-Nusra was subject to orders from outside Syria and may act unilaterally according to the different concerns of those involved in Jihad in Syria. However, Jabhat Al-Nusra has remained much closer to the national Jihadist groups compared to the Islamic State's stance toward them. For instance on 26 September 2013, Jabhat Al-Nusra signed a statement with another eleven national Jihadist groups disregarding the National Coalition and any foreign-based opposition.[605]

While the Islamic State and Jabhat Al-Nusra have the same main founding ideology, doctrines and aims, such as Al-Tawheed, *Al-Walaa-Wa-Al-Braa*, and establishing a cross borders Islamic State, they adopt different strategies on the ground, as described below:

---

605 "Islamic fighters refuse the opposition, and call for an Islamic Leadership", Akhbaar.org, 26 September 2013. http://www.alakhbaar.org/home/2013/9/154830.html, viewed on 1 June 2014.

Al-Nusra. Its strategy focuses on making changes from below by educating people, mingling with them, and offering social services for their communities. It concentrates heavily on the hearts and minds battle. Jabhat Al-Nusra provides some public services such as health and education services in the areas that it does control or has a foothold in.[606] While they are heavily involved in attacking the regime, they avoid clashes with the secularist and pro-Western brigades in the Free Syrian Army. This strategy led to huge numbers of Syrian youths joining the group. Trabulsi, a fighter from Damascus, and based in its suburbs very close to Jabhat Al-Nusra, stated, “The youths of Jabhat Al-Nusra are very good-mannered people, very dedicated, and very brave. Everyone likes them; they have the knowledge to beat every one in any subject practically in topics like the invalidity of democracy and the legitimacy of Jihad.”[607]

In July 2016, Jabhat Al-Nusra declared its split from Al-Qaeda. its name was changed to Fatih Al-Sham. The split was as al-Jawlani stated to confirm the moderate approach of this armed group, and to emphasize on its mission on fighting the Syrian regime only, so the West will give up striking it under the pretext of Al-Qaeda affiliation. I think Jabaht Al-Nusra leaders have been approached by some regional actors such Qatar and Turkey to give up their Al-Qaeda links and integrate fully with the moderate armed opposition. al-Jawlani has been on Aljazeera TV many times criticizing the Islamic State and respecting the rights of ethnic and religious minorities in the Syria. Therefore, I think his group was contained and will be used to impose any potential political conciliation on the ground between the regime and the opposition, and moreover, to be used to fights ISIS and weaken its religious legitimacy among the Syrian people. Fatih Al-Sham changed its name again to Hay’at Tahrir Al-Sham in January 2017. Such changes imply great regional influence on al-Jawlani to adopt new approach. He went even further with the guidance and the

---

[606] Today’s Meeting, television program, Aljazeera, 19 December 2013.

[607] Interview with the author over Skype on 25 May 2013.

permission of Turkey to form the Syrian Interim Government to run the area he controls. Apparently, he wanted to copy Hamas case in Gaza, so this group has changed upside down since its establishment. it became an oppressive authority in some parts of Idlib but not a populist group, its behavior of treating the people was not so different from the Assad regime igniting a public resentment. Its main concern not fighting the Assad regime anymore, but to collect money through investment and through imposing taxes on people. Moreover, it has become a tool in some regional countries hands for some political gains for both sides.

The Islamic State. With a fundamental strategy to impose its ideology from above, the Islamic State always wanted to impose itself as a proper state governing the areas that control and rule the people because managing or ruling the areas and the people is more important than liberating them. The Islamic State imposed the Sharia law on people with no concessions and without great concern for public opinion believing that applying the Sharia law would eventually make the people happy, satisfied, and safe. They changed the school curriculums according to the Islamic principles and the Islamic teachings. In addition, they opened the Islamic courts and setting up a penalize system according to the Sharia law. They imposed charity (*Zakat*) on the people and distributed it to the needy families through a sophisticated system. Also, they asked people to close their shops at the time of prayers, and smoking was totally and strictly banned within its territories. However, the Islamic State did not pay great attention to the cultural differences between its people claiming that Islam would melt all different cultures among people. For instance, having some Tunisians or Libyans on the check points in Syria has created many problems with the local people undermining its popularity and prevalence. Meanwhile, the Islamic State spared no time and no effort fighting other Islamic and non-Islamic groups that were trying to undermine or restrict its extending influence. It has adopted a confrontation strategy, perceiving all such groups as penetrated by foreign agents and constituting possible seeds for future Awakening

Councils (*Sahawat*),[608] so the Islamic State intends to liquidate them before they get stronger and constitute a more significant threat later.

In general, Akkram Hijazi revealed that the Islamic State imposed what he called the "Jihad of elites," where foreign veteran fully equipped (ideologically and militarily) Jihadists constitute its backbone in Syria in terms of fighting and policing the controlled areas. Contrary to this, Jabhat Al-Nusra was successful in forming what he called the "populist Jihad" in Syria through its benign contacts with Syrian people, and understanding its special nature of being predominantly influenced by Sufism for a long time.[609]

The Islamic State adopts the Jihad of elites and was successful in building its own state or quasi-state according to Sharia law. In contrast, Jabhat Al-Nusra has compromised Sharia law in order to satisfy people and some other Islamic groups. As a result, Jabaht Al-Nusra was in a big dilemma as it was not able to win the people's satisfaction all the time nor was able to rule and govern according to the Sharia law. I think, the brave military operations of Jabhat Al-Nusra against the Syrian regime were the real ground for winning some popular dimension. Moreover, the Islamic State wanted to impose itself on the international system by force and intimidation on the ground as a great power in the region, which the whole world must respect and be scared of. It carried out many vicious terrorist attacks on many countries such as France, Britain and Germany as a retaliation for their involvements in the war against it and as intimidation. In addition, Al-Nusra, as the vast majority of the Islamic groups in Syria, contrary to ISIS, do have great regional and international links, and such links hugely influenced their combatant and non-combatant activities, which made the struggle and the whole situation in Syria in the hands of regional and international powers. Therefore, Syrians in the regime and in the opposition (armed and political opposition)

---

[608] Awaking Councils (Sahawat) are groups from Sunni tribes in Iraq. The have been established by the US and Saudi Arabia after the invasion of 2003 in order to fight Al-Qaeda.

[609] In depth, television program, Aljazeera, 3 March 2014.

cannot solve the crisis or reach any kind of conciliation in the country without these foreign powers.

Finally, while the Islamic State transformed from a group into a state or quasi-state, Jabaht Al-Nusra became a fragmented and disorganized group, so local branches in Daraa, Damascus, Idlib and others seem to have different strategies and different goals, making an impression that Jabhat Al-Nusra is no longer a united group, but a divided body able to gather itself again in Idlib after their defeat in other parts of the country.

Mr. Ismael, a veteran Jihadists from Syria, summarizes the core difference between the state and Al-Nusra: "Al-Qaeda precedes the Muslim people by twenty years in understanding the real global battle against Muslims and its horizon and foreseeing the future, but the Islamic State precedes Al-Qaeda itself by another twenty years."[610]

THE COST OF IDEOLOGY

Resorting to violence to counter the regime's cruelty has been manipulated by the regime for more violence against the revolutionaries and their public supporters or public shelters. Yet, resorting to ideology has been manipulated by the regime more effectively, and in many ways that helped it domestically, regionally and globally. In addition to a more violent response from the regime, the Islamization of the revolution has consolidated the regime even further through restoring the minorities' support. All minorities have concerns over Islamism in the country, so the regime has used it effectively to mobilize the Shia communities in the region to protect the holy Shia sites in the country from the threats of Takfiris (Jihadists). Great numbers of Iraqi Shia traveled to Syria for this purpose.[611] One Hezbollah leader made it very clear on many occasions that he is committed to fighting Takfiris

[610] Interview with the author on Skype on 16 June 2014.

[611] "The foreign fighters siding the regime, who are they?" Asharq Al-Awsat, 19 February, 2014, http://classic.aawsat.com/details.asp?section=45&article=761991&issueno=12867#.U7LlUo1dUVg. Viewed on 13 June 2014.

in Syria.[612] In response, renowned Sunni scholars from many different countries met in Cairo on 13 June 2013. With the endorsement of President Morsi, they declared Jihad in Syria against the Syrian regime and its Shia allies such as Hezbollah and the Iraqi Shias militias.[613] Such a declaration has mitigated the difference between moderate Islam and radical Islam. Both trends called for the use of violence against the Syrian regime and all other militias fighting the Syrian people. Moderate Islamists have always proclaimed themselves to be non-violent Islamists. Therefore, ideology has led to more of an identity crisis not just in Syria, but also across the region and the Islamic world. Moreover, the Islamization of the Syrian Revolution and the spread of Jihadist groups in Syria have helped the Syrian regime's discourse for fighting terrorism; it also validated the regime's thesis, and thus helps justify its repression. The regime portrayed itself as a rock in front of Jihadist groups protecting other regimes in the region. Waleed Muallem, the then Syrian foreign secretary, warned the Arab regimes of the implications of a regime collapse in Syria. He stated, "The Jihadists who want to establish the Islamic Khilafa would not stop within the Syrian borders. We are defending Jordan, Lebanon and Turkey."[614]

Finally, the spread of Jihadism in Syria has reduced the possibility of international support and backers to moderate groups fighting against Bashar Assad as this support may fall into the hands of wrong people as has been claimed.[615] In fact, there was no great international support for the revolution even before the its Islamization.

[612] euronews, Hasan Nasrullah is ready to go to Syria to fight Takfiris. Posted on 16 August 2013, https://www.youtube.com/watch?v=m_cVVx1XqJs.

[613] AljazeeraMubashar, The Muslim Scholars declare Jihad against the Syrian Regime. Posted on 14 June 2013. https://www.youtube.com/watch?v=ZtYdAP6gae4.

[614] Al-Sham the Headquarter of Islam, al-Muallem warns of establishing Al-Khilafa if Bashar Assad fell. Posted on 24 June 2013, www.youtube.com/watch?v=MxDmPQien2k&feature=share

[615] Clinton: Arming Syrian rebels could help Al-Qaeda, CBS, 27 February 2012, viewed on 13 June 2012. http://www.cbsnews.com/news/clinton-arming-syrian-rebels-could-help-Al-Qaeda/.

The international efforts have been diverted completely in principle to fight ISIS within a great international alliance including the Assad regime and Iran. The Iranian militias under the name of Al-Ḥashd Ash-Sha'bī (Popular Mobilization Forces) constituted the main ground forces in this international alliance.

THE FORMATION OF THE SUPREME MILITARY COMMAND (SMC)

Despite the overwhelming trend toward Jihad at this stage, a great part of the Syrian Revolution's activities and supporters, secularists and some moderate Muslims alongside the political opposition, did not want the situation to develop into Jihad. In fact, they wanted the struggle with the regime to be kept within the revolution framework for two main reasons: First, their adherence to secularism, which is anti-Islamic discourse. Second, they do not want Jihad to be a burden on the revolution as Jihad is associated with terrorism in mainstream media and think tanks around the world. Therefore, the revolution flag stayed their symbol for the revolution all through.

When resorting to violence after the peaceful phase of the revolution, the leadership of the battalions and brigades was from the public, and had some military experience gained through serving in the national army. However, it was not the qualified military leadership that was needed to combat the regime forces. Such a situation has created disorganization and chaos, as the Free Syrian Army failed to transfer itself from being an idea for the violent struggle against the regime into a proper united military formation. The lack of unity has made cooperation and coordination difficult on the battlefield, and has limited the effectiveness of rebel operations.[616] Moreover, the great numbers of officers that have defected from the army needed to be invested and employed in the battlefields in a way that would serve the revolution against Bashar

[616] O'Bagy, op, cit.

Assad. Therefore, the need was urgent to form a hierarchical united military structure formally representing military struggle against the regime. After many aborted attempts, on 7 December 2012 the formation of Supreme Military Command was announced. The establishment of this body may have been to achieve three main goals: 1) It has created a formal body representing the military side of the revolution, so the outside world can deal with it in terms of coordination and support; 2) It was intended to form a military bloc made up of defected Syrian officers, and able to preserve and control the military institution in the country if the regime were to collapse. It was an attempt to avoid the Iraqi scenario, where a vacuum was created after the military institution collapsed following the fall of the regime in 2003, plunging the country into total chaos and disorder. 3) Monopolizing military resources can bring many of the scattered groups under this umbrella, and more importantly can weaken the various Islamic groups across the country. The formation of SMC in this phase was a great attempt to unite and organize the Free Syrian Army, but could not dilute the overwhelming Islamic inclination of the Syrian Revolution that spread in this phase.

THE SYRIAN NATIONAL ARMY

The Syrian National Army (SNA) was established on 30 December 2017 as an official part of the Syrian Interim Government (SIG). It replaced the Free Syrian Army and aimed to include all the opposition armed groups in one formal hierarchal armed body to be the sole opposition armed group fighting Assad, the Kurdish militias and ISIS with direct support from Turkey.

It has two main branches in the Aleppo countryside and in Idilb, and consists of many legions and armed groups from different parts of the country, most importantly Asham Legion in Idlib in addition to the First Legion, the Second Legion, and the Third Legion in the countryside of Aleppo. Most of these factions received great support from the United States to combat ISIS.

THE CLASHES WITHIN

Clashes from within started to spread due to different ideologies, different identities and different interests. Therefore, the revolution trajectory became more complicated when the conflict between the revolutionaries and the regime fragmented into four or more other conflicts: the Free Syrian Army against the Kurdish Democratic Union Party (PYD); the conflict between the Free Syrian Army and ISIS; the conflict between ISIS and other Islamic groups against the PYD; and more viciously, the conflict between ISIS and other Islamic groups, including Jabhat Al-Nusra and the Islamic Front. After the withdrawal of Syrian forces from major Kurdish areas in northeast Syria in July 2012, and handing it over to the PYD, the Free Syrian Army and different Islamic groups believed that some undeclared alliance between the regime and the PYD was talking place.[617] Therefore, fighting the PYD was part of fighting the regime. On the other hand, the PYD has a great interest in purging the region from the Free Syrian Army and the Islamic groups in order to establish a local Kurdish authority in the territory. Moreover, there are great interests for all parties to control of this part of Syria. Gaining this province is of particular importance due to its acquisition of strategic wealth, such as oil, gas, cotton and this wealth in the eyes of the FSA and the Islamic groups is the money and weapons, while among the Kurds it is a strong ground for local government.[618] Controlling this territory also means capturing its border towns such as the border town with Turkey, Ras Al-Ain. The town and its border post are of high strategic importance, allowing whoever is in control to determine what supplies can cross the border, generating revenues through imposing taxes on travelers crossing the borders.[619] The ISIS wars against both some Free Syrian Army groups, and some Islamic groups, can be attributed to many different causes, but ISIS aims for

---

[617] Khorsheed Dally, "The Kurds and the Free Syrian Army between understanding and collision", Aljazeera.net, 11 April 2013. http://www.aljazeera.net/knowledgegate/opinions/2013/4/11, viewed on 1May 2014.

[618] Ibid.

[619] Democratic Union Party [PYD], Global Security.org, unknown date, www.globalsecurity.org/military/world/para/pyd.htm, viewed on 3 June 2014.

one ultimate goal, which is eradicating all opponents in order to extend its solitary control and influence over the land. However, ISIS's leaders claim that their war against some groups in the Free Syrian Army such as Ahfad Al-Rasoul[620] and Asefat Al-Shamal[621] was a pre-emptive and defensive war against the Western manipulated groups (Sahawat)[622] wanting to target ISIS through Western support.[623] Meanwhile, the clash between ISIS and some Islamic groups, including Jabhat Al-Nusra, refers to ISIS's strategy and its wrong policies,[624] as al-Jawalni stated. He added that this fighting is a *Fitnah*[625] between Muslims, and must be stopped.[626] In fact, the problem is more complicated. The Islamic State proposes itself as a legitimate state and all other factions must follow or at least not involve themselves in the fighting against it. The groups that opposed this proposition or involved in the fighting against the Islamic Stated were labeled by it as *Sahawat, Murtaddeen*[627] (Apostates) and traitors hinting at Jabhat Al-Nusra, so fighting them was a priority as the Islamic State believed.[628] In turn, the Islamic State were labeled by the others as Khawarej,[629] and must be fought and eradicated, and

[620] It was centered in A'zaz in North Aleppo; its fame came mainly from holding some Hezbollah members as hostages for months.

[621] It has been established by a coalition of some tribes from the Golan such as Al-Nuaimi, Al-Fadel, and Al-Refaea, and had spread to many areas across the country. They enjoyed good support from the Gulf governments.

[622] Sahawat (Awaking Councils), which was established in Iraq by the American support after the invasion in 2003, and was led by different Sunni leaders to fight Al-Qaeda members in the country.

[623] The Eagle Banner, Allah be with you the oppressed State. Posted on 30 September 2013, https://www.youtube.com/watch?v=n13iymaJOdw

[624] aljadeedonline, a statement for al-Jawlani, about the recent events Posted on 7 January 2014, https://www.youtube.com/watch?v=ds9K7aVICvQ.

[625] Fitnah means in this context a dispute, discord, or fighting among Muslims.

[626] Ibid.

[627] Murtadeen, meaning Apostates, this term is used mainly against the people who refuse Sharia law. It was first used during the first caliphate (Abu Baker) fighting people who refused to pay Zakat.

[628] Hafiz, op, cit, p.200.

[629] Al-Khawarej, it is mainly used to depict the people that want to overthrow the rulers, and used first on the group that rebelled against the forth caliph Ali (the Prophet's cousin) during his war with Muawiyah.

fighting it was a priority, too, as they believed. Many *Fatwas* have labeled ISIS as the Khawarej of this time.[630] Such a situation has made the conflict between them have an ideological dimension, and hence more violent and more vicious. The revolution at this point, where fighting between the different Islamic groups is increasing to unprecedented levels, enters a new fourth phase, and can be called the clashes from within phase, in which Bashar Assad and his supporters were the sole beneficiary.

CONCLUSION

Overall, during this phase, the revolution in Syria turned into a Jihad, not just to overthrow the regime, but also to establish an Islamic state in Syria for the national Jihadist groups, and across the borders for global Jihadist groups. Abu Hamza, an independent Jihadist, stated, "The revolution against the regime has finished, Jihad has started now after the whole world kept silence toward the regime's brutality against our civilians; against women and children. This Jihad is to attain justice through the establishment of our Islamic state."[631] There are three main disintegrated groups that can be found among the revolutionary side in this phase: 1) Secularist revolutionaries and the political opposition including moderate Islamists such as the Muslim Brotherhood, who adopted the independence flag; they became a minority in this phase; 2) National Jihadists with a national Islamic agenda; 3) Global Jihadists.

The concept of Jihad is dominant now among the revolutionaries in Syria after being an alien concept for decades or more. The recurring scenes of carnage and bloodshed with no active international stance, and the influence of national and global Jihadists on the people, have diverted their attention from

---

[630] Jaish Al-Islam, the statement of Zahran Alloush before setting out to liberate Mida'a village from Al-Khawarej. Posted on 2 July 2014, https://www.youtube.com/watch?v=h7miPdaMzwE. The Syrian Islamic council also issued a Fatwa supporting the fight against ISIS, and describes their approach as Khawarej. http://eldorar.com/node/51191, viewed on 5 June 2014.

[631] Interview with the author over Skype on 14 May 2013.

the concepts of freedom and democracy to the concept of Jihad as the right path to topple the Syrian regime and to establish the Islamic State, where Sharia law is to be implemented. However, the clashes within the Jihadist groups have made the revolution trajectory more complicated, and served the regime's cause and tactics, and made its collapse even more difficult. However, the clashes within the Jihadist groups has made the revolution trajectory more complicated, and served the regime's cause and tactics, and made its collapse even more difficult. In fact, the regime in this phase started to recapture areas that were lost in the past, taking advantage of the fierce clashes among the Jihadist groups. In fact, the regime in this phase started to recapture areas that were lost in the past, taking advantage of the fierce clashes among the Jihadist groups.

The international coalition against the Islamic State changed the game in the region. Shia fighters and many Sunni Jihadists in Syria were united under this coalition to fight the Islamic State. In fact, the Iranian-backed Shia militias and Kurdish militias turned out to be the ground forces for this coalition leading the way to defeat the Islamic State with a big massacre committed by the coalition on its last stronghold in Bāghūz in March 2019, where many civilians have been killed by the coalition by different sorts of weapons, including phosphoric attacks.

Chapter Six

THE SYRIAN REVOLUTION VIS-À-VIS INTERNATIONAL RELATIONS

INTRODUCTION

This chapter focuses on international relations toward the Syrian Revolution, and how these relations contributed to the complexity of the Syrian Revolution through Russian and Chinese vetoes in the Security Council condemning the Syrian regime, and through the American veto on arming the opposition with anti-aircraft missiles. I discuss the position of the most important states and sub-state actors toward the Syrian Revolution. Also the use of chemical weapons, the war on terrorism, and questioning the notion of a proxy war in Syria is also included in the discussion.

THE INTERNATIONAL DIMENSION OF REVOLUTION IN SYRIA

Revolutions may happen within a particular state, but its implications would never be limited within the borders of that state. This is what Katz has explained more precisely: "Revolution does not just change things inside one country. It can disrupt international relationships throughout an entire region or even the world."[632] This fact drove different states and sub-state actors regionally and globally, for different reasons but mainly national

[632] Mark Katz, "The International Relations of the Arab Spring", The Middle East Policy, Summer 2014, volume XXI, Number 2.

interests, to interfere directly or indirectly to support the revolution in Syria and push toward its success, or to hinder it and push toward its failure. Unfortunately, the fate of extended internal armed struggles in the third world rely heavily on foreign actors as the conflicting parties need military and non-military supplies in order to sustain and continue. In June 2014, Ajnad Asham, the armed group, complained about the lack of food and military supplies coming from abroad, which affected their operations in Ghouta, east of Damascus,[633] as Khalid, one of its members has claimed. Likewise, continuous Iranian and Russian support were always crucial for the regime's survival since the beginning of the uprising in 2011. Moreover, the involvement of foreign Shia groups was vital for the regime to recapture certain areas in Homs, Aleppo and suburbs of Damascus.[634] Syria is not an isolated or marginalized country in the Middle East. In fact, the vital importance of Syria derives first from its geopolitical position, which makes it a center for regional and international struggle. Secondly, its importance is also derived from its distinctive regional and international strategy, a strategy that has been adopted and consolidated for decades, which transformed Syria into a key regional country in Middle Eastern politics. Syria is a country still formally at war with Israel, adopting resistance and passive resistance strategies against Israel, and supports Hezbollah, Hamas and resistance factions. This has made Syrian regional and international relations very complicated.

Syria cannot be isolated from the historic Greater Syria. Although Greater Syria is now divided into several independent states, the security of present-day Syria is still being considered on the Greater Syria scale. Therefore, any ruler of Syria would not feel safe if he did not look at the concerns of Greater Syria.[635] Hence, Syria had to achieve regional security in order to guarantee its internal security. Wasel Chamali, an independent Syrian politician, argues that one of the reasons for Hafiz Assad's

[633] Interview with the author over Skype on 8 June 2014.

[634] "The Russian Weapons and the Iranian Support", Ashams, 22 April 2014. http://www.ashams.com/art/145703, viewed on 15 August 2014.

[635] Patrick Seal. A lecture at BRISMES Conference, LSE, March 2012, London.

intervention in Lebanon in 1976 and after was to dominate the country in order to secure and consolidate his sway over Syria as Lebanon has been safe haven of the opposition,[636] where they can pose a real threat for the regime.

A great importance for Syria as such has given great weight and extraordinary effects for the Syrian Revolution in the region of Middle East. Since day one, the revolution in Syria has had great regional and international dimensions, causing the uprising to develop into a new struggle for Syria. One of the greatest and most dangerous implications of the Syrian Revolution was to shake the foundations of Middle East politics through threatening the collapse of the Sykes–Picot system. In June 2014, ISIS announced the diminishing of borders between Iraq and Syria after gaining control of provinces across the two countries. Such developments created more insecurity in the region by threatening the survival and security of many regimes in the region, and hence, threatening the national interests of great powers, who wanted a stabilized Middle East and in particular the Gulf region in order to secure the oil flow.

Since 2012, we can recognize three groups of states, and also include sub-state actors in relation to the Syrian Revolution: 1) Friends of Syria Group claiming the support of Syrian people; 2) The direct supporters for the regime in terms of logistics, military and politics. I call this latter group Friends of the Syrian Regime Group. The third group involves states which formally decided to distance themselves from the crisis.

Friends of Syria Group

This group was formed from more than 100 countries around the world in February 2012 as a reaction to the first Russian–Chinese veto in October 2011,[637] obstructing a Security Council resolution

[636] Interview with the author on 1 April 2011.

[637] "Fiends of Syria: Conferences and Decisions", Aljazeera, 7 July 2014. http://www.aljazeera.net/news/reportsandinterviews/2012/7/7/, viewed on 19 July 2014.

condemning the Syrian regime.[638] However, this group contracted dramatically, forming what is known as the Core Group and which consists of eleven countries; the United States, France, Britain, Germany, Italy, Turkey, Saudi Arabia, Qatar, the United Arab Emirates, Egypt and Jordan.[639]

Although friends of Syria or the Core Group have agreed that ousting Bashar Assad is the cornerstone for a proper solution in Syria, their help and support to the opposition and to the fighters on the ground does not lead to that aim. Ghalioun has expressed his disappointment in the friends of Syria Conference in Tunisia in February 2012.[640] More than two years later, Abd al-Ilah al-Bashir, the new leader for the Supreme Military Command (SMC) in the Free Syrian Army, appealed for support from friends of Syria in order to deter the regime forces in Aleppo and ISIS forces in Deir ez-Zur.[641] Such a statement can confirm the widening gap between what is needed in Syria and what the friends of Syria are actually willing to do.[642] The main reason behind the weakness of the friends of Syria appears to refer mainly to the United States' and Saudi Arabia's positions toward the revolution in Syria. Below, I analyze the position of the main countries in the Core Group.

It is very important to say that the components of this group are not consistent; it is a strange, suspicious mixer of democratic and dictatorship countries. While people may be deceived by the democratic countries' rhythm and discourse about their support for a democratic change in the Arab world, dictatorships such as

[638] Russia and China have vetoed resolutions in the Security Council condemning the Syrian regime in four different occasions since October 2011 until April 2014.

[639] "The Rise And Fall Of The "Friends of Syria" Group", Moon of Alabama, 22 April 2013. http://www.moonofalabama.org/2013/04/the-rise-and-fall-of-the-friends-of-syria-group.html, viewed on 19 July 2014.

[640] "After a disappointing conference, Davutoğlu meets with SNC", Syrian Opinion, 27 February 2014. http://www.spo.sy/news/2953/www.moex.gov.sy/www.moex.gov.sy/www.parliament.sy, viewed on 19 July 2014.

[641] Anas Kadour, Al-Bashir calls on Friends of Syria to support the Free Army. Posted on 5 June 2014.https://www.youtube.com/watch?v=tyj_O8o_pXQ.

[642] Yezid Sayigh, "The friends of Syria's credibility Gap", Carnegie Middle East Centre, 2 May 2014, viewed on 19 July 2014. http://carnegie-mec.org/2013/05/02/friends-of-syria-s-credibility-gap/g398

Saudi Arabia, Qatar, Jordan or UAE should not be able to deceive people because they are ruthless dictatorship countries and under no circumstances would support a revolution from below in any part of the world.

The United States

The US always expressed its supportive stance to the Syrian people in their struggle for freedom and democracy, and Barak Obama called on Bashar Assad to step down in August 2011.[643] However, Obama's call on Bashar Assad was not comparable in any way to George W. Bush's call on Saddam Hussein to step down before the American invasion of Iraq in 2003. George Bush invaded Iraq in order to topple Saddam Hussein, while the perceived moral and ethical responsibility of the United States obligated President Obama to adopt a "red line" policy in the Syrian conflict. Obama set a (flexible) red line for Bashar Assad, which is the use of chemical weapons against the Syrian people.[644] However, Bashar Assad crossed Obama's red line, and used chemical weapons many times, and one of them was on a large scale in Ghouta, east Damascus, in August 2013, where almost 1400 people died immediately, many of them children and women.[645] Still, the United States did not intervene or strike Syria. Instead, it was more important for the United States that Bashar Assad sign the Chemical Weapons Convention (CWC) and commit to handing over Syria's chemical weapons stockpile for decommissioning.[646] The result was that Bashar Assad became a partner, and his stay in power was essential for the disarmament process to be successfully completed. Oliver Thränert argued,

---

643 ThinkProgress6's channel, Clinton: Assad must go Posted on: 18 August 2011, https://www.youtube.com/watch?v=p2WuJeaoscs.

644 The Telegraph, US President Barack Obama in "red line" warning to Syria over chemical weapons. Posted on 21 August 2012, https://www.youtube.com/watch?v=avQKLRGRhPU.

645 Violations Documentation Centre in Syria 22 August 2013. http://www.vdcsy.info/index.php/ar/reports/chemicaldamascussuburbs#.U8rAOoBdUVg

646 http://www.telegraph.co.uk/news/worldnews/middleeast/syria/10320221/Syria-how-Bashar-al-Assads-chemical-arsenal-became-a-strategic-liability.html

> The disarmament of chemical weapons has led to a paradoxical result: namely, since over the course of the inspections Assad has again become an international partner, he's been somewhat strengthened as a leader. And this is based on his having employed poison gas against his own people.[647]

On 7 October 2013, the US Secretary of State John Kerry praised Bashar Assad for cooperating fully with the international disarmament experts sent by the UN. He stated: "I think it's also a credit to the Assad regime that they complied rapidly."[648] Such a statement posed an important question about American moral responsibility and its real position toward the Syrian Revolution. Three phases of the American position since the beginning of the Syrian Revolution can be observed:

1. The Syrian uprising as an aspect of the Arab Spring, a public and peaceful movement seeking freedom and democracy, was not in line with the national interests of the United States in this region. Once democracy is installed in Syria or any Arab country, it would spread regionally. Such a scenario is very dangerous to the United States' interests in the region, so the fear is from the revolution itself, and also from exporting the revolution to other countries. Noam Chomsky pointed out that the US and its allies would do anything they can to prevent authentic democracy in the Arab world because there is an overwhelming majority of the population in the region who regard the United States as the main threat to their interests. The US does not want to see governments there which are responsive to the will of the people. If that happened, not only would the US lose its control over the region, it would be

[647] "Assad, an international partner again, expert says", DW, 10 October 2013. http://www.dw.de/assad-an-international-partner-again-expert-says/a-17148703

[648] Elise Labott. "John Kerry's praise for Bashar al-Assad on chemical weapons destruction raises eyebrows", CNN, 7 October 2013, viewed 7 October 2013. http://security.blogs.cnn.com/2013/10/07/john-kerrys-praise-for-bashar-al-assad-on-chemical-weapons-destruction-raises-eyebrows.

thrown out entirely.[649] The US may call for or support more democratic practices in the Middle Eastern countries in order to put pressure on the regimes, but not to the extent of supporting democratic movements to take control of these countries. I think the US support for dictatorships in the region such as Saudi Arabia, Egypt and Algeria, and the US's uncooperative position toward the Arab Spring, can support this view.

2. When the situation inside Syria developed into an armed struggle between the regime and the armed opposition, the US military support through its regional allies (Saudi Arabia, Jordan, Qatar, and Turkey) to some fighting groups in the opposition was accompanied by imposing a veto on anti-aircraft missiles or MANPADS or heavy arms to reach these groups,[650] creating a situation of stalemate between the regime and the armed opposition. The United States allowed anti-tank missiles to reach the opposition armed group, but these were ineffective against the aircrafts, the most dangerous weapons in the hands of Assad, which killed the people and destroyed the country. The US favored such a situation as long as the struggle was contained in Syria and did not threaten regional security. Many voices in the US such as Edward Luttwak consider such a strategy to be in the core interest of the US and must persist as much as possible. He argued:

> The Obama administration should resist the temptation to intervene more forcefully in Syria's civil war. A victory by either side would be equally undesirable for the United States. At this point, a prolonged stalemate is the only outcome that would not be damaging to American interests.[651]

---

[649] MIT ESA Q&A on Egypt with Noam Chomsky, Oct 2013, Posted on 8 October 2013, http://www.youtube.com/watch?v=zLPYN82xHck.

[650] Ziyad Majed, "the American veto on anti-aircraft missiles to reach the opposition is the biggest service for Bashar Assad, Al-Asr", 8 April 2014. http://alasr.ws/articles/view/15067, viewed on 16 July 2014.

[651] Edward Luttwak "In Syria, America Loses if Either Side Wins", The New York Times, 24 August 2014. http://www.nytimes.com/2013/08/25/opinion/

I agree with Stephen Walt when saying: "The US administration does not want to play a visible role in the conflict, so no boots on the ground, no 'no-fly zones', and no big, highly visible shipments of US arms. Instead, Washington can use Qatar and Saudi Arabia as its middlemen."[652] However, the aim was still to perpetuate the struggle, but not to end it. Some might argue that President Obama, who withdrew American forces from Iraq and who set in motion a plan to withdraw those stationed in Afghanistan by 2014, would not involve the US in Syria militarily unless the situation there begins to threaten the security of the region. However, Obama's support or leading from behind for international military intervention in Libya in 2011 to topple Gaddafi can refute such an argument.

3. When Jihadism spread in Syria, and extremist groups, namely ISIS, became strong in the country, American national interest was more toward combating terrorism rather than supporting the armed opposition against the regime. The emergent terrorism danger in Syria and Iraq poses a threat to homeland security,[653] as Robert Ford claimed. I think the United States used some armed groups in the Syrian opposition to fight the Islamic State under the name of fighting terrorism. Such an aim would meet with other Islamist groups' interests, such as the Army of Islam, who always stress that fighting Al-Khawarej is a priority.[654] The Syrian regime will seize this opportunity to prove its commitments in the war against terrorism, so its attacks against the Islamic State will increase significantly. At this

sunday/in-syria-america-loses-if-either-side-wins.html?_r=0, viewed on 20 May 2014.

[652] Stephen Walt, "What is the U.S. REALLY doing in Syria?", Foreign Policy, 22 May 2013. http://www.foreignpolicy.com/posts/2013/05/22/what_is_the_us_really_doing_in_syria, viewed on 10 May 2014.

[653] TheHistoryTV, Obama administration's Syria policy a failure - US Ambassador Ford. Posted on 4 June 2014, https://www.youtube.com/watch?v=ElXPt9NXZgw.

[654] Shada Alhuria, A Statement of Zaharan Alloush About the ISIS.
Posted on 25 February 2014, https://www.youtube.com/watch?v=XnNpKvt6feo

> stage, we can find the United States, the Syrian regime, and some armed groups from the opposition including some Islamists in a direct or indirect coalition against the ISIS. Furthermore, Iran and Russia were on the side of the United States in the international coalition against ISIS. The Iranian militias constituted the ground forces for the coalition in this war.

Regardless of these three phases, Robert Ford expressed the American stance from the beginning through what is known as Ford's three noes: no to military solution, no to military intervention, no to no-fly zone over Syria, stressing always on a vague political solution to the crisis. However, the US coordinated so closely with the Russians, and the Russian military intervention in Syria in 2015 was the outcome of such cooperation to prevent the fall of Assad's regime in a way that would endanger US interests, which includes the security of Israel.[655] In addition, the US was watching closely the situation of heavy weapons when fallen in the hands of the armed opposition in order to seize them, so they would not be used against Assad or against Israel. For instance, a special unit coordinated with some opposition fighters in Ghouta in late 2012 to seize S200 missiles that were situated in Al-Iftris military base, and moved them outside Syria to Jordan.

Trump, in contrast, was more offensive vocally and in action toward Assad, calling him an animal. He launched missile attacks on some Syrian military bases associated with chemical weapons capabilities as a response to Assad using chemical weapons in Duma, April 2018. Trump accused Obama of not dealing rightly with the Syrian Crisis. In addition, the Trump administration

[655] See the testimony of the former senior Pentagon official Andrew Exum, the deputy secretary of defense for Middle East policy under the Obama administration. He provided candid testimony to the Congressional Committee of Foreign Affairs on America's strategic orientation vis-a-vis the Middle East on 9 May 2019. https://www.congress.gov/116/meeting/house/109455/witnesses/HHRG-116-FA13-Wstate-ExumA-20190509.pdf

adopted the Caesar Act[656] imposing some economic sanctions on the Assad regime. However, the sanctions have affected the Syrian people badly, but not the Assad regime, putting the Syrian people on the brink of starvation. I think such regimes can somehow escape the real implications of the economic sanctions, but people would suffer and pay the ultimate price of the consequences.

Overall, Trump has used the same strategy in response to chemical attacks in 2018 by destroying the tools of the crime rather than punishing the criminal. It is clearly the official strategy for the United States to preserve Assad against the revolution and against the Islamists.

Turkey

Turkey was hoping for President Bashar Assad to carry out some serious reforms and to respond to the people's demands. Mr. Ahmet Davutoğlu, the then Turkish foreign minister, visited Syria many times in between April and August 2011, trying to convince Bashar Assad to make serious political changes and stop spreading violence. It was an indication of a good understanding from the Turkish government to the new wave of public revolt in the region. However, the relationship weakened considerably when Turkey hosted defected Syrian officers on its soil and opened its hospitals to treat injured Syrian revolutionaries. The borders were open between the two countries since 2010 and Turkey welcomed the Syrians after March 2011 as guests, but not refugees, making the burden on the Syrians themselves to face the difficulties and exploitations in Turkey with no rights apart from health and education. Nevertheless, thousands of Syrians have been granted Turkish nationality on different grounds.[657]

President Recep Tayyip Erdoğan condemned the heavy use of violence by the Assad regime against its own people. He stated,

[656] Caesar Act was the American response to the Caesar Report showing leaked pics of tortured detainees to death in the Assad's prisons.

[657] Some of them were granted citizenship on higher education qualifications, on investments or on ethnic background, particularly Turkmen.

"We will not allow another Hama in Syria."[658] The Turkish position concerning the Syrian Revolution was based on cultural and historical bonds, and on humanitarian principles. According to Gol, those who are analyzing the Turkish stance from the Arab revolutions should not ignore the shared history between the Turks and Arabs.[659] Also, Turkey under Erdoğan always wanted to be known as a vital Muslim country standing for Muslims values and standing by persecuted Muslims around the world. In 2009, Erdoğan accused China of committing genocide against the Uighur Muslim minority in Xingjian province.[660] Similarly, in January 2012, Turkey called on international organizations to intervene in Myanmar to stop the violence against Muslims that was occurring there.[661] Moreover, Erdoğan comes from Muslim Brotherhood roots and has very close ties to the current Muslim Brotherhood in the Arab world, who tried to override the Arab Spring revolutions. Therefore, a great relationship between the Arab Spring countries and Turkey was one of the great achievements for the revolutions.

Allowing their relationship with Turkey to deteriorate, I think, was the greatest miscalculation in Syrian foreign policy after the uprising. The Syrian regime underestimated the role of Turkey in buttressing the revolution. Turkey is a large, powerful democratic neighboring country, so freedom of speech, movement and gathering are respected in the country. Syrians enjoy free entry to Turkey, which made it very easy for the opposition as well as for activists to hold their meetings and activities in the county. Turkey also opened its lands for the first time for opposition activities, both political and military. Most of the opposition conferences and meetings have been and still are held in Turkey.

[658] Erdoğan's Statement, the Turkish prime minister "We will not allow another Hama in Syria", 10 June 2011.

[659] Mohammad Zahid Gol, "The Foreign Influence on the Syrian Crisis", a paper was presented at the International-Arab Relations Formula Conference, Doha 2012.

[660] Turkish leader calls Xinjiang killings "genocide", Islamic City, 10 July 2009 http://www.islamicity.com/forum/printer_friendly_posts.asp?TID=15034, viewed on 10 May2014.

[661] "Turkey calls on intervention in Myanmar", AsiaNews, 17 July 2012 http://asianewslb.com/vdcj8yev.uqeyizf3fu.html, viewed on 15 May 2014

Moreover, Turkey was also the gateway for Jihadists to enter Syria, and a center to support the Free Syrian Army with weapons coming from different parts of the world. Furthermore, thousands of international humanitarian aid convoys have entered Syria through Turkey since the beginning of the uprising. Turkey also supported the seizure of the FSA on the borders between Syria and Turkey, which caused a serious blow to Syrian sovereignty. However, Turkey placed many important defected Syrian officers under house arrest in a dedicated camp, and prevented them from participating in any kind of military actions against Assad. It was a suspicious policy.

The imbalance of power between Syria and Turkey on the one hand, and Turkey being a member of NATO on the other, made the situation more complicated and in favor of Turkey's position. However, the Syrian regime has the ability and tactics to cause great damage to Turkey: namely through the Kurdish Issue and the Alawi minority in Turkey.

The Kurdish Issue. Syria has resumed support of the Kurdish Worker Party (PKK) and the backing of its affiliates the Kurdish Democratic Union Party (PYD). This move encouraged the Turkish government to a ceasefire deal with the PKK in March 2013.[662] As a result, the PKK has diverted its main operations to focus on the Jihadist groups and the Free Syrian Army in the north of Syria. Meanwhile, with backing from Damascus, PYD has a free hand to repress Syria's Kurds and exercise a state-like power in the Kurdish region of Syria,[663] as Savelsberg claims. The PYD's announcement of self-rule in the Kurdish region in Syria was a provocative move, which created concerns in Turkey and among the Syrian opposition too.[664]

---

[662] "Turkey Kurds: PKK chief Ocalan calls for ceasefire", BBC, 21 March 2013. http://www.bbc.co.uk/news/world-europe-21874427, viewed on 21 July 2014.

[663] Eva Savelsberg "With backing From Damascus, PYD has a free hand to repress Syria's Kurds", World Politics Review, 23 August 2013, viewed 3 September 2013. http://www.worldpoliticsreview.com/articles/13185/with-backing-from-damascus-pyd-has-free-hand-to-repress-syria-s-kurds.

[664] "Turkey warns Syrian PYD against seeking autonomy", Today's Zaman, 19 July 2013. http://www.todayszaman.com/_turkey-warns-syrian-pyd-against-seeking-autonomy_321293.html.

The Alawi community. The majority of the Alawi and Alevi community in Turkey,[665] which constitutes almost 15–20% of the population,[666] is against the government's policy concerning the Syrian Revolution, and they pose a great political challenge to the government. The Arab Alawis in Hatay are more anti-government in this respect, so the regime in Syria was able to recruit people from that community to cooperate with regime forces in anti-Free Syrian Army actions. Moreover, Turkish investigations have confirmed the involvement of Arab Alawis from Turkey in the explosion, which occurred in Reyhanli in south Turkey in May 2013.[667] Reyhanli is one of the main centers in Turkey for Syrian refugees.

The Syrian forces shot down a Turkish fighter jet in June 2012,[668] and many Turkish villages have been targeted by the Syrian regime's artillery attacks, killing dozens of Turkish citizens.[669] Turkey has retaliated on many occasions by firing back at the Syrian regime's forces. However, the Turkish reaction was considered to be weak, and a strange, cowardly position. Despite Turkish military superiority over Syria, Turkey was never interested in engaging in a real war with Syria due to the regional and international implications this would have. Although Turkey is not interested in entering a direct mutual war with Syria, it always supported an international military intervention to topple the Syrian regime, particularly after the use of chemical weapons in August 2013.[670]

---

[665] It is very important to make a difference between Alawis and Alavis. The Alawis are Arabs, while Alavis are Turkish, Balkans and Kurdish. Both names are derived from Ali, the prophet's cousin, but their religious practices are different. Both defined themselves as minorities and were historically persecuted by Sunnis.

[666] Documentary Film, television program, Al-Arabiya, 1 June 2013.

[667] Turkish detectives confirm the involvement of Ural Group in Reyhanli explosion, Almustaqbal, 24 May 2013, viewed on 10 March 2014. http://www.almustaqbal.com/v4/Article.aspx?Type=np&Articleid=572303.

[668] "Turkey: Jet downed by Syria in international airspace', BBC, 24 June 2012. http://www.bbc.co.uk/news/world-middle-east-18568412, viewed on 10 March 2014

[669] "Turkey fires on Syria after deadly shelling", CBS News, 03 October 2012. http://www.cbsnews.com/news/turkey-fires-on-syria-after-deadly-shelling/, viewed on 10 March 2014.

[670] "Turkey would join coalition against Syria, says foreign minister", Reuters, 26 August 2013. http://www.reuters.com/article/2013/08/26/us-syria-crisis-turkey-idUSBRE97P05C20130826, viewed on 10 March 2014.

In 2015, Turkey started to change its position gradually when implying its acceptance for Assad to stay in power, forcing the opposition to attend dialogue conferences with the regime in Astana. Those conferences appeared to be surrender talks with the regime as the regime gained more and more lands as a result. Moreover, Turkey imposed an entry visa on all Syrians to enter Turkey by air or sea in January 2016, and starting shooting dead Syrians trying to cross the borders fleeing the war. Hundreds of people were killed by shooting or torture by the hands of the border guards (Gendarmerie), including women and children. It was a cruel move to shoot dead someone crossing the borders fleeing the war while they were allowed to enter the country freely a few years ago. Thereafter, Turkey started to build a wall between the two countries to prevent people crossing over the borders.

The fall of Aleppo, the largest city in the country, to the hands of the Assad regime in December 2016, was a major setback in the battle against Bashar Assad and a big blow to the revolution. On the contrary, Bashar Assad hailed the fall of Aleppo, calling it a historic victory and a watershed between two periods. Turkey played a big role in such a major setback through instructing its loyalist from the Free Syrian Army groups to withdraw from Aleppo in 14 days and head toward Al Bab to fight ISIS. It was a big shock as Aleppo was a huge city and would take years to fall if the situation went to street-to-street fighting with the regime.

By 2018, Assad had recaptured most of the lands and the armed groups were defeated and forced to move to Idib in the north by green buses, so the green bus has turned to be a sign or a symbol of the opposition armed groups' defeat and humiliation. Meanwhile, Turkey has been investing in the armed groups in Idlib and North Syria in general, subjecting them to its control, including Jabhat Al-Nusra. Furthermore, Turkey have deployed some of its troops in North Syria in order to fight the Kurdish militias and terrorists, as it was claimed, but in fact, another main purpose was to control the opposition fighting against the Assad regime.

Turkey invested more in the Syrian war and from controlling the armed opposition in Idlib and North Syria, it was able to recruit some of them to fight for Turkey in Libya and Azerbaijan, turning some Syrian revolutionaries into mercenaries for its own interests. Moreover, some Syrian armed groups backed strongly and directly by Turkey, mainly Turkmen such as Sultan Murad, Suliman Shah and Zinky, tried to seize the houses of many Kurdish people and force them out in Afrin and some other areas in an attempt to bring about demographic changes.

Syrian people inside Turkey (the guests) have been affected hugely by the changing position of Turkey, they were victim of hate crime due to increasing hate speech that was adopted by some government media outlets. Also the government imposed on them severe restrictions on movements, and started to deport many Syrians to Idlib randomly and in a very cruel way.

While we are writing these words in March 2023, Erdoğan is making massive diplomatic efforts to meet Assad, but Assad is declining. A meeting is to take place between the deputy foreign secretaries along with the Russians in May 2023.

Saudi Arabia

Saudi Arabia was faced with a great dilemma regarding the outbreak of the Syrian Revolution. Many great factors have influenced its stance. The first factor is that Saudi Arabia has never had any interest in supporting revolutions from below against ruling regimes. As a dictatorship, supporting a public revolution is not a rational decision for the Saudi leadership and inconsistent with its identity. However, if regime change occurs through Western intervention, Saudi Arabia would support it, with a previous example being the Iraq scenario in 2003. And the second factor concerns the Islamists as the potential prevailing power in Syria following the hypothetical collapse of the regime, making Saudi Arabia more reluctant to assist in a regime change struggle bringing Islamists such as the Muslim Brotherhood to power. Moreover, the global Jihadists who are fighting in Syria are the greatest enemy of Saudi Arabia. Their strength means real threat to its security.

Saudi Arabia, in coordination with the United States, has supported certain Salafi battalions and brigades which adopted traditional Salafism, such as the Jaish Al-Islam all over, in order to shift the balance on the ground against global Jihadists in Syria. On the other hand, Saudi Arabia also has a significant influence on the Supreme Military Command (SMC) and the National Coalition. Such influence has been another great factor in undermining the national framework of the Syrian Revolution.

Supporting traditional Salafi fighters in Syria can achieve several significant goals for Saudi Arabia. First, creating a front can absorb the passionate young Syrian people who want to be part of a Jihad against Bashar Assad before getting recruited by the Jihadists fronts that antagonize Saudi Arabia and the Arab regimes such as Jabhat Al-Nusra and ISIS. Second is creating a strong front parallel to the Jihadist groups. This front is a traditional loyal Salafi front, and can enjoy public credibility, and more importantly is able to fight Jihadists when it is asked to do so. Third, controlling the mainstream struggle against the Syrian regime, Saudi Arabia wanted to be the main player controlling the political as well as the armed opposition, and make the decisions for their advances and withdrawals according to its interests. Fourth, protecting the region from ISIS and Al-Qaeda and their affiliates and twins that consider the ruling regimes illegitimate ones. Therefore, Saudi Arabia was an essential pillar in the international coalition against the Islamic State.

Saudi Arabia hosted the Riyadh Conference in December 2015; it was an important conference for the Syrian armed and political opposition. It was declaration of a new phase in Syria where the opposition expressed their readiness to negotiate with the Syrian regime. I think the assassination of Zahran Allosh soon after (on 25 December 2015) by the Russian air strike was a direct obvious outcome of this conference. Saudi Arabia's behavior since this conference went to the surface and was more with the regime than with the revolution. In fact, Saudi Arabia has already encouraged Russian direct military intervention in Syria prior to the Riyadh Conference in order prevent Assad's fall. Saad Aljabri, a former spy chief, who is in hiding in Canada, mentioned that Bin Salman gave a covert green light for Russia's intervention in Syria.[671]

[671] "Saudi strongman 'encouraged' Russia intervention in Syria, lawsuit claims", The Guardian, 16 August 2020.https://www.theguardian.com/world/2020/aug/16/saudi-strongman-encouraged-russia-syria-intervention-lawsuit-claims.

Overall, the alleged support of Saudi Arabia to the Syrian revolution against Bashar Assad had a backlash and a very negative impact on the cause and the legitimacy of the Syrian revolution worldwide, especially among socialists and human rights activists. The Saudis have suspicious international alliances and a dark record of human rights. They never stood by people, but by dictators and occupiers. They did not support any revolution in the Arab Spring, not even in Libya against their foe Gaddafi, so in what respect would they support the revolution in Syria against their relative and friend Assad!

Qatar

Qatar is a relatively small Gulf state, but its role in the region of the Middle East has grown significantly since 1995, when Amir Hamad seized power from his father. His foreign policy never had an ideology, but he was always seeking a large regional role. Qatar has counted on its wealth from natural gas to boost its leverage in the region, and on its Aljazeera satellite channel, the most powerful channel in the Arab world. Some important countries in the region such as Egypt, Tunisia, Libya, Yemen, Saudi Arabia and others[672] did not welcome the growing Qatari role and influence in the region. Therefore, when public uprisings erupted in some of those countries in 2011, Qatari officials reacted to the Arab Spring with expressions of declaratory and material support. On the contrary, when the Syrian uprising erupted, Qatar acted cautiously, and Al Jazeera, the Qatari-owned television channel, was criticized for downplaying the first protests.[673] I think, downplaying the first protests in Syria was due to the great relationship between Syria and Qatar before the uprising, so Qatar had no interest in regime change in Syria. However, when Bashar

[672] Kristian Coates Ulrichsen, "Qatar and the Arab Spring", Open Democracy, 12 April 2011, viewed on 12 March 2014. http://www.opendemocracy.net/kristian-coates-ulrichsen/qatar-and-arab-spring.

[673] Roula Khalaf and Abigail Fielding-Smith, "How Qatar seized control of the SyrianRevolution"FTMagazine,17May2013.http://www.ft.com/cms/s/2/f2d9bbc8-bdbc-11e2–890a-00144feab7de. html#axzz 37P57n5Np, viewed on 11 March 2014.

Assad was determined to use violence against the people, Qatar's position changed dramatically and decided to side and back the uprising in all forms: diplomatic, media, humanitarian, financial and military, so Doha is considered to be the main Arab capital for meetings of Syrian opposition parties.[674] Moreover, Qatar was the only country in the world to open the Syrian Arab Republic embassy representing the opposition and not the Assad regime. Qatar also exerted extremely strong efforts to offer Syria's seat in the Arab League to the opposition.[675] On the ground, Qatari tried to identify the armed groups in the opposition that should be supported, so various groups have enjoyed Qatari support, but others were ignored, and, hence, diminished. In sum, the Qatari position toward the Syrian Revolution can be considered as advanced politically, but cooperative with the US and in line with its strategy militarily. This inconsistency between the political and military involvement of Qatar has always posed a big question mark. But the statement of Hamed Bin Jasim, the former prime minister, about Qatari involvement can be interpreted that their effort was to infiltrated the arm groups and the opposition in order to empower and support the right people who accept Military Operations Center's agenda and liquidate those who does not.[676]

Jordan

Jordan is part of the so-called historical Greater Syria (*Bilad Asham*), so the bonds between Syria and Jordan are dense. Moreover, many tribes are divided in between Daraa and Jordan, so the early events in Daraa had its public impact on the people in Jordan, but on the formal level Jordan was in a double dilemma

[674] Khalid Haroub, "Qatar and the Arab Spring - Conflict & Intl. Politics", Heinrich Boll Stifung, 3 March 2014, viewed on 11 March 2014. http://lb.boell.org/en/2014/03/03/qatar-and-arab-spring-conflict-intl-politics.

[675] "The Syrian Opposition occupies Syria's Seat in the Arab League", NOW, 26March 2013. https://now.mmedia.me/lb/ar/gulf/, viewed on 20 July 2014.

[676] Charlie Rose, Interview with Sheikh Hamad bin Jassim bin Jaber al-Thani, the former prime minister of Qatar, 12 June 2017. https://charlierose.com/videos/30589.

when it came to the Arab Spring and in particular the Syrian uprisings. It is a dictatorship vulnerable to public movement, and has relatively strong Islamic opposition. Therefore, Jordan did not welcome the Syrian uprising, and tried to contain it, and tame the opposition in accordance with its interests. I disagree with Khalid Mahmoud when saying that Jordan until mid-2012 wanted the Assad regime to stay, and would prefer it to Islamic rule in Syria.[677] In fact, that is not the core stance for Jordan before and after 2012. Jordan never supported the uprising, but manipulated it in every possible way, including the humanitarian aids.[678] A democratic rule in Damascus would shift the balance toward the Islamic opposition in Jordan. Yet, the growing influence of ISIS and its twins in Syria and Iraq, undoubtedly, is a great threat to the very survival of the regime in the country. Jordan tried to play a balanced role, reflecting developments on the ground. While Jordan decided to admit thousands of Syrian refugees and train some armed groups in the opposition, mainly non-Islamic,[679] in preparation for the situation if the Assad regime collapsed, it still preserves its diplomatic relationship with Syria, and still opposes any control of the borders between the two countries by the Free Syrian Army. This balanced position reflects the great fears of Jordan from the implications of backing the losing party in the Syrian conflict.[680]

The European Union

Most of the European Union countries have denounced violence in Syria from the outset and have announced sanctions against the

[677] Khalid Mahmoud, "where Jordan Stands from the Crisis in Syria", Aljazeera, 19 September 2013, viewed on 18 July 2014. http://www.aljazeera.net/knowledgegate/opinions/2013/9/10/.

[678] Jordan use to deduct a share from all aids coming to the Syrian refugees in Jordan up to 40%

[679] Jordan allowing training Syrian opposition to deter the Salfis, ElKashif News, 10 March 2013. http://elkashif.net/site/news/2092, viewed 20 July 2014.

[680] Shafiq Shuqair, "Jordan's position on the Syrian crisis: ambiguity or contradiction?", Aljazeera Centre for Studies, 10 February 2014, viewed on 20 July 2014. http://studies.aljazeera.net/reports/2014/02/201421010290736845.htm.

Syrian regime; they are a great part of the friends of Syria group. Their activities revolve primarily around humanitarian aid. But, the European Union imposed an arms embargo on the Free Syrian Army, causing a huge impact on the Free Syrian Army's capability to semi-balance the Syrian regime's capability, and hence defend the civilians in Syria. The embargo was eventually lifted in August 2013.[681] However, lifting the embargo did not allow the Free Syrian Army to get arms freely from the European market. In the words of Captain Adham, an officer in the Free Syrian Army, "The Europeans lifted the embargo, but they do not allow us to get the arms that we need. We cannot access the market."[682] Brigadier General Salim Idris, the former head of the Supreme Military Command (SMC), has pledged to overthrow the Syrian regime within six months if the needed weapons were secured.[683]

Scrutinizing the Saudi, Qatari, and Turkish Support

With the beginning of 2012, the Assad regime started losing its control over Eastern Ghouta in Damascus. Some vital military bases and Damascus International Airport fell in the hands of local independent Free Syrian Army groups. At this very critical point, Qatar and Saudi Arabia started to approach some armed groups in the name of supporting the revolution against Assad. They established and sponsored some armed groups financially and militarily. The aim was evident which was to penetrate, control, and direct those armed groups in accordance with the Military Operation Centers' agenda. Some groups have accepted such support, but they lost their autonomy and the decision making. The supported groups fought the regime on many fronts

[681] European Union to lift arms embargo on Syrian opposition, FoxNews, 28 May 2013, viewed on 20 July 2014.

[682] Interview with the over Skype on 20 September 2013.

[683] "The Free Syrian Army Pledge to Overthrow the Syrian Regime if Weapons were Secured", Al-Arabiya, 15 June 2013, viewed on 22 September 2013. http://www.alarabiya.net/ar/arab-and-world/syria/2013/06/15.

and for few years, but they never posed a real threat to its survival nor to any vital military base in the area. Meanwhile, the adamant groups who refused such support and declined to exchange the support for their autonomy have disappeared gradually as they could not sustain. As a result, the regime regained its control on the area slowly and gradually, and eventually forcing those groups out towards Idlib in February 2018. For instance, Damascus International Airport went out of Assad's control in November 2012 by the hands of the early genuine resilient revolutionaries, but the airport was regained by the Assad's forces in 2015 at a time when the Saudi and Qatari supported groups such as Jaish Al-Islam and Failaq Al-Rahman were dominating the area. Turkey has played the very same role in north Syria enabling the Assad regime to regain vast territories, villages, towns from the Free Syrian Army. The same tactics and same outcome have been applied and reached all over the country which eventually led to the retreat of the revolution, and thus, the remaining of Bashar Assad. The Syrian people were cheated and stabbed in the back by those countries.

The Coast region and the Western Ghouta in Damascus have never been out of Assad's military control, so there was no needs for such Saudi, Qatari, and Turkish involvement. The Western Ghouta is surrounded by many military bases in Al Moadamyeh mountains and by the adjacent Mazeh military airport. However, the excessive Assad's brutality there was to bring about a massive destruction and eventually to force people out of their land in order to pave the way for a demographic change in Damascus and in the country as a whole. Meanwhile, the Coast region is dominated by the regime's social base and its overlapping interests and influence.

Friends of the Syrian Regime

Many states such as Russia, Iran and Iraq have provided the Syrian regime with different kinds of support: diplomatic, political, military, logistic and financial, making the regime more able to sustain and survive.

Russia

Russia has adopted a very hardline policy toward the Syrian Revolution since day one, and embraced the regime's discourse. Like China, Russia also vetoed many resolutions condemning the Syrian regime's behavior. Moreover, Russia is still supporting the Syrian regime politically and militarily. I think this hardline policy, which has led to huge numbers of civilian casualties in Syria and created a humanitarian crisis in the region, has no strong foundation in Russia's national interests, leading many observers to question the authenticity of Russia's position. Nikolay Khuzanv, from St. Petersburg State University, stated, "I have no explanation for this strong Russian position supporting Assad's regime."[684] However, al-Nufaisi believes that Russia is different from the USSR. While the USSR policy used to support popular movements and popular interests around the world, Russia's behavior reflects its national interests only, so there is little to no difference between Russia and the United States. Both of them act according to their national interests.[685] Roy Allison tried to figure out those interests to help understand Russian support for the Syrian regime. He argues that material interests,[686] geopolitics and political order in the Middle East, the Islamic threat, and Russian anxieties about regime change by foreign powers, can provide a sustainable explanation to the Russian position.[687]

The Syrian–Russian relationship in the past few years (post 2005), have been good, but not so good as to explain the present Russian hardline position. Unlike the USSR during the Cold War, Russia is not a traditional ally of Syria. In fact, Russia now has a much better relationship with Israel than with Syria, and is more pro-Israel than pro-Arab. During his visit to Israel in June 2012,

[684] Nikolay Khuzanov, "Russian Support of Assad's Regime: Driving Factors of Bilateral Cooperation and its Limits", a paper was presented at the Center of Syrian Studies in St. Andrews, Scotland 12–19 June 2013.

[685] In Sum, television program, Russia Today RT, 28 March 2014.

[686] Material interests such as keeping the base in Tartus, the weapons deals between the two countries, and the Russian oil companies deals in Syria.

[687] Roy Allison, "Russia and Syria: explaining alignment with a regime in crisis", International Affairs, Vol. 89, No. 4 (July 2013), pp.795–823.

Putin visited the Kotel and stated: "Here, we see how the Jewish past is etched into the stones of Jerusalem."[688] Moreover, the Israeli lobby has a big influence in Russian business as well as in Russian politics.[689] Russia is supporting the regime in Syria against the Free Syrian Army and the Jihadists, but not against the Israeli threat or not to defend the regime against the increasing Israeli offensive attacks on Syrian soil. The S300 missile deal between Russia and Syria was suspended due to Israeli concerns,[690] and Russia only displayed concern, but not support, when Israel launched a series of devastating missile attacks on Damascus on 3 May 2013. Lavrov, the Russian foreign minister, declared his opposition for a Sunni State in Syria,[691] sharing this with the US, Israel and the West in general. In Katz words: "If an Islamic fundamentalist regime does replace Assad's, American, Israeli, and Russian interests will all suffer."[692] Supporting the Assad regime against the revolutionaries and the Jihadists means that Russia and Syria are facing common enemies: public revolt and the Islamists, and ironically, their defeat is also wanted by the US and its allies. Here we can recall Katz again when saying that the US needs a strong relationship between Russia and Syria in order to protect it from the Islamists.[693]

In September 2015, Russia decided to involve militarily, launching direct airstrikes on the opposition and ISIS under the pretext of fighting terrorism. In fact, Russian involvement was to

---

[688] "Arab Rage: Putin Recognized Jerusalem's Jewish Past", Arutz Sheva, 28 June 2012, viewed on 20 July 2014. http://www.israelnationalnews.com/News/News.aspx/157332#.U884SYBdUVh.

[689] Faisal al-Kasim, "The Israeli Russia", Bawabat Al-Sharq, 22 September 2013, http://www.al-sharq.com/Detail/articles/82/, viewed 23 September 2013.

[690] "Russia suspends Syria S-300 missile deliveries", NOW, 4 September 2014, https://now.mmedia.me/lb/en/nowsyrialatestnews/russia-suspends-syria-s-300-missile-deliveries, viewed on 19 July 2014.

[691] TRENDJLoiiiJI2 Lavrov's comments warning of a Sunni rule in Syria Posted on 25 March 2012, https://www.youtube.com/watch?v=3LTxmdifjCA.

[692] Mark Katz, "Putin's Foreign Policy Towards Syria", 2006, Mason Archival Repository Service, https://hdl.handle.net/1920/3024.

[693] Mark Katz, "Mideast Watch: A Russian-Syrian Alliance?" 5 September 2005, http://www.upi.com/Business_News/Security-Industry/2005/09/05/Mideast-Watch-A-Russian-Syrian-Alliance/UPI-79891125934110/#ixzz2Kr496nM0, viewed 13 April 2013.

back up the Syrian regime's military assaults on the armed groups and their social base in the areas outside the regime control. The aim was to eliminate all the obstacles that prevent the regime's advances in the country through a shock and awe strategy against the regime's enemies, so its strikes were indiscriminate and very effective. Ironically, the United Arab Emirates (Friends of Syria member) have funded the cost of the Russian operations in Syria since 2015 according to many different resources.

Russia, in addition, took control of negotiating with the armed group to give up their arms and surrender or to move to Idlib. The regime, with the help of the Russian strikes, was able to recapture large areas that Assad lost for years. However, the Russian direct heavy involvement has marginalized Bashar Assad's role and his regime in the war in Syria, so if Bashar Assad was killed, I think the Russians would protect the regime from collapsing. Hundreds to thousands of civilians were killed from Russian attacks including children, and many civilian institutions such as schools and hospitals were destroyed.

Finally, the Russian hardline policy and its brutality against the Syrian people have provoked Muslims around the world. Mevlut Altintas, a Turkish off-duty police officer, has shot dead the Russian Ambassador to Turkey Andrei Karlov in Ankara in December 2016. However, such dangerous and critical development was somehow downplayed in comparison to the killing of the American ambassador to Libya John Stevens in September 2012 by some Jihadist groups.

China

China vetoed many Security Council resolutions condemning the Syrian regime's behavior against its people. China is not a strong ally of the Syrian regime, but it does stress the importance of sovereignty. China did not support, but rather abstained from UN Security Council Resolution 1973 that gave the way for a military intervention in Libya in 2011. Moreover, non-democratic and oppressive regimes, such as that of China, would not support any public uprising in any event. Recently, China did not denounce the Russian intervention in Ukraine. In fact, its stance is more inclined toward the aggressor, Russia.

Iran

Iran has adopted a discourse strategy demonizing the Syrian Revolution and stating that it is part of a Western, Zionist and imperialist conspiracy designed to destroy the Axis of Resistance in the region.[694] It has provided the Syrian regime with every financial, economic, logistic and military aid possible.

Captain Abd al-Nasser Shmer, a defecting officer, and later the leader of the Al-Rahman Legion which captured 48 Iranians in 2012 stated: "Iran is sending revolutionary guards, specialists in cyber technology and expert snipers to Syria to train the regime forces. Most of them have their own motivations for helping the Syrian regime."[695] He refuted the official Iranian and Syrian claim describing the Iranian captives as pilgrims. Captain Shmer argued, "How can someone going on a pilgrimage not to have enough money to cover his expenses for one day in Syria?"[696] However, a deal was struck by Qatar to release them.

Iran's behavior since day one of the revolution has been based on a realist point of view. It does perceive the revolution in Syria as a threat to its survival as a regional power in the Middle East. The collapse of the Syrian regime would be a major setback for its regional ambitions. Iran is using and manipulating every possible element in this struggle: identity, ideology and material support. It has mobilized its proxies and loyalists in Syria and in the region as a whole. Shia villages in Idlib and Aleppo such as Fou'a and Kafrayya have been provided with a wide range of support from Iran to fight their Sunni neighbors and fellow citizens,[697] who in turn are engaged in the fight against the regime in Syria. However, Shia–Sunni neighbors had never been at odds prior to the revolution. Playing on the long-lasting historical disputes between

[694] Robin Pomeroy, "Iran sees ally Syria surrounded by U.S., Arab 'wolves'", Reuters, 15 August, 2011. http://in.reuters.com/article/2011/08/15/idINIndia58790020110815?feedType=RSS&feedName=everything&virtualBrandChannel=11709, viewed on 22 July 22, 14.

[695] Interview with the author over Skype on 20 February 2013.

[696] Ibid.

[697] Who Killed Al-Husain? Documentary, television program, Orient, 5 April 2013.

the Shia and Sunni doctrines, Iran mobilized all its loyalists. This strategy was not confined to Syria; in fact, Iran has mobilized great numbers of loyal Shias in Lebanon, Iraq, Bahrain, Yemen, Pakistan and Afghanistan in order to protect the holy shrines in Syria.[698] I think for Iran, its survival as a regional power is greater than any shrine. Many claims have accused Iran to be behind the al-Askari Shrine bombing in Iraq in 2006. It was an act that erupted a vicious sectarian war in the country.

Many fighters in the opposition believe that their struggle is with Iran, and not with Bashar Assad. They believe that Bashar Assad is not more than a picture, and that Iran has the upper hand in the country.[699] However, the Russian military intervention has undermined the Iranian influence in some areas to some extent.

While sparing no effort to preserve Bashar Assad, Iran is also preparing for the post-Assad situation in Syria and in the region. According to an academic study by Will Fulton, Joseph Holliday and Sam Wyer in the Institute for the Study of War,

> Iranian strategy seeks first and foremost to preserve the Assad regime for as long as possible. Iran's hedging strategy aims to ensure, however, that it can continue to pursue its vital interests if and when the regime collapses, using parts of Syria as a base as long as the Syrian opposition fails to establish full control over all of Syrian territory.[700]

Iraq

The relationship between Syria and Iraq has also been totally reversed, but in the opposite way to Syria's relations with Turkey and Qatar. Syria and Iraq became allies after having been bitter enemies

[698] Some Shias fighters have been captured possessing Iranian passports, addressed Passport to Paradise http://www.youtube.com/watch?v=mrQW3IBlojY.

[699] Al Arabia, Riyad Hijab: Syria is occupied by Iran and run by Sulimani, Posted on 14 February 2013, https://www.youtube.com/watch?v=MfRkVx9x5QE.

[700] Will Fulton, Joseph Holliday, and Sam Wyer, "Iranian Strategy in Syria", The Institute for the Study of War, Washington DC, May 2013, viewed 10 October 2013. http://www.understandingwar.org/sites/default/files/IranianStrategyinSyria-1MAY.pdf.

for years. Iraq has supported the mission of some Iraqi Shia militias to fight alongside Syrian regime forces all over the country, especially in the suburbs of Damascus. More than 15,000 fighters representing almost 14 Shia factions from Iraq are said to be operating in Syria.[701] These fighters claim to have been deployed to protect Set Zaynab, a shrine in the south of Damascus, from the *Takfiris*.

The dramatic switch in the relationship between Iraq and Syria can be attributed to many factors: 1) The sectarian element, the Iraqi prime ministers and Assad belong to the Shia sect framework;[702] 2) The Iranian influence over the Iraqi government, pressuring it to support the Syrian regime; 3) Both regimes are non-democratic and hence oppose popular movements; 4) The global Jihadists are a great threat for both regimes; the Islamic State (ISIS) operated in both countries, and gained control over large territories in Syria and Iraq.

States and Sub-state Actors Decided to Show Formal Neutrality

Some regional states decided formally to distance themselves from the struggle in Syria for domestic concerns, such as Lebanon, or for regional and international consideration, such as Israel. Similarly, sub-state actors such as Hamas decided to distance themselves from the struggle in Syria for their own future.

Israel

Although Israel shows neutrality and non-involvement in the conflict in Syria, it is one of the countries most concerned by the situation in Syria, and its national interests support one of the conflicting parties to win the war in Syria. Zisser claims:

> Upon the outbreak of unrest in Syria in March 2011, many Israeli principals and academics made no secret of their fear that the downfall of Bashar Assad's regime would undermine

[701] In Depth, television program, Aljazeera, 2 June 2014.

[702] A Lebanese Shia cleric Mousa al-Sader who considers Alawis part of the Shia sect.

> the stability along the Israeli–Syrian border and perhaps in the entire region.[703]

Although Syria and Israel are still formally at war, destabilizing Syria created three primary concerns in Israel, the most immediate being the infiltration of Jihadists or Free Syrian Army forces across the Syrian–Israeli border. This has resulted in Israel building an electronic wall along its borders with Syria, equipped with very sophisticated devices able to detect any movement.[704] Another concern is the stock of chemical weapons which the regime in Syria has been holding and developing for decades in an attempt to maintain a balance of power with Israel, so chaos and disorder in Syria would make chemical weapons in the country very accessible to the Jihadists and some other enemies of Israel. Finally, Israel was also concerned about the increasing cooperation between the regime in Syria and Hezbollah in Lebanon. Israel claims the regime has shipped heavy military weapons and missiles to Hezbollah during the crisis.

Israel has launched many direct attacks against Syria during the uprising and is to this day. One of the largest attack was on 3 May 2013, when Damascus came under direct Israeli missile bombardment. The aim of this attacks is still unclear. However, Israel continues to claim that it will never allow Syria to ship dangerous missiles to Hezbollah or the existence of the Iranian Revolutionary Guards in Syria. The implications of attacking an organization such as Hezbollah are far less serious on the regional and international level than attacking a sovereign state. In other words, Syria is a sovereign independent country, while Hezbollah is a proxy militia and considered by many as a terrorist group. Therefore, I think the Israeli attacks on Syria to prevent it from shipping missiles to Hezbollah is not a persuasive reason, because

---

[703] Eyal Zisser, "Threats and Opportunities for Israel" Academia.edu, unknown date, viewed on 13 July 2013. http://www.academia.edu/3112352/The_Crisis_in_Syria_Threats_and_Opportunities_for_Israel.

[704] "Israel Build the most sophisticated wall in the world on the border with Syria", Al-Arabiya, 4 February, 2013, http://www.alarabiya.net/articles/2013/02/04/264314.html, viewed on 20 July 2014.

attacking these missiles in Hezbollah territory is less defiant to United Nations' rules.

Since the beginning of the revolution, the leadership in Syria had balanced between the external threat (Israel) and the internal threats (uprising). They decided to align with Israel implicitly in order to face internal threats. Syria has withdrawn the majority of those of her forces that, since 1974, had been stationed on the Israeli border, and deployed them inside the country to fight the revolutionaries, putting the national security of Syria under imminent threat from Israel.[705] Realism is no longer prevailing as the doctrine, dictating the relationship between Syria and Israel despite frequent Israeli attacks on Syria. In fact, I think, since Jihadists gained a stronghold in Syria, collective security against Jihadists and the war on terrorism would constitute the heart of the relationship between them. Many Israeli principles have expressed their concern over the replacement of current regimes in the region by Islamic elements.[706] On the contrary, the Syrian demand for S300 missiles from Russia to deter future Israeli attacks vindicates realism and makes it the persistent doctrine that rules the relationship between Israel and Syria.

In general, there are three approaches to the management of the Syrian conflict prevailing in Israel: the first approach is the downfall of Bashar Assad; a development that would undermine Iranian influence in the region and ensure the demise of Hezbollah, and eventually bring about the end of the so-called Resistance Axis. The second approach prefers that Bashar Assad remain in power. The collapse of the Syrian regime would create a vacuum that could only be filled by Islamists. Noam Chomsky explains the Israeli approach:

> Israel could mobilize considerable forces in the Golan Heights. If they mobilize forces in the north, the Syrians

[705] "The Syrian Army withdraw its soldiers from the borders with Israel", 8 April 2013, PalPress, viewed on 22 July 2014. http://www.palpress.co.uk/arabic/?Action=Details&ID=81637

[706] Saleh al-Na'my, "Israel and the Scarecrow of Islamists in aftermath of the Arab Revolutions", unknown date, http://www.naamy.net/view.php?id=1145, viewed on 23 August 2014.

> would be compelled to respond by mobilizing their own forces. But they are not doing it, which can only mean that they do not want the regime to fall.[707]

The third approach prefers that the conflict in Syria continue for as long as possible. This scenario would render Syria a very weak state, were it to survive division and partition. According to Amos Harel, Israel can stand to gain from Syria's civil war, as long as it avoids interfering. The emerging situation in Syria now (long war) is in their favor. Syria at this stage is not a bleak image from their perspective.[708] I think the Israeli leaders want a weak Bashar Assad in the face of Israel, but very strong in the face of the Islamists, and particularly the Jihadists. In other words the Islamist fear drives Israel to support Assad's survival.[709] But also Israel wants Bashar Assad without the Iranian Revolutionary Guards after they have been used to rescue the Assad regime from the revolutionaries and the Islamists. A study by the Arab Center for Research and Policy Studies concluded its evaluation of the Israeli position toward the events in Syria by saying:

> As regards the Golan, Israel is very comfortable with the current Syrian regime, and there is a fear in the Hebrew state that a new leadership would lead to the end of the calm on this front. Any new regime in Syria will take a stance that is hostile to Israel because it will be in need of domestic legitimacy. On the other hand, the current regime (if it remains) will be in need of external legitimacy and would have to relax its position toward Israel.[710]

---

[707] Noam Chomsky, "Sykes–Picot is falling", Al Akhbar, Beirut, 16 June 2013, viewed 19 June 2013. http://english.al-akhbar.com/node/16132

[708] Amos Harel, "Israel can Stand to Gain from Syria's Civil War, as Long as it Avoids Interfering", Haaretz, 29 May 2013, viewed on 15 June 2013. http://www.haaretz.com/news/diplomacy-defense/israel-can-stand-to-gain-from-syria-s-civil-war-as-long-as-it-avoids-interfering.premium-1.526512.

[709] Sheera Frenkel and Roger Boyes, Islamist fear drives Israel to support Assad survival, The Times Middle East, 17 May 2013, viewed on 30 July 2014. http://www.thetimes.co.uk/tto/news/world/middleeast/article3768370.ece.

[710] "The Israeli Position towards the Events in Syria", Arab Center for Research and Policy Study, Doha, 02 February 2012, viewed on 19 October 2012. http://english.dohainstitute.org/release/cbdbcfb5-d8dd-43c2–9c06–76ea0044d4e7.

Lebanon

The Syrian Crisis has seen Lebanon divided into two parties; one supporting the regime and the other the revolution. Officially, Lebanon has decided to distance itself from the events in Syria. This position was adopted in an attempt to prevent Lebanon from descending into a civil war as a result of the struggle in Syria. However, when it came to condemning the Syrian regime's behavior in the Arab and international forums, such as those set up by the Arab League and the International Assembly, Lebanon repeatedly either abstained from or objected to all suggested motions,[711] and this was due to the great influence of the pro-Syrian regime inside Lebanon. Indeed, the actual Lebanese position was under the influence of Hezbollah, the strongest element in Lebanon. The leadership of Hezbollah decided to enter the struggle and support the regime militarily, ignoring calls for distance and detachment from the Lebanese president. In the Battle of Al-Qusayr in Homs, Hezbollah involvement was crucial to the taking of the town from the Free Syrian Army. It was very difficult for Hezbollah to declare its involvement, but its leadership preferred survival to maintaining the legitimacy of its existence. Legitimacy was derived from defending Lebanon against Israel, and survival would be through supporting the Syrian regime. Hezbollah tried to gain legitimacy for its involvement by adopting the regime's discourse about a new American, Israeli and *Takfiri* conspiracy against Syria and Palestine. In fact, the decision to become involved was very difficult. If the revolutionaries were to win the struggle, it would mean Hezbollah's termination. There is a logic behind Hezbollah's involvement.[712]

The overt involvement of Hezbollah in Syria is a sign of three developments in the struggle. Firstly, there is the weakness of the Syrian regime, as the regime had to rely on foreign allies and proxies in the war against its own people and international Jihadists elements. Secondly, the Syrian National Army had become exhausted as a result of the non-stop defections and the

[711] Al- Arabia, Riyad Hijab: Syria is occupied by Iran and run by Sulimani, Posted on 14 February 2013, https://www.youtube.com/watch?v=MfRkVx9x5QE.

[712] Chomsky, op, cit.

continuous struggle. And thirdly, the struggle in Syria was becoming particularly divisive, so ideological fighters were more reliable and more steadfast at this stage.

Hamas

Hamas tried to distance itself from the struggle in Syria, calling for both parties to arrive at a peaceful reconciliation. The regime in Syria did not accept this stance, coming as it was from a movement that has been receiving Assad's support and protection for years. The strong relationship between Hamas and Qatar played a destructive role in the relationship between Hamas and the regime in Syria. Eventually, Hamas left the country.[713] The deteriorating relationship with Hamas has turned out to be a substantial blow to the Axis of Resistance, as Hamas, along with Hezbollah, constitutes its head. Such a development can be considered one of the most important changes in the international politics of Syria after 2011. The regime now is seeking an international legitimacy, so abandoning such movements would help its aim. On the other hand, this development was damaging to the Syrian regime's image, a regime that always relied on the Axis of Resistance for domestic and regional legitimacy. However, the legitimacy of the resistance of the regime was somewhat restored after the direct Israeli strikes against Syria. The regime was successful in polarizing the support of nationalist, socialists, Nasserists and Marxist parties in the Arab world against Israeli attacks. Such support has boosted the regime's confidence.

After 2020, Hamas showed a big interest to resume its relationship with Assad through Iran mediation, but the regime is not responding positively.

The Role of the Arab League

The Arab League introduced a political initiative to stop the bloodshed in Syria and sent a convoy of inspectors to monitor the situation on the ground in January 2012. However, the Arab

[713] "Tension with the Syrian Authorities: Hamas left Damascus", 21 December 2011, http://www.arabs48.com/?mod=articles&ID=87766, viewed on 22 July 2014.

League was incapable of achieving any kind of solution in Syria. Mr. Anwar Malik, one of the Arab inspectors, attributed the failure of the initiative to the lack of genuine interest: "The League did not organize our mission properly, our drivers were from Syria, probably from the security services, and our cars were brought from Iraq. We did not have proper equipment such as pens, paper and bags, so we had to rely on the Syrian regime."[714] Most Syrian people were expecting the League to play a role similar to that it took on in Libya in 2011, or in Lebanon in 1984, when Arab forces intervened in the country during the civil war.

The United Nations

Many resolutions have been adopted by the UN Security Council regarding the situation in Syria. Those resolutions tried to address the humanitarian aids, the violence, the use of chemical weapons and ceasefire. However, none of the adopted resolutions hold Assad responsible for the violence in Syria and denounce his war crimes against civilians. Here are some of the most important resolutions:

Resolution 2118, 27 September 2013. Adopted after the chemical weapons attack on Ghouta, east Damascus, in August 2013, and constituting the framework for elimination of Syrian chemical weapons. This resolution came after the US failed to punish Assad for using chemical weapons on civilians in an obvious breach of Obama's red line on Assad. This resolution was no more than a farce, so instead of punishing the perpetrator and the criminal it has been decided to take away and withdraw his criminal means. Moreover, this resolution proved to be ineffective after the Assad regime used the chemical weapons again on civilians in Duma in April 2018.

Resolution 2254, 18 December 2015. This resolution has stressed the unity of Syria, and called for ceasefire in the country to protect civilians, and support a political solution in the country, encouraging negotiations between the two parties in order to reach a political transition in the country though an election supervised by the UN. This resolution was

[714] Interview with the author over Skype on 24 July 2013.

a good step to end the conflict and the bloodshed in the country, but it was born dead due to the recent direct military intervention for Russia to support the regime and to crush the armed oppositions.

Needless to say, a UN Security Council resolution would mean nothing if there is no willingness from the great powers, particularly the US, to implement it. For instance, resolutions 242, 338 had been taken against Israel for decades but never implemented.

MILITARY OPERATION CENTERS

The United States embarked on forming two military operations centers (or rooms) in Turkey and in Jordan in order to identify and control the armed opposition groups. Those centers included Jordan, Turkey, Saudi Arabia, Emirates, France and Britain. Their aims were to prevent any kind of threat to Israeli borders by the armed groups, prevent the armed groups from approaching the Druze area in the south and the Alawi areas in the coast, controlling the battles with Assad' regime in terms of place and time and weapons used, and finally, fight terrorism and namely ISIS. Ironically, Assad's regime shares most of these aims and protecting his Alawi social base was the secret factor for its survival.

THE CHEMICAL ATTACK CATASTROPHE

The chemical attack issue touched this book directly. On 21 August 2013, at 2:30am (Damascus time) I was Skyping with Bassam, a Free Syrian Army fighter, stationed on the Jobar–Zamalka Front in the east of Damascus. Shortly after beginning the conversation, Bassam said that he wanted to terminate the conversation immediately, explaining: "I have to go, there is a warning announcement on the walkie-talkie saying that we are under chemical attack from the regime."[715] The attacks have targeted many areas; Zamalka and Ein Tarma in east Damascus, and Al Moadamyeh in west Damascus. However, the attack on Zamalka was the strongest and has caused excessive and dreadful causalities. Almost 1,400 people died immediately, most of them

[715] Interview with the author over Skype on 21 August 2013.

children. The chemical attack was followed by heavy airstrikes from the Assad's forcers in order to inflect more harm and more suffering on the people. The tragedy has created an overwhelming chaos and mayhem. People were rushing into the streets screaming, crying, and praying. The already ill-equipped medical centres were awfully flooded with victims and casualties, and the dedicated medics were overwhelmed and exhausted. Dr. Karim stated that no one can cope with such dismal situation.[716] It was like the Judgment Day as someone has described it. Families were separated and many children got lost in the streets and in the medical centers after the collapse or the death of their parents. Some people including children were buried alive thought to be dead. Dozens of families have been vanished and wiped out entirely. Scholar Rashad Chams was killed inside his house along with his pregnant wife and all of his children.

The regime initially denied the incident and accused the armed opposition of fabrications.[717] However, Buthaina Sha'ban afterward accused the armed opposition of kidnapping children from Latakia villages (Alawis) and gassing them in Ghouta.[718] The international condemnation of the regime following this event was so strong that even the United States was perceived to be prepared for military action against the Syrian regime. However, the United States changed its stance and ruled out the military option when the Syrian regime decided to give up its chemical weapons, an initiative that was accepted by Russia. Giving up the chemical weapons also benefited Israeli security. The Security Council adopted this initiative on 27 September 2013 under resolution 2118, and stressed the need for a political solution in Syria based on the Geneva Communiqué of 30 June 2012.[719] The international community dealt with the chemical weapons catastrophe from a very realist point of view, and

---

[716] Interview with Dr Karim on Skype 25/08/2013.

[717] SYRPRESS's channel, the Minister of Information denies incident of Chemical Weapons in Al-Ghouta. Posted on 21 August 2013, https://www.youtube.com/watch?v=nINsa7sIxAQ

[718] Saleh Ali, Buthaina Sha'ban impugns America. Posted on 03 September 2013, https://www.youtube.com/watch?v=3o0B3cesDyE

[719] Geneva Communiqué 30.06.2012 can be found on this link: http://www.un.org/News/dh/infocus/Syria/FinalCommuniqueActionGroupforSyria.pdd. It was suggested to constituted the base for Geneva 2 Conference, which took place

in the interest of Israeli security, but was not motivated by ethical or moral responsibility. The use of chemical weapons could have been exploited by the international community and made to form the basis for punitive military intervention based on the responsibility to protect. Antony Lang argues, a "punitive military strike combines moral, legal, and even strategic logics in a way that might contribute to a resolution of the current crisis and reinforce norms concerning prohibited weapons and the protection of civilians."[720]

The British government had some plot to play in this matter as the British Parliament voted for no military action against Assad, which paved the way for President Obama to find a pretext to thwart the US military plan, if it ever existed. A British Labour government in 2003 was able to win the Parliament vote to invade Iraq, but ironically, a conservative British government was not able to win the Parliament vote to attack the Syrian regime for using chemical weapons against its own people.

That was not the first or the last time that Assad attacked the Syrian people with chemical weapons.[721] According to a study by Schneider and Lutkefend from GPPI:

> Our research found that there have been at least 336 chemical weapons attacks over the course of the Syrian civil war—significantly more than has commonly been known. Around 98 percent of these attacks can be attributed to the Assad regime, with the Islamic State group responsible for the rest. Approximately 90 percent of all confirmed attacks occurred after the infamous 'red line' incident of August 2013.[722]

22–24 January 2014, but the conference failed to reach a political solution between the regime and the political opposition.

[720] Antony Lang, " Syria: The Case for Punitive Intervention", Carnegie Council, 30 August 2013, viewed on 23 July 2014. http://www.carnegiecouncil.org/publications/articles_papers_reports/0169.html.

[721] For more information see the report made by the Arm Control Association showing the timeline of Syrian Chemical Weapons activity from 2012–2022. https://www.armscontrol.org/factsheets/Timeline-of-Syrian-Chemical-Weapons-Activity.

[722] T.Schneider&T. Lutrkefend, "Nowhere to Hide: The Logic of Chemical Weapons Use in Syria", 17 February 2019.https://gppi.net/2019/02/17/the-logic-of-chemical-weapons-use-in-syria.

Here are some of images for child victims of the chemical attack in Zamalka, August 2013.[723]

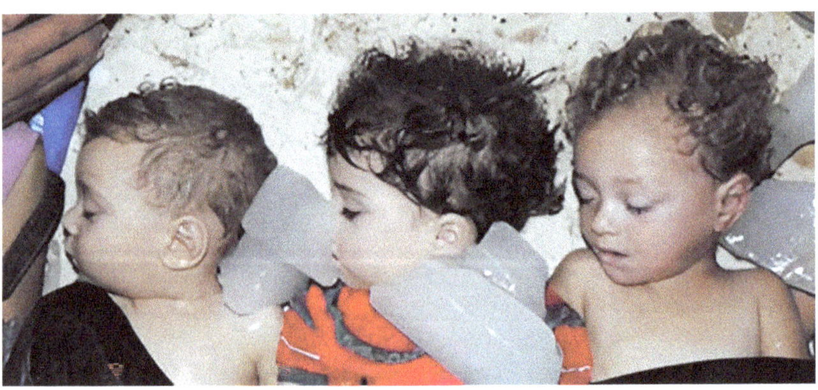

[723] More media materials about this chemical attack including interviews with survivors and witnesses can be found on the internet.

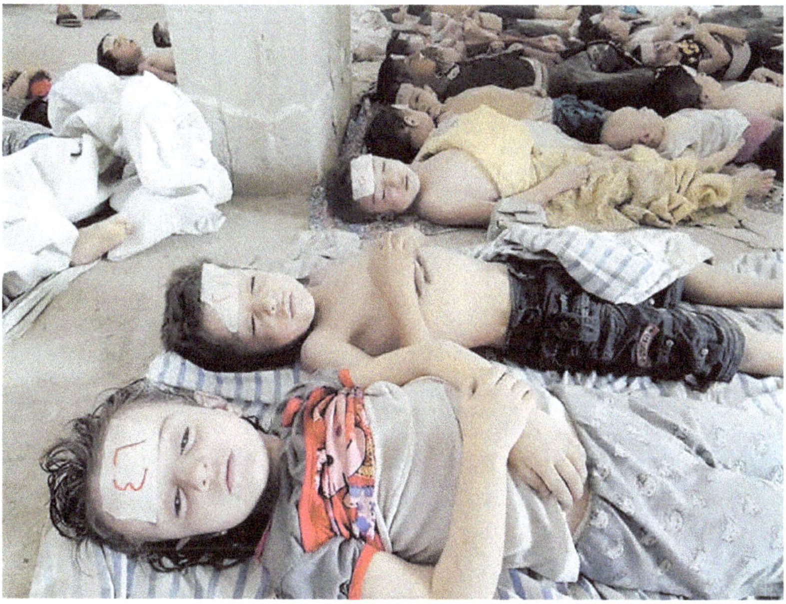

PROXY WAR

Understanding the structure of the contemporary international system is very important if one wishes to understand the real stance of the international community toward the Syrian Revolution. Ethan Kapstein and Michael Mastanduno explain, "The structure of the contemporary international system is unipolar. The United States leads its competitors by a wide margin in overall military capabilities and the ability to project its forces globally."[724] It is a US-centered international system. Therefore, international engagement in any crisis or war around the world has to reflect these unipolar politics. After the end of the Cold War, such politics were reflected in many cases, for example in Yugoslavia and Iraq. The international stance toward the Syrian Revolution portrayed the international system as moving toward a bi-polar system: Russia against the United States. However, this portrayal is debatable. Russia is not the USSR, and does not have the capability to undermine the United States' will.

The Syrian uprising, like all Arab Spring uprisings, has never enjoyed strong support from any Western state claiming support for democracy in the Arab world. When the revolution in Syria became a holy war, the regime had more legal international support for its violent campaign against the Free Syrian Army, the Jihadists, and the people, leading to the portrayal of the conflict in Syria as part of the global war on terrorism. The Islamic State and Jabhat al-Nusara were the most powerful forces operating against the regime in Syria, and are considered to be terrorist groups by the United States and the international community.

The conflict in Syria has become a proxy war indeed, but I am unable to agree with Paul Rogers' portrayal of it. He stated:

> Within months there was a strong element of a proxy war [in Syria], with Iran backing the regime and Saudi Arabia and

[724] Michael Mastanduno and Ethan Kapstein, "Realism and State Strategies After the Cold War", in *Unipoar Politics,* Michael Mastanduno and Ethan Kapstein(eds), Colombia University Press, New York, 1999, pp.1–27.

> Qatar backing the rebels, complicated further by an unusual double-proxy element; Western states backing the rebels against the regime, but Russia supporting the regime.[725]

Such a statement does reflect the widespread poor understanding of the Syrian war. The conflict in Syria is not a balanced proxy war in which each patron gives its client the same level of support. While the friends of the regime (Russia, Iran, Iraq and China) offer great support in all fields, by comparison friends of Syria have offered so little to the opposition groups in the midst of such conflict, instead stressing on a political solution to the conflict. No amount of Saudi or Qatari military support was enough to fully liberate the provinces of Idlib or Aleppo. Ahmad, a member of an Islamic brigade, reported, "The support that we get is very limited, and for more than a year now in Aleppo, we could not liberate the whole city, and the city of Idlib is still under the regime's control."[726] Salim Idris once stated: "We cannot confront Iran and Hezbollah in 10% of our actual military needs."[727] Additionally, the American veto was on the opposition but not on the regime to get anti-aircraft weapons. Therefore, we are not in front of proxy war in principle.

Syria is not a chessboard on which the United States and Russia can compete head to head or through their proxies. Nor is it a battlefield where Saudi Arabia and Iran compete on a regional level for dominance. This is not the true nature of the struggle in Syria. The struggle in Syria after March 2011 is actually between its people, who want to regain their control over their own country, and the great world powers, who have been supporting dictators such as Assad and brutal regimes in the Middle East and other parts of the world for decades. These powers have no

[725] Paul Rogers, "War in Syria: The Proxy Elements" Oxford Research Group, 11 July 2013. http://www.oxfordresearchgroup.org.uk/publications/briefing_papers_and_reports/war_syria_proxy_element.

[726] Interview with the author over Skype 17 September 2013.

[727] "Idris: we cannot face Iran and Hezbollah in %10 of our military needs", Okaz, 26 September 2013, viewed on 22 July 2014, http://www.okaz.com.sa/new/Issues/20130926/Con20130926641603.htm

interest in seeing a real democracy in Syria and in the Arab world, and will do their utmost to abort any popular uprising in the region.

Syrians still remember the statement of Anders Rasmussen, the former NATO secretary general, when stating the reasons for the NATO intervention in Libya. He said: "Our goal is to protect civilians and civilian populated areas from attack by the Gaddafi regime."[728] However, Bashar Assad killed civilians hundred times more than what Gaddafi has done, but blind NATO did not see it, or they actually saw it but do not care. A retired colonel and analyst, Safwat al-Zayyat, divulged his views on Western unwillingness to alleviate the suffering of the Syrian people. He argues,

> NATO installed the Patriot Missiles System in south Turkey in January 2013 to protect the Turkish civilians from the attacks of the Syrian regime. NATO can extend the range of these missiles to cover North Syria, protecting the civilians, and may establish a Safe Zone, but they do not want to do it. It is very strange![729]

Finally, friends of Syria, friends of the regime and the formally neutral countries considered ISIS, and its affiliates, as the real enemy, and the real new threat for their national security, so great collective security efforts were needed to defeat them in a new battle of the war on terrorism. "Fighting terrorism is becoming a much more frequent and important topic than fighting the regime in all our meetings with so-called friends of Syria. Their real problem was always with ISIS, but never with the Syrian regime,"[730] as one member of the National Coalition, who asked to remain anonymous, disclosed. Moreover, some armed groups in the opposition have been recruited to fight ISIS and have been

---

[728] Andre Rasmussen, "NATO Security General's Statement on Libya", 27 March 2011.

[729] SanSyria, Colonial al-Zayyat divulges America Europe, and Turkey. Posted 6 April 2014, https://www.youtube.com/watch?v=sMclcfsaBjk.

[730] Interview over Skype with an anonymous member of the National Coalition.

supplied with the necessary military equipment and training courses in Jordan and Qatar.[731] Some other armed groups have been asked to fight ISIS as a precondition to provide them with arms to fight the Assad regime,[732] but after the defeat of ISIS the armed opposition groups were betrayed by the US and its allies and heavy weapons were never provided to fight Assad. Therefore, all of these incidents totally refute the notion of a poxy war in Syria, so any talks about the Syrian war as proxy war is no more than hearsay or misleading

GENEVA MEETING

A conference was held in Geneva, 30 June 2012, to support a political solution. Many countries participated in the meeting, but ironically there was no Syrian attendance neither from the regime nor from the opposition. The conferees agreed to find a solution to the war in Syria beginning with an immediate cessation of violence from both sides, and establishing a transnational governing body made up of elements from both the regime and the opposition. The future of Bashar Asad was not clear, and everyone has a different interpretation of it, so the opposition has refused its outcomes. However, huge international efforts exerted on the opposition to accept an invitation for a Geneva II meeting in January 2014. The majority of the opposition declined the invitation by voting against it, but contrary to the National Coalitions's rules the opposition decided finally to accept the invitation, after receiving assurance from many countries that Bashar Assad was leaving power.[733]

[731] A report by Vice News.

[732] Omar Salem, The west to the Free Syrian Army: fighting the Islamists for getting the weapons. Posted on 17 February 2013. https://www.youtube.com/watch?v=fchAvuhQiHg.

[733] According to the bylaws and the rules of procedure agreed upon by the opposition in Qatar, taking any decisive decision requires the approval of two-thirds of the members, so when voting on Geneva II, 44 out of 121 members withdrew, which made the meeting taking any decisive decision illegal. However, Haytham Al-Maleh, head of the legal committee, with the objection of the other committee members Hussein al-Sayyid, Marwan Hajjo and Hisham Marwa, but

However, no considerable outcomes were reached from the meeting, but led to consequence meeting till 2014 with the meeting of Geneva III.

Overall, Geneva was a failure in all aspects apart from dragging the opposition to accept a dialogue with Bashar Assad directly or indirectly after a long refusal by the opposition. I think that was the major achievement the international community wanted to reach, paving the way toward the Russian route dialogue between the regime and the opposition in Astana.

ASTANA MEETING

In the aftermath of Aleppo's fall in December 2016, Turkey called for the Syrian opposition meeting in Ankara in January 2017, putting a pressure on them to accept the Russian route talks and dialogue with Assad's regime in Astana with heavy involvement of Turkey and formal participation of Iran. The Syrian delegation team included representatives of many armed groups within the national army.

Astana had many rounds, but the core was always the de-escalation areas, between the regime and the armed opposition. Russia and Turkey played the role of guarantors for both parties on this commitment. Four zones were proposed in the de-escalation areas:

Zone 1: Parts of Idlib province, as well as parts of northeastern Latakia province, western areas of Aleppo province and northern areas of Hama province.

Zone 2: Eastern Ghouta, in the Damascus countryside.

with the support and endorsement of the Muslim Brotherhood, Imad Al-Rasheed and Ahmad Al-Jarba blocs, he permitted voting by two-thirds of the attendees instead of two-thirds of the members in order to make the decision to go to Geneva II to pass. It was clear fraud and rigging. For more information see this interview with Wasel Chamali on Aljazeera https://www.youtube.com/watch?v=LQVmMtBLSoI.

Zone 3: The Rastan and Talbiseh in northern Homs province.

Zone 4: The rebel-controlled south along the border with Jordan that includes parts of Daraa and Al Qunaitra provinces.

While Turkey were involved in direct military presence in some points in these areas to secure the opposition commitments to halt fighting against the Assad regime, Russia supported Assad's recapture of most of theses zones. Turkey, in fact, fooled and failed the opposition, and Astana was a great achievement for Russia and Assad and a big setback for the armed opposition in terms of losing lands and losing arms. In fact, the opposition was not able to make any achievement, not even getting one of their captives of the Assad regime released.

The SYRIAN REFUGEE CRISIS

I think the United States and the international community has apparently listened to the Israeli advice that Assad must stay, and the Syrian people who revolted against him must leave their country. As a result, millions of Syrian people have left their county in all directions, fleeing Assad's brutality. Emptying Syria of its Muslim people was a great step towards bringing about the old-new massive demographic change in the country, where the traditional Sunni Arab majority are not a majority anymore as the Iranian Shia seize terrains, towns and properties in Syria with the support of the international community.

The Syrian people crossed the lands and the seas in their travel, fleeing the war for safety and security. However, thousands could not make that journey, dying tragically on the way; drowning in the Mediterranean Sea, or getting killed viciously and relentlessly by the Turkish border patrol, or by many other different cruel means while crossing the borders in Europe on foot.

Turkey played a big role in facilitating the illegal immigration of Syrians to Europe and hence emptying Syria from its people. Moreover, the United Nations also launched a big scheme of relocating the Syrian people from neighboring countries (Jordan, Lebanon, Egypt and Turkey) to Europe and North America. It was a major international agenda and a big international conspiracy against the Sunni Muslims in Syria.

It is known that the suffering of some people is somehow an investment for others in our current brutal international system, so the treatment of refugees in hosting countries has varied according to the national interests of each country, but in general, the Syrian refugees were victims of exploitation and hatred mainly in Turkey and Lebanon and have suffered severely from a devastating culture shock in Europe and North America. On the other hand, the Syrian refugees were somehow a good solution for the inherent demographic and aging problems in Sweden, Canada and Germany. Meanwhile, the UN relocation scheme was a great investment opportunity for many local authorities in the UK and their different partners, and a vital resource of funds and benefits. Many businesses have been established and supported in the name of supporting the Syrian refugees. However, cases of negligence, discrimination, and exploitation have been observed and were evident.

Great success stories have been made by Syrian refugees in many countries such as Egypt and Germany, giving a good impression worldwide that the Syrian people are a hard-working and multi-skilled people who never wanted to be refugees or a burden on any county or economy, but rather to return to their blessed land and live in their country without the Assad family.

CONCLUSION

The uprising in 2011 and its outcome has turned the situation upside down in Syrian foreign policy; Qatar and Turkey have become the greatest enemies of the regime after being Syria's closest allies for almost a decade, while Iraq has become a very close ally, a considerable reversal as it became an opponent of Syria in the aftermath of the American occupation of Iraq in 2003. Iran has sustained its alliance with Syria by providing the regime with a wide range of support.

International relations vis-à-vis the Syrian Revolution could not help its cause. In fact, it contributed to its complexity. Friends of Syria are anything but friends of the uprising. Their verbal support for the uprising was and is still belying their actual actions. Meanwhile, friends of the regime demonstrate an admirable example of a beneficial alliance between states in the international arena. They have provided the regime with every kind of support. Such a situation refutes the claim of a double proxy war in Syria. While friends of the regime help the regime's sustainability and its military superiority, friends of Syria help the struggle to continue, creating a massive and unprecedented humanitarian catastrophe in the country. Moreover, while Security Council Resolution 2254 was meaningless after the Russian intervention, Security Council Resolution 2118 was not than a gateway for Bashar Assad's survival after using the chemical weapons.

The spread of Jihadism in Syria and Iraq also added more concerns to the Syrian Revolution regionally and globally; it has united the friends of Syria and the friends of the regime in combating terrorism in the region. Moreover, identity polarization was at its peak during the Syrian Revolution, where all Sunnis in the region supported the Syrian Revolution, but Shias decided to be with the regime. Ironically, the majority of Sunnis support for the revolution was labeled as a terrorist activity so was restricted, but the Shia support to the regime was allowed, and without limits or restrictions.

Chapter Seven

CONCLUSION

After the independence, authoritarianism has been entrenched deeply through many elements in the Arab world, and became the prevailing governing system in those countries. However, authoritarianism was exhausted internally, and became somewhat archaic in the face of globalization forces. Therefore, upgrading the form of authoritarianism in the Arab world was vital and crucial in order for the regimes to be sustained and to stay in power for longer. Ironically, authoritarian upgrading led to revolutions from below. Popular uprisings erupted in Tunisia and spread to Egypt, Libya, Yemen, Bahrain and Syria respectively. These Arab Spring revolutions aimed to alter the status quo and the long resolute political system of the Middle East and North Africa.

The causes related to these revolutions were almost identical, and although they were mainly political in nature, the entrenched economic and social issues cannot be underestimated. However, both economic hardship and political oppression were great aspects of the present as well as of the past in those countries and were always causing unpleasant social outcomes. Therefore, explaining the Arab Spring revolutions required a new analytical approach.

For decades, Arab countries were governed by authoritarian regimes, but after the end of the Cold War, these governments changed notably in order to secure themselves through the adoption of open economic policies, and the implementation of cosmetic political reform. However, the regimes later decided, despite moving ahead radically in terms of economic openness, to recede back to political authoritarianism. The political cosmetic developments in the Arab countries diminished, even though neo-liberalism was flourishing. Privatization was perpetuated within most sectors, creating levels of unprecedented inequality in society. Meanwhile, public political participation was retreating. The parliamentary elections in Egypt in 2005, for instance, were more democratic and more transparent than the elections in 2010. Similarly, local elections in Syria in 2003 were less Baathist-dominated than the elections in 2007. Political freedom in Syria between 2000–2001 was clearly placed on a higher pedestal than it was in 2006 and afterward.

In Syria, upgrading authoritarianism was extremely crucial for the inheritance of power to be accomplished in 2000, and for Bashar Assad to consolidate his grip over the country. Moreover, it was needed to face the external challenges in between 2003–2007, so foreign policy was also employed to serve this goal. However, since 2007, the regime began retreating to authoritarianism and its political concessions were mainly recalled, and the reform rhythms found no public attentions anymore. Meanwhile, neo-liberal policies were in full swing, and benefiting the regime's men and their loyalists, but increasing mass grievances in society. The Syrians fell in between the harsh social and economic implications of neo-liberalization policies, and reproduced political oppression. Such a situation created a fertile field for a popular uprising in the country, and the revolution became a matter of time, waiting for a spark and the barrier of fear to break down.

The Syrian Revolution in 2011 was supposed to be another great aspect of the Arab Spring. This revolution may stem from similar causes to other Arab Spring revolutions, but its trajectory was unique, due to the internal circumstances within the country, and to the international positions. It started as a peaceful revolution from below like other revolutions in the Arab Spring countries, but developed into internal war after the revolutionaries decided to adopt violence as a reaction to the regime's brutality against them. The defections from the army helped this transition to violence, plunging the country into internal war, so the country was divided between a pro-regime coalition presenting the vast majority of the country versus an anti-regime coalition, and others decided not to be involved in this conflict, and to wait for the winner to emerge and take control of the country. The conflict developed further into Jihad after the concept of Jihad developed in the minds and the feelings of the revolutionaries, due to the needs of continuous fighting and great sacrifices to defend themselves and their lands, and has been reinforced after the arrival of foreign Jihadists to fight and settle in Syria. Foreign Jihadists became the overriding power in the anti-regime coalition posing a great threat to many other factions fighting the regime, and also posing a great threat to regional states and to international security. Their agenda was not limited to deposing the Syrian regime, but also aimed to establish the Islamic caliphate in the region.

Indeed, a caliphate was declared in July 2014, and controlled territories and oilfield across Syria and Iraq, so that the borders between Iraq and Syria were removed. However, the borders were reinstated after the defeat of ISIS in 2017 with the retreat of ISIS in front of the international coalition.

Overall, to wage war against a regime that possesses superior capacities has led to guerrilla warfare, prolonging the conflict further. However, when the concept of Jihad dominated the struggle against the regime and its allies, where ideas, symbols and beliefs became so influential, the struggle then is bound to last longer, and spread much more widely in the region. The Jihadists have only two possibilities in such circumstances: claiming victory or claiming martyrdom, and not acknowledge the borders between Muslim countries.

This prolonged and complicated trajectory of the Syrian Revolution can be attributed to many factors: First and foremost is the concrete structure of the inner core of the regime. The regime core is an Alawi regime, and the power is concentrated in Assad's family and their close relatives. The Yemeni scenario of a top military leader from the inner core defecting proved to be very unlikely in Syria. The inner core was getting stronger and more coherent since the beginning of revolution in March 2011. In fact, the whole Alawi community generally proved to be very loyal, as the regime employed all means possible to guarantee its ultimate support.

The fragmentation of Syrian society was also a great obstacle for mass mobilization in Syria, and was the first indigenous challenge to the Syrian uprising. Such an obstacle did not exist heavily in other Arab Spring countries. The spirit of solidarity among the people of Tunisia and Egypt during the uprising was absent from the Syrian people during the uprising. While the regime in Syria is brutal, coherent and Alawi compact, Syria is a country of fragmented and disintegrated groups. Such realities thwarted the chances of a peaceful uprising managing to undermine Bashar Assad directly, or to ignite a revolution from above. Syria is a very divided country in terms of ethnicity, religion and ideology. These divisions caused tension and problems for and among the people as well as the revolutionaries. Identity was a dividing factor between Syrians, while ideology was a dividing factor among the revolutionaries and the opposition. Salafis, Sufis, the Muslim Brotherhood, secularist, national Jihadists and global Jihadists are now dividing lines within the revolution movement. This situation made the revolution trajectory very complicated.

The demobilization of Damascus and the failure of the revolutionaries from outside the capital to reach it also had a great impact upon the revolution's trajectory. The regime succeeded in aborting large public rallies and demonstrations to take place in the city of Damascus. In fact, the regime strengthened its grip over the city and portrayed the city as loyal to the regime, unlike the situation in Tunisia and Egypt, where the revolutionaries have occupied the main streets and squares in the capital cities, leaving no other option for Bin Ali and Mubarak but to leave or step down. The incapability of the revolutionaries to break the regime's grip over the capital, Damascus, played a great factor for prolonging the struggle in Syria.

The lack of independent and strong civil society organizations in the country, and the weakness and deep divisions of the opposition, prevented the revolution in Syria from progressing at speed, unlike the situation in Tunisia, Egypt, Yemen and Bahrain, where civil society organizations had a great role in the public uprisings in these countries. Ideological differences, irredentism, foreign penetration and corruption were all big factors that rendered the Syrian opposition's institutions defunct. They failed to form a strong and independent united body that could represent or lead the revolution, or even constitute a real alternative to the regime. Instead, the formal opposition hijacked the revolution and was representing the will of some regional countries, in particular Saudi Arabia, Qatar and Turkey.

Primary international actors never showed a real intention of supporting the revolution, so while Russia and Iran provided great support for the regime, the friends of Syria group never put its verbal support to the Syrian Revolution into real actions. The regime enjoyed great military and political support from Russia, Iran and somewhat from China in confronting internal threats, and in defeating the revolutionaries and Jihadists. Moreover, the involvement of Iran made revolution seem like a far-off prospect and it complicated the battle for the Free Syrian Army. Meanwhile, the Free Syrian Army or the national Jihadists suffered from a lack of support from the United States and its allies in the region, such as Saudi Arabia, Qatar and Turkey. Many leading figures in the Free Syrian Army complained frequently about the lack of support they needed to defeat Bashar Assad. The arms embargo, which was imposed on the revolutionaries by the Western powers in the early days of the armed struggle, weakened the potential of the revolution, and hence influenced the revolution's trajectory by prolonging certain stages of it. The role of force was very important in the revolution's trajectory and its outcomes. The international community ruled out any possibility of military intervention even after the chemical weapons catastrophe as long as Bashar Assad complied with Security Council Resolution 2118, and as long as the conflict in Syria did not pose a threat to the region as a whole. In fact, evidence can be found that demonstrates an international interest in the continuation rather than termination of the struggle, but guaranteeing the regime's superiority.

The outcome on the ground showed that the US and its allies were actually opposing the Arab Spring revolutions, including the Syrian Revolution against Assad. While they aborted all attempts to topple Assad, they were involving heavily in the counter-revolution process in Tunisia and Egypt, bringing back the old regimes with a much stronger grip on power and a crueler policy toward the people. It was like revenge against the people who opposed the establishment and started the revolutions.

The US and the international community had no problem keeping Assad in power, encouraging more than 15 millions Syrians to leave their country fleeing Assad's brutality to be refugees in the countries around the world or to live in tents and camps in difficult conditions near the Turkish border or in the desert near Jordan such as Al Rukban Camp with no food or water, and no basic services either. The same scenario has happened before with the Iraqis after the American invasion in 2003 and with the Palestinians after the Israeli occupation in 1948. However, the Syrian tragedy is not comparable on all aspects.

I think the West has missed a great opportunity of winning Syria and the Syrian people when they failed to support or at least protect them from the mass killing that is still conducted by Bashar Assad's regime. The international community, particularly the United States, has the power, but lacks the will, to put pressure upon Bashar Assad to stop the ongoing massacres in the country even after the use of chemical weapons against the civilians in August 2013.

Finally, this study tried to answer two very intertwined questions: Why is there revolution in Syria? And why is the revolution in Syria taking a long time and enduring such enormous complexity compared to other Arab Spring revolutions? After exploring the possible motivations for revolution in Syria through concentrating on authoritarianism and upgrading authoritarianism and their aspects in the country, I have tried to look at the revolution or the war in Syria from a different angle through dividing its trajectory into three main phases: revolution from below, internal war and Jihad. There were also phases within these phases, where I have tried to sketch out and reveal their details through interviewing people involved when possible. I believe this book is the first study to reveal the full facts in detail with deep analysis of the situation in Syria between 2011 and 2018. This study also tried to answer many questions which are still vague or unanswered concerning the Syrian Revolution such as the demobilization of Aleppo during the peaceful phase of the revolution, the factors behind the failure of peaceful resistance and moving to violence, the reasons behind military defections in the national army, and last but not least the transition from a popular non-ideological uprising into Islamism.

Labeling the war in Syria as a civil war is a broad and somewhat misleading term, so this is the first book to look at the Syrian war as an internal war. I tried in this book to be very precise and to offer a specific and fair study on the Syrian Revolution which developed into a vicious internal war with great regional and international affects.

The following photos perhaps best sum up the revolution from below in Syria in 2011:

Bashar Assad's pictures and Baath Party's symbols have been dumped in a dumpster, April 2011.

Hafez Assad's statue, June 2011.

And the photo below perhaps best sums up the three phases of the Syrian Revolution:

This picture was taken in the town of Hobait in Idlib province in June 2013.

THE FUTURE

Assad must stay, as Israel once declared openly, regardless of any costs.[734] The US and the international community worked on this plan from the beginning. Many Western politicians have warned implicitly and explicitly that Assad's fall and having the Black and White Flag flying over Damascus means that within months Lebanon would fall and Jordan would fall, and then ISIS would make its drive toward Europe.[735] Russian also warned that Assad's fall means a powerful Sunni state in the region which would change the whole shape of the Middle East and pose a real threat to the international system. Dr. Hijazi stated once that the Alawi regime in Syria is one of the most important formidable pillars for the international system, hence, Syria has to be ruled by an Alawi leader, but as no other figure than Bashar can rally Alawis behind them, so there is no choice but to support him to stay in power. This is why Bashar has liquidated all possible figures among the Alawi community that might compete with him, such as his brother-in-law Asef Shaukat. The Alawai community is like the military institution in Egypt, where presidents have to be solely from their wombs.

The US and the international community wanted the whole country to go back to Assad's control apart from the northeast and east, where the American military is seizing the oilfields, and lurking for ISIS to preempt its revival. Turkey is putting lots of pressure on the civil society and the armed groups under its control in northwest Syria to accept dialogue and conciliation with Assad, but they are refusing any dialogue or any kind of cancellations with Assad. They have no solution but to remove Bashar Assad. Such good will and resilience would cost them bloodshed and misery in the future.

---

[734] "Israel says Assad must stay", THE TIMES, 18 May 2013.

[735] Syrian News Free Press, U.S. Sen. Richard Black: "If we stop training, arming jihadists, the war will end", posted on Sep 27, 2015, https://www.youtube.com/watch?v=utjJRWfmcdM.

There was a lack of support to the people in northwest Syria following the earthquake which struck the area in 06 February 2023, where no proper equipment or professional search teams have been provided to help the desperate people in their search for survivors under the rubble. Not even trained dogs were provided to help in this catastrophe. In addition, borders with Turkey closed for a few days in a time where delivering aid and equipment was urgent to save lives. Such cruel actions imply somewhat that the international community, including the United Nations, wanted the people to die under the rubble. Such behavior from the international community reflected their real intentions toward the Syrian people, who are refusing to conciliate with Assad and decline going back under his rule again.

Syria, the geopolitical entity we all knew before 2011, will never come back again as the already frail social contract between its people has been broken beyond repair. Ethno-nationalisim and ideologies have divided the people and the country too deeply. Turkmen wanted to be part of Turkey and the Kurdish wanted to be in the sought-after Kurdistan State. Islamists against secularists and Sufis against Salafis. Christians are leaving the country, meanwhile, Druze are trying to isolate themselves as an independent district. Above all, Iran, with the support of the regime, are seizing the properties of Muslims in Damascus and Aleppo in order to complete the demographic change in the country in favor of Shias over Sunnis. The influence of the Iranian Shia is well noticeable in Damascus. Their desecration of the Muslims sites is taking place every day, including mosques and graves. Moreover, the majority of Muslims who went through all different kinds of tragedies (killing, imprisonment, torture, rape, property destruction and displacement) by the hands of the tiny minority of Alawis would not accept living side by side with them, and if that happened it would be like the fire under ashes.

More than 10 million Muslims (Sunnis) have left the country, and to return to it without a regime change is impossible. In fact, this demographic change was planned and was on purpose in order to dilute the heavy Sunni presence and influence in the country. The new generations of the Syrian refugees in diaspora would have no strong bonds and connections with their mother country, Syria, so it is a matter of time that Syria will have no Muslim majority. The time element is well exploited in this struggle.

The future is bleak not just for Syria, but for the whole region. Counter revolutions in Egypt and Tunisia have defeated the Arab Spring and the old system was reborn again from the womb of the deep military state; a well-established system, with a direct or indirect support from the West, Russia and China. Anti-regime sentiments again surround the old regimes and their supporters, so the situation will explode again in the future, but will be more vicious and much more violent than the Arab Spring. All of these developments come with the worsening situation between the Palestinians and Israelis, especially in the Al-Aqsa Mosque, creating a high level of concern and passion across the Arab and the Islamic worlds. In addition, Lebanon is on the brink of bankruptcy and chaos and maybe a bitter civil war is a matter of time. The situation in Turkey is also not stable internally and regionally with the prolonged struggle with the Kurds. The Shia in Iraq are resuming their sectarian war against the Muslims. Meanwhile, ISIS is reviving and regrouping again in between Syria and Iraq. Such developments and challenges would create more unrest, violence and chaos in the region in the future, threatening the nation-state system in the region and bringing about the collapse of Sykes–Picot, leading eventually to the collapse of the current international system.

While writing this conclusion, news broke with the story of Saudi Arabia inviting Bashar Assad to attend the Arab Summit in Riyadh in May 2023. Meanwhile, Turkey is planning to discuss normalizing its relationship with Assad with the support of Moscow. **The Game is Over!**

The following images are from Caesar Report.

Resource: www.aljazeera.net

Resource: www.aljazeera.net

Resource: www.aljazeera.net

Index

K

L

P

Milton Keynes UK
Ingram Content Group UK Ltd.
UKHW051829010224
436980UK00001B/12

9 781803 815831